WAS WAL

Essays in me

WAS WALES INDUSTRIALISED?

Essays in modern Welsh history

John Williams

GOMER

First Impression—October 1995

ISBN 1 85902 139 5

This volume is published with the support of the Arts Council of Wales.

Printed in Wales by
Gomer Press, Llandysul

Contents

PREFACE

At one Oxford conference I attended, a popular lecture was given in a too-small, too-stuffy ground floor room with the windows open. When the speaker had finished the Chairperson was issuing the usual invitation for questions and comments when the door opened at the back and a young man entered with his hand raised to signal his wish to speak. In a charming Irish brogue he began: 'I haven't just come in, I've been outside listening . . .' It seems to sum up my present relationship to Welsh economic and social history; although I have only marginally participated I haven't just come in but have been listening intently outside.

It still requires some justification for someone who has recently written very little on Wales or Welsh history to offer even a slim book of essays on the subject. To an exercise which is inherently egotistical I must seem to have added the extra ingredient of effrontery. There is no escape from that; instead of, probably futile, attempts at justification, it may be better briskly to indicate the broad criteria used in determining what to include. Essentially these were relatively simple and straightforward. The first was chronological: to attempt to impose some cohesion by confining the offerings to essays dealing with the late nineteenth and early twentieth centuries. It is also hoped that the pieces selected address issues which are still of some concern to historians and, more crucially, that some of them raise questions which still have some pertinence for contemporary Wales. It also seemed desirable that a few pieces which had not previously have been published should be included, if only as a leavening, since they had been prepared as talks and were rather less formal in their presentation.[1]

If these criteria have not been uniformly applied, that is not because to my other misdemeanours has been added, consciously at least, that of self-indulgence. Partly it simply reflects incompatibilities between different criteria. The title-piece, 'Was Wales Industrialised?', spills over the selected chronological corset, but attempts to raise the issue of whether, in the British context, there was anything distinctive in the Welsh industrial experience. And, by implication, to suggest that this carried consequences for the present and future.

It does not seem appropriate in this Preface to provide a kind of Cook's tour of the individual pieces: those who are interested will read and judge for themselves, those who are not will not be enticed by summaries of what are already summary essays. But it may be more helpful to indicate what, to the author at least, are some of the recurring themes. The aim here, beyond alerting the reader as to what may be expected, is to suggest some ways in which the agenda of Welsh historiography could be extended. If some of these ways sound rather work-a-day, at least to those unwilling to leave the so-called high ground of national politics and culture, they are essential to understanding and can generate their own exciting re-interpretations.

One such theme is that of structure and structural change. The particular form in which this appears and re-appears in these essays relates mostly to the changing ways in which Welsh men and women earned their living. But if the stress is on industries and occupations because the census returns offer an accessible entry to these issues, the hope would be to stimulate interest in a broader range of, especially, social structures. This is also a theme which, in its nature, is impossible to contain within the generally imposed chronological limits. Structural change is relatively long-run but if its effects are slow they are not imperceptible as the essay on the 'Rise and Decline of the Welsh Economy' tries, in part, to demonstrate. Structural shifts also raise large issues of women's history which were little touched on when these pieces were written and are now being fruitfully pursued by a number of enthusiastic present historians. What women did constitutes an important segment of that enterprise of rescuing women from their marginalisation in Welsh history. What does it tell us of progress and liberalisation that many of the vast army of nineteenth century female domestics did much the same work in public institutions in the twentieth century, or that low paid sweated seamstresses became low paid, part-time component assemblers in Japanese-owned factories?

As a by-product of probing these themes, it should be clear that there are important issues which require some attention to a quantitative approach if they are to be comprehended. It may be fortunate that Welsh history has avoided the excess of cliometrics—the attempts to give a literal application of, mostly static, orthodox economic models to the, essentially dynamic, processes of history. But if it would be undesirable to see the pages of the *Welsh History Review* dominated by equations, correlations and regressions, it is equally undesirable that they should be largely innocent of tables, figures and basic statistics. One of the unpublished essays, 'Figures in Welsh History' constitutes an explicit plea to this effect.

Not surprisingly, given the period mostly concentrated on, much attention is given to mining and miners. If the structural story is accepted, no apology is necessary for this. The incidental object is to suggest the centrality of institutions, those of the coalowners as well as the miners; to stress the importance of the generally invisible implementation of the law as well as the very visible Acts of particular legislation; to suggest the need to try and understand some broad economic trends. One essay, on miners' solidarity, was written to make some of these points in the wake of the triumphalism of the early 1970s: it was unsurprisingly, not well received. Several of the articles on mining also serve to point up my increasing conviction that the 1890s represent in some central respects a turning-point in the economic and social development of modern Wales. They, with other essays, also serve to emphasise ways in which the Welsh experience was both tied to, and diverged from, that of Britain as a whole.

Such preoccupations will strike many people as too mundane and unambitious. So be it. In defence it could be said that there has been too much absorption with the issue of 'who are we?' No doubt such a reflection partly stems from a personal inability—philosophically, linguistically and temperamentally—to wrestle with the metaphysical problems of defining what constitutes Welshness or the state of being Welsh. It is not intended to devalue such struggles but rather to suggest that, especially for recent times, other questions clamour for equal prominence. A century ago there was a general air—the rural heartland might have been an exception—of vitality and confidence; as we approach a new millennium these qualities—the corridors of the Welsh Office might be an exception—have for some time been missing. It is a frankly personal value judgement that it is a matter of some significance that this intervening period should be rescrutinised to ask what happened to (and in) Wales, and how has that experience affected those, whoever they be, who live in Wales.[2]

[1]The presentation of a collection of essays necessarily raises some problems. These are mostly of interest only to the author and his/her ego: but a few impinge on the reader and perhaps require a brief explanation. A basic decision was to reproduce the pieces in their original form—essentially no updating or revision. It does mean that the reader has to endure a few repetitions. Nor, in general, has there been any attempt systematically to include references which have appeared since any of these essays were first written, although very occasionally a note is made at the end of a more recent work that is of specific relevance to the topic.

In dealing with such matters I am grateful for the comment of the two anonymous readers to whom the text was submitted. One of these also helpfully suggested an ordering which was much more coherent than my previous attempt. As a result the first four chapters now cover, and raise some broad issues in the recent economic and social history of Wales; they are followed by a further four essays which deal with various aspects of what I contend is a neglected theme in modern Welsh historiography—namely, the functions and behaviour of the coalowners. Essays 9, 10 and 11 are more directed to the concerns of workers, the first two dealing with particularly significant 'moments' of unrest (1898 and 1910), and the third with the effects on Wales of a generally UK shift towards organising unions amongst 'untraditional' categories of workers. The book ends, as it began, with a few essays with a wider focus. Essay 12 uses the broad experience of Wales in the 1890s to point to some ways in which the Welsh experience was distinctive from that of Britain as a whole. The penultimate essay covers the structural changes in the occupations of Welsh people over the 120 years before 1970, whilst the final essay questions facile notions of miners' solidarity in order properly to appreciate the obstacles to common action, and the extent to which they were overcome.

[2]In this, as in many other respects, the starting point is now the awesomely comprehensive account recently made available in John Davies, *Hanes Cymru* (1990), and (in English translation) as *A History of Wales* (1993).

1. WAS WALES INDUSTRIALISED?

It is largely accepted that, within the general context of the British economy, Wales was industrialised comparatively late. Sir Frederick Rees long ago indicated that by the end of the classical British Industrial Revolution period around 1830, industrialisation in Wales was still confined to a few, localised pockets. And he asserted that the process only became generalised, even in South Wales, when the demand for coal became the main driving force.[1] The implication is that once that happened, and especially once the demand for steam coal began to gather pace in the 1830s, industrialisation then came rapidly and decisively. The present purpose is to question this assumption: to ask whether Wales, even then, became industrialised. Indeed, the immediate object is to pose the question, even for 1914: was Wales industrialised? So stark a formulation might suggest that what is contemplated is a dramatic, even brash, exercise in revisionism. The ultimate intention is more suitably modest: in wrestling with this question it is hoped to obtain some purchase on a more complex issue: namely what was the nature of the industrialisation process in Wales before 1914 and what peculiar features did it assume?

It is worth giving some thought to the *ways* in which industrial development affected Wales because preconceptions about this are central to many of the most crucial debates about Welsh history in the half century or so before 1914. How did industrialisation affect the pattern of internal and external migration? What was the relationship between industrialisation and religion? Did the development of industry initially encourage the spread of nonconformity? and then later lead to a general under-mining of religion? In what ways was the socialism engendered by industrialism coloured by the religious environment? Why was there no nineteenth century Welsh T.U.C? Were Welsh language and culture given a new lease of life by industrialisation, or were they under-mined by the crude universal necessities of commerce? In all too many of the debates around such issues industrialisation is taken for granted, both as a factual occurrence and in the presumption that it is not necessary to specify what the term connotes.

Industrialisation clearly is an amorphous, portmanteau word capable of various shades of meaning. It is even more obvious that its exact specification at any given time and place will always be peculiar to that time and place. As a preliminary to such a specification for Wales it is proposed to take a few generally accepted characteristics of industrialisation and enquire how prominent were these traits in Wales during the second half of the nineteenth century.

Various indicators of industrialisation have been proposed. Michael Hechter, in his far-ranging book on *Internal Colonialism*, suggested seven such criteria.[2] And since an important part of the book addresses itself specifically to Wales this might seem a useful point of departure. However, a couple of his yard-sticks, the marriage-rate and the proportion of the population aged over 65, seem mostly to have been included because there is some statistical correlation between them and the existence of industrial countries. That is, there seems to be no organic or causal reason for linking them to industrialisation: impressionistically, they seem more likely to be associated with relative affluence and as characteristic of New Zealand or Denmark in the first half of the twentieth century as of Britain or Germany. And three of Hechter's other indicators—the proportion in non-agricultural occupations; in manufacturing; and in commercial and professional occupations—seem essentially to be sub-divisions of one general criterion, the distribution of the occupied population. With such considerations in mind, the present study has concentrated initially on three broad indicators: the degree of urbanisation of the population; the distribution of the occupied population; and the nature, methods and means of production. The last of these three criteria does not appear in Hechter's list, partly no doubt for the very good reason that it is not readily amenable to quantitative testing, but it is hoped to demonstrate that its importance justifies the loss of precision.

The basic facts about urbanisation in Wales can be simply and shortly stated. Before doing so, however, it is necessary to stress that the use of the word 'fact' conveys a misleading impression of certainty. The 'facts' in question relate to the proportion of the total population which was living in towns at various dates. A town is not, however, an objective phenomenon: definitions of towns or urban communities have an elusiveness of their own and the problems tend to multiply in making comparisons over time because, for example, the boundaries shift—but not at the same pace as the realities. Fortunately the use we presently wish to make of this data is at a general, aggregated level, where the rough conclusions are not seriously threatened by the limitations of the material. What has been done, therefore, is to take the census population of those boroughs, municipal boroughs, urban sanitary districts, urban districts etc. having a total population of 5,000 and above. This qualification rules out a few communities that in formal status and in a Welsh context might seem undoubtedly to be towns—thus in 1911 it excludes Beaumaris, Mold, Porthcawl and Chepstow—but it facilitates comparison with Britain (or England and Wales) as a whole.

On this basis, rather less than 20 per cent of the population of Wales lived in towns in 1851, just under 50 per cent in 1891 and nearly 60 per cent by 1911. Despite the various qualifications already mentioned, these figures seem robust enough to point towards two well-founded conclusions. In the first place they suggest that, as late as the middle of the nineteenth century, Wales was only lightly urbanised, which would support Sir Frederick Rees's contention that development, even in the South, was sporadic until the extension of the demand for coal in the 1860s and 1870s. None the less by the end of the century—and certainly by 1911 with the vast immigration from the West of England in the 1890s and 1900s—there was no doubt that the population of Wales was significantly, and perhaps predominantly, urban. In the second place, it is equally clear that the urbanisation of Wales lagged to a significant, but declining, extent behind that of England and Wales as a whole. Already by the mid-nineteenth century one out of every two of the population of England and Wales lived in towns of over five thousand population (compared to less than one in five for Wales). By 1911 the relative proportions were that 4 out of 5 of the population in England and Wales lived in urban areas, compared to 3 out of 5 in Wales. Thus, in so far as urbanisation is a reasonable index of industrialisation, the conclusion on this basis would seem to be that although Wales continued to lag substantially behind England, Wales *had* become industrialised by about 1900. This positive conclusion is reinforced when it is borne in mind that, even in 1920, the United States—by then easily the world's major producer of industrial goods—only had half of its population living in towns of more than two and a half thousand.

There would, however, be at least one reservation to attach to such a conclusion. It may be, as so often happens, that an essential element has eluded the arithmetic.[3] The 113 thousand inhabitants of the Rhondda U.D. in 1901 were not necessarily town-dwellers in anything like the same sense as Cardiff's 164 thousand. Geographical conditions partly dictated the difference, but it was under-lined and given an additional dimension by the social and economic basis of urban development in the valleys. So much of life centred around, or was conditioned by, the pit that each of the pits tended to spawn their own communities, as well as adding to the aggregate population of the valley. Many would argue that the human and cultural reality lay in the relatively small communities which straggled along the valleys, and that the large numbers contained in the Urban Districts merely reflected administrative convenience or statistical definition. It was not, of course, as clear-cut as that but the peculiarities of the industrial structure in Wales and its geographical location probably means that the figures exaggerate the pace of urbanisation before 1914.

The information on occupational distribution is more complex but we shall be content to peel just a few of its layers.[4] One of the rare relatively safe generalisations in this area of study is that, as economic development proceeds, it is accompanied by a decline in the proportion of the population engaged in agriculture and that this decline tends to be accelerated with the onset of industrialisation. Wales before 1914 certainly conforms to this pattern, which, again, would seem to confirm its essentially industrial status. The occupational census of 1851 was the first which was both reasonably reliable and in a form facilitating comparisons with later years. At that time 35 per cent of the occupied men in Wales were engaged in agriculture: by 1911 only 12 per cent were similarly occupied. On this basis, indeed, it might seem that Wales was not simply an industrial nation, but a highly industrialised nation, by the First World War. The percentage engaged in agriculture did not for example, fall to a similar level (12 per cent) in the United States until 1950. And if the United States in the mid-twentieth century was not industrialised then the word has little meaning. Indeed, few analysts would doubt even that France was an industrial country by 1950: but in that year 29 per cent of the occupied males in France were still engaged in agriculture.

Placed in this context, the dramatic decline in the proportion engaged in agriculture in Wales—the proportion of occupied women in agriculture similarly fell from 27 per cent in 1851 to 9 per cent in 1911—is evidence which constitutes a powerful indicator. Nor is there any doubt about the direction in which it points: it points decisively towards viewing Wales as an industrialised nation. Such evidence is powerful and persuasive but not necessarily conclusive. The exodus from agriculture is undoubtedly important but, in the context of the present discussion, it is claimed that some part of its significance depends on the destinations of the migrants: into what jobs and industries did the men and women who left agriculture go? An investigation of this issue throws up two basic findings—one negative and one positive—which are pertinent to the immediate problem. In the first place, they did not go into manufacturing. The proportion engaged in manufacturing was virtually unchanged at about 23 per cent in 1851 and 1911 (though this is not to say that they were doing the same things in the same ways at the two dates).

The low and stagnant proportion of the occupied workforce which was engaged in manufacturing in nineteenth century Wales might seem to lend strong support to the basic contention that Wales was not industrialised. It cannot, however, be made to bear such weight. It is not an aspect which distinguishes the Welsh experience from that of countries which were obviously industrialised. Indeed, the relatively modest and stable share of the occupied population directly engaged in manufacturing in industrialising countries is a reasonably general phenomenon. The redistribution of the occupied population away from agriculture tends to go more to trade, distribution, government, services and transport than to manufacturing industry. Hence the stagnant proportion of the Welsh workforce in manufacturing cannot be taken as significantly qualifying the effect of the sharp relative decline in agriculture. It may, however, be of some significance that the actual proportion of the work-force in manufacturing in Wales was, and remained, significantly below that of Britain as a whole (23 compared to 33 per cent).

The second finding about the re-distribution of the occupied population is both positive and crucial. The sector which gained most was that of Mining and Quarrying. Between 1851 and 1911 the absolute number employed in this sector rose by nearly 200,000 whilst its proportional share of the total occupied population increased from 17 to 32 per cent. It is, of course, precisely this phenomenon which it is customary to put at the centre of the industrialisation process in Wales. The present contention is that it could (perhaps should) be made instead the central basis for querying whether this process took place at all in Wales in the nineteenth century. At all events, if the huge shift into mining and quarrying is looked at from this quite different perspective it might help to focus attention on, and to clarify, the specific nature of the process in pre-1914 Wales.

Much of the current literature on under-development lays stress on the extent to which such countries are primary producers, with the—sometimes implicit, sometimes explicit—contrast to industrial countries. In particular it is emphasised that the exports from such countries are heavily dependent upon the export of primary produce. This empirical observation has been the basis for many comments upon, and debates about, the differences between the rich (industrial) nations and the poor (primary-producing) nations. The connection has been made in the specific case of mining. Thus a far from radical work, published by the World Bank, asserts that: 'There is no doubt that the mining industry can also have adverse effects, directly or indirectly, on the economy of a developing country. By their very nature, mineral export projects have remained enclaves, better integrated with the outside world than with the host economies, and have allowed little backward integration. The enclave industry label is well deserved.' The same point is driven home by their judgement that the 'record of the world mining industry in responding to the needs of the developing countries is dismal. The industry's total effort has been directed to obtaining sufficient supplies for the consuming countries, namely the developed countries . . . Only recently has the industry even shown awareness of the needs of the developing countries . . .'[5] At a still more general level, Paul Prebisch made the heavy dependence of under-developed countries on primary production the starting point for his argument (first formulated in the 1950 United Nations report on *Economic Development in Latin America*) that the terms of trade between industrialised and primary producing countries were inherently biased against the latter. It is an argument, and a case, which is clearly relevant to those who claim that Wales was exploited by being locked in to its nineteenth century occupational structure. Neither the generality of the analysis, nor its possible particular application to Wales, is central to the question of the industrialisation of Wales before 1914. It is, however, highly pertinent to notice that Prebisch, in common with many other commentators, drew the line not between agricultural and industrial, but between primary producing and industrial: copper mining in Chile was as much a badge of under-development as beef-raising in Argentina. It is a distinction to which writers seeking to define industrialisation often turn. Thus Phyllis Deane, in struggling to identify the characteristics of industrialisation, includes in her short list: the 'movement of labour from activities concerned with the production of primary products to the production of manufactured goods and services'.[6]

Looked at in this light, the really striking feature of the nineteenth century Welsh economy was the extent to which it was dominated by primary production—agriculture, coal, lead, slate. In particular, it would need to be emphasised that this dominance was persistent: it was a major feature of the economy throughout the period up to 1914. In 1851 over half (52 per cent) of the occupied population was engaged in the two basic groups of primary production, Agriculture and Mines and Quarries: in 1911 these two groups still accounted for nearly half (44 per cent) of a much enlarged workforce.

Another illuminating aspect emerges when the development is viewed in this way: in terms of a relationship to primary production, rather than just to agriculture, there seems to have been a general economic experience which was more or less common to Wales as a whole. One of the persistent problems in writing about modern Wales is that any comments derived from aggregates are likely to be more or less misleading because all these aggregates are distorted by the numerical dominance of a few counties in the south—Monmouthshire, Glamorgan and, perhaps, Carmarthenshire. Nearly everything that has been said so far has, for example, been influenced by this consideration if it rested on any sort of, direct or indirect, quantitative element. But the preponderance of primary production is not simply an aggregate illusion. Not merely for Wales but for (almost) every Welsh county the occupational structure was dominated by primary producers both in 1851 and 1911.

But is it justifiable to bundle mining and quarrying into the same box as agriculture? Briefly, it seems reasonable enough on two basic counts. Firstly, the products of these industries were primary in the basic sense that they were not manufactured. This was especially true of the major mining activity of coal where the processing carried out within the mining industry was mainly confined to washing and sizing the coal—and even these activities were still far from universal before 1914. Nor was there much processing even outside the industry apart from some coke production and the manufacture of a little patent fuel. Secondly, the coal was only to a limited extent directly used as a basic raw material within Wales. It was not, that is to say, industrial in the sense of acting mainly as the foundation for other industrial enterprises. It was so used, of course. Indeed, in the mid-nineteenth century the local iron, tin-plate and copper industries had been major sources of demand for Welsh coal. But these demands had-relatively-declined by 1914 and they had not been significantly replaced by other local industrial uses: the outstanding feature of the Welsh coal industry in the half-century before 1914 was the increasing proportion of its output which was shipped outside Wales. Nor was this all. These exports of raw coal totally over-shadowed all other shipments from Wales. Finally, the slate industry of North Wales displayed similar characteristics, although on a smaller scale. At its peak, around 1890, about one-fifth of the slate (73 out of 352 thousand tons) was exported.[7] Thus nineteenth century Wales had a major characteristic in common with many currently under-developed countries: its exports consisted of one (or a small range) of primary products.[8]

Indeed, the relevance of the dominance of mining in the Welsh economy may be even more significant, and again in a way that is commonly found as a feature of contemporary developing countries. Change, of course, affects all industries. But mining is inherently transitory. Whatever it is that is being mined, once it has been dug up it has gone for ever. So there is no necessity for an economy based on mining to give rise to a continuing industrial society.

This leads us to a more general consideration of the methods and means of production. Thus the process of industrialisation is crucially associated with the development and application of new sources of power. This is a common-place of the text-books on the Industrial Revolution: it has survived even the frequent, and occasionally frantic, revisionism of the 'new' economic historians in recent years. Thus, whether we look at Toynbee writing the first-ever set of lectures on the Industrial Revolution a century ago, or at Mantoux's classic written in the first decade of the present century; or at Landes's more recent—and more general—volume, there recurs some such phrase as: 'the use of motive power other than the muscular strength of men or of animals is one of the essential features of the modern factory system'.[9] Indeed, the comprehensive two-volume attempt to use the approach of the new economic history to re-interpret the modern British experience still contains, in an excellent chapter by Donald McCloskey on 'The Industrial Revolution, 1780-1860', the statement that: 'In textiles . . . the inventions harnessed non-human power, initially the power of falling water and later steam'.[10] In the nineteenth century the relevant motive power was certainly steam-power. On the face of it Wales was exceptionally well-placed to participate in a process at the heart of which was steam-power. Wales was well-endowed with coal and, as it turned out, the coal in a significant portion of the major coal-field in South Wales was especially suitable for steam-raising purposes. It seemed likely to be a connection which would boost industrial development in South Wales.

The connection was, to some extent, made. Welsh coal was used as a source of power for Welsh industries in the nineteenth century, but such use was restricted by the particular structure of industry which developed in Wales. There was an under-representation of the kind of mills and work-shops for which steam was the all-pervading pulse of life. In the iron, and other metal-making, industries coal was used as a raw material, not as a source of power—although, of course, steam-engines were used to strengthen the blast at the furnaces, and were prominent in all the finishing processes, in the forges, foundries and rolling mills. The tin-plate rollers were driven by steam but they were fed and re-fed by human muscle. Above all, there was the coal industry itself, easily the largest user of manpower. The industry did make extensive use of steam power. Mining had, indeed, been the industry which had originally provided the forcing-ground for the development of the steam engine and its special needs continued to demand some of the largest and most powerful of these. There were engines to pump water from the pits and to drive the compressed air machines which reduced—but never fully replaced—horses and men and boys as the power for underground haulage. There were enormous engines to drive the ventilating fans, whilst the coal—and the miners—were wound up the deepening pits by steam-driven machinery. And steam locomotives hauled the long black caravans of coal down to the ports. But the essential business, the business of coal-getting, was and remained a handicraft absorbing vast armies of human labour. In relation to the dominant part played by the new sources of power in shaping the new industrial societies it is a fact of the highest importance that mechanisation made virtually no inroads into the dominant Welsh industry before 1914, and its influence was muted in the most important part of the Welsh manufacturing sector—that of metal-making.

The relative lack of mechanical methods of production pointed towards another significant way in which the progress of industrialisation in Wales differed from that of England. The characteristic unit of organisation for an industrial society is taken to be the factory. Mantoux, indeed, subtitles his book on the Industrial Revolution: 'an outline of the beginnings of the Modern Factory System in England'. And, again, this central feature of the substitution of the factory system for the domestic system—the 'all-prominent fact' as Toynbee termed it[11]—recurs in most of the literature on the subject. 'The Industrial Revolution', to quote just one commentator, 'was characterised by the rise of the factory to the centre of social as well as economic life'.[12] Indeed, it is not difficult to carry away from some of the texts a strong impression that in the nineteenth century all English industry—or at least all manufacturing industry—was organised on a factory basis. It was not, and the vast majority of workers were still employed outside factories.[13] Equally, it is possible to carry from the much sparser writings on Welsh industrial development a strong impression—Dodd would be a prominent exception—that factories did not exist in nineteenth century Wales. This would be equally mis-leading. The Factory Inspector's report for 1911, for example, shows that factories—there were 5,304 of them—were more numerous than coal mines. It is important therefore, to keep some perspective. However, even if one proceeds with a proper caution it seems reasonable to assert that the factory was, if not the characteristic, then the symbolic unit of organisation in nineteenth century England, but it was not so in Wales: that the factory worker formed a significant, though never a majority, part of the occupied urban inhabitants in many parts of England, but he (or she) did not do so in many parts of Wales.

And the significance of this difference is more far-reaching than a mere divergence over the characteristic type of work-unit. We have already seen that it connoted a difference in the degree of diffusion of mechanisation. The development of the factory system also vastly quickened, though it did not initiate, two other trends associated with the rise of industrial societies: the extent to which the workers became divorced from the ownership of the means of production, and (some would say consequently) their lack of any control over the nature and conditions of their work. The increasing need for relatively expensive machinery—and, moreover, machinery which could not be effectively housed in the workers' cottages—meant that workers characteristically contributed only their labour to the production process. In addition, the demands of factory organisation required a heightened discipline to provide these expensive machines with regularity and constancy of attention and use.

The first of these trends, the inability of the workers to own the means of production, was equally marked in Welsh industrial development. It was as pervasive in the mine and the quarry as in the factory. Indeed, in one sense the creation of a proletariat owning none of the means of production was an even more obvious feature of mining. Mining—clearly—had never been a cottage craft and, as Nef indicated long ago, had been a capitalist industry well before the eighteenth century. None the less there was one general constraint on the full operation of the capitalistic process. In mining—and in quarrying—the basic cutting tools, the tools actually used at the face, were normally owned by the worker. The collier provided his own picks and mandrils and, for much of this period in many pits, he had his own lamp—as he had earlier often provided his own candles. Part of the ritual of a strike or lock-out was tied in with the process of the men bringing out their tools from the pit. The slate quarrymen similarly provided their own hammers and chisels and crowbars. The significance of these residual property stakes in their work is not easy to assess. Did it, to any meaningful degree, differentiate their industrial experience from that of the factory workers who brought nothing but their labour and were, as Hobsbawm has pointed out,[14] significantly known as 'hands'? Or did it merely reduce somewhat the amount of capital that the owner needed to invest? Or was it mainly, but not merely, psychological—conferring a greater involvement in the work process or giving a whiff of independence? It is difficult to escape the conclusion that the significance was mostly marginal. The Welsh experience over the ownership of the means of production was essentially similar to that of Britain as a whole.

The similarity, however, was much less obvious in the case of the other trend associated with the emergence of the new forms of organisation, and especially of the factories—that is, the tendency for workers to lose control over their working conditions. In recent years there has been a heightened realisation of the crucial necessity of training a distinctly industrial labour force, and of the traumatic nature of that experience during the early stages of industrialisation. What was required was the imposition of great 'regularity and steady intensity' to the work process in order to ensure the accurate repetition of a very limited operation or operations.[15] In the new factories work rules, often of incredible detail, were the norm. They were enforced by a mixture of sticks and carrots (mostly sticks) against a formidable degree of opposition from below. But much of the rationalisation behind this process emanated from the necessity to subject labour to the rhythms of the new machines. The machines were unremitting, so this characteristic was imposed on the workers; the machines performed limited repetitive tasks, and this was carried over to the operators; the machines were relatively expensive, so it was thought to be essential that the workers should tend them with great care and regularity over long hours. And much of the possibility of imposing these changes on labour arose because in the factories it was feasible to subject the workers to a strict supervision. The open workrooms were, and were designed to be, easy to oversee allowing the labour force to be constantly surveyed.

Conditions in the dominant Welsh industries were perceptibly different. And most of the difference derived from two fundamental considerations: the basic cutting operations resisted mechanisation; and close supervision was inherently difficult in mining and quarrying operations. Of course, discipline and regularity were necessary ingredients in running mines and quarries as well as factories. Moreover, in the South Wales coal industry in particular, the constant recruitment of mainly agricultural labour must have involved countless individual traumas of adjustment. But there was more elasticity and scope for personal judgement. In many small pits and drift mines the miners, or at least the face-workers, retained some margin of control over their starting-time, they were not subjected to the rigid domination of the clock, to the minute and enforced by a stringent system of fines, which characterised the factories. Some variation over leaving-time was even more general and survived longer. In the slate quarries, often unfenced and with a wide ease of access, such practices were still more common. As Merfyn Jones has recently pointed out: 'Not only the actual work of slate-quarrying but also the hours and days worked were only tenuously controlled by the management.'[16] A degree of irregularity of working was, in any event, part of the normal operation of the steam-coal trade. There was virtually no stocking of coal. Thus even a temporary failure of demand soon showed itself in short-time working—and it was short-time working, rather than unemployment, that was the characteristic response of the industry to fluctuations. Even a storm at sea could lead to days lost because it interrupted the smooth flow of the coal from the pit-head, into the railway wagons, down to the ports and into the ships. The open slate quarries—especially given their locations—were even more susceptible to interruptions from the elements. Besides these involuntary irregularities the miners and quarrymen managed to cling more successfully to the celebration of St. Monday., By the end of the century it had become only a monthly holiday and it had been secularised as Mabon's Day but the owners had been unable to shift—and, indeed, had to give formal recognition to—this monthly holiday which was so much at odds with the whole ethos of the new industrialism.

More importantly, when he was at his work, the collier performed a wide range of functions: under-cutting, driving bore holes, loading, removing clod, listening to the roof, putting up props, loading the gob. And these were not, could not, be performed in any simple invariable sequence. The seam varied, the roof and floor changed. There was a constant need to exercise judgement and this need was reinforced by the impossibility of providing any continuous supervision in a labyrinth of ill-lit, dusty passages where the actual working-places often involved stooping or lying, perhaps in water. There was discipline, but much of it was self-discipline—and the piece-rate, the cutting rate per ton, often acted as the most effective equivalent of the factory foreman. The freedom to organise their own work was still more marked amongst the quarrymen. Once each crew of three or four had made its 'bargain' with the management they expected to be left to work as they thought fit.[17] And both miners and quarrymen were very conscious of these differences from factory work and cherished, and exaggerated, the greater independence it conferred upon them. In the mid-eighties the Dinorwic quarrymen fought tenaciously against the attempt to introduce even a very mild version of factory rules by a new Manchester-trained manager. And their resistance stemmed not only from a feeling that the rules were inappropriate and unjust, but also—as they explained in a pamphlet issued during the struggle—from a rejection of the conditions of 'slavery' with which they explicitly associated factory discipline.[18]

It needs to be added that the latitude available to workers in mines and quarries was coming increasingly under attack before 1914. In slate-quarrying this was symbolised by the Dinorwic lockout of 1885-6 which all sides recognised as being more about how the enterprise was to be run than about the rate for the job. In coal-mines, too, the deeper more capital-intensive pits made it more necessary and more possible to impose stricter controls on working hours. Moreover many previous customs were challenged and eroded as managements disputed the right of men to take time off for a funeral or leave the pits on the occasion of a fatal accident. In this, as in so many other respects, the decade or so before 1914 saw radical changes, not least in the shifting and hardening of attitudes. None the less the process of whittling-down the independence of workers was still constrained by the limited progress made by mechanisation and the persisting problems of imposing a close supervision. Thus, despite their high significance for aspects such as industrial relations, the management onslaught on working customs and practices before 1914 had only a very limited relevance for the general question of the nature and extent of industrialisation in Wales.

Of much greater relevance are several more broadly-based criticisms of the general theme being argued here. Thus, for example, it could reasonably be asserted that the differences already indicated over the degree to which men controlled their work, or variations in work-satisfaction, are essentially minor considerations. It could reasonably be argued that the essence of the workers' situation was that, with the loss of any effective ownership of the means of production, they were governed by the wage-nexus. The forms taken by this and the policies within which it was expressed might, of course, vary. Thus in the conduct of industrial relations attitudes tended to swing between the 'identity of interest' approach, emphasising the necessarily co-operative aspects of the connection between Capital and Labour (since both were needed in the production process), and the 'inherent antagonism' involved in sharing out the product. Nonetheless, it is argued, the basic reality was that in an industrial society the labourer simply sold his labour to an employer in return for a wage. And there was no doubting that that reality reigned in all branches of Welsh—as in British—economic activity well before 1914.

At an even higher level of generality it has been said that the 'one basic change in the industrial revolution was the establishment of a market economy'.[19] What was meant by this, what gave it its significance, was that fundamental decisions about how society was organised and how its resources were used, were made through the mechanism of the market. The force and the relevance of this for our purposes is that Wales undoubtedly became integrated into the British market as a whole in the nineteenth century. In this fundamental respect, therefore, it could be said that there was little that was distinctive about the industrialisation process in Wales. There were lags and (for some goods and in some areas) there were minor differences in prices because of imperfections in the market, but the essential fact was that almost every aspect of Welsh society felt the tug of market influences that were affecting Britain as a whole. More than this: because trade was so important to Britain and because coal made the Welsh economy heavily export-orientated it was often world-prices which had to be responded to. This may have been a consequence of industrialisation but it affected much more than industry. The fall—partly produced by the steam locomotive and the steamship—in world corn prices in the 1870s, for example, required profound adjustments in Welsh agriculture. Moreover the argument about markets could be countered as being too wide-ranging. Certainly the implied connection between the influence of the markets and industrialisation could be used to demonstrate that most under-developed countries are industrialised because their economies have been so heavily drawn into world markets through their high dependence on exporting primary products.

Despite such reservations it would be foolish to deny that, at this broad conceptual level, it becomes much harder to differentiate the Welsh experience from that of Britain as a whole. In part this simply reflects and recognises that, in many respects, there was no separate Welsh economy and that this is, in itself, an important point to make about the process of industrialisation in Wales: the more general the treatment the more forceful is the reality that Wales was simply part of the British economy.

Acceptance of this does not, however, invalidate the exercise that has been undertaken. Despite occasional incautious remarks to the contrary it was never the intention to construct an argument to abolish the nineteenth century. The main thrust was always meant to be more modestly directed towards indicating what was peculiar, or at least different, about the Welsh industrial experience as it had developed by 1914. It is claimed that it is possible to identify some distinctive features, such as the persistent dominance of primary production, the relatively modest spin-off to manufacturing, and the continued ascendancy of methods and means of production which were inherently resistant to factory-type management and discipline. It is further claimed that such features carry important implications. With that apologia the question in the title—Was Wales Industrialised?—is perhaps best left hanging in the air. Or perhaps it can be deflected as was done by a Harvard law professor who visited friends in a small Maine sea-coast town at the end of the nineteenth century and who found himself on the edge of a heated argument about the efficacy of baptism. He tried to stay inconspicuous, knowing that any intervention was likely to make enemies of half the town. But it was of no avail. He was cornered and asked point-blank: 'Do you, or do you not, believe in baptism?' After a brief hesitation, he replied: 'Do I believe in it, sir? Why, I assure you, I've seen it done.'

(This essay formed the basis of an address given to a conference at Aberystwyth in the early 1980s, and has not previously been published. Serious discussion about how 'de-industrialisation' affects Wales has hardly started: when it does it might be sensible to have some information on the nature of the industrialisation that was presumed to have taken place in the past.)

Notes

[1]J.F. Rees, *Studies in Welsh History*, Cardiff, 1947, Ch. IX.

[2]Michael Hechter, *Internal Colonialism: the Celtic Fringe in British National Development, 1536-1966*, 1975, Ch. 7.

[3]The urban experience in Wales is most fully explored in H. Carter, *The Town in Wales*, Cardiff, 1966 and H. Carter (ed.) *Urban Essays*, Cardiff, 1970. Some of the measurement problems are made evident in C.M. Law, 'The Growth of Urban Population in England and Wales, 1801-1911', *Trans. of Institute of British Geographers*, 41 (1967), pp. 125-44.

[4]A fuller analysis is offered in L.J. Williams and T. Boynes, 'Occupations in Wales, 1851-1971', *Bulletin of Economic Research*, Vol. 29, 1977.

[5]R. Bossom and B. Varnon, *The Mining Industry and the Developing Countries*, Oxford 197, pp. 7, 11.

[6]P. Deane, *The First Industrial Revolution*, Cambridge, 1965, p. 1,

[7]J. Lindsay, *A History of the North Wales Slate Industry*, 1974, p. 253.

[8]Of course this could have been offset by the traffic passing by land to England. Wales could have been exporting substantial quantities of manufactures, and importing raw materials, in this way. But although there is little hard evidence on this, it seems unlikely, and what evidence there is—of GWR traffic, for example,—tends to reinforce the picture painted by the port statistics, at least in terms of exports.

[9]P. Mantoux, *The Industrial Revolution in the Eighteenth Century*, 2nd ed., p. 318. Another more recent, and equally perceptive, French commentator on Britain's industrial revolution judged that it 'consisted of a complex series of technological innovations based . . . on the exploitation of a new source of energy, steam' and these development 'led to a rapid transformation of the methods and structure of industry.' F. Crouzet, *The Victorian Economy*, 1982, p. 2.

[10]Toynbee, *op.cit.*, p. 69.

[12]R.L. Heilbroner, *The Making of Economic Society*, 4th ed., p. 81.

[13]The point is effectively driven home in R. Samuel, 'Steam power and hand technology', *History Workshop*, Spring 1977.

[14]E.J. Hobsbawm, *The Age of Revolutions.*

[15]There is an excellent discussion of the struggle to create a labour force of this type in Britain during the industrial revolution period in S. Pollard, *The Genesis of Modern Management*, Ch. 5.

[16]R.M. Jones. *The North Wales Quarrymen, 1874-1922*. 1981. Cardiff, University of Wales Press, p. 88.

[17]*Ibid.*, p. 86.

[18]*Ibid.*, p. 101.

[19]Karl Polanyi, *Origins of Our Time*.

2. 1890-1930: THE RISE AND DECLINE OF THE WELSH ECONOMY

The course taken by the Welsh economy in the half century preceding 1930 is simple and straightforward: it is one of rise and fall. But the direct statement, whilst accurate enough, disguises the nature of both the growth and the decline. The scale of each was of dramatic proportions. Indeed, the tragedy embodied classical elements in that the seeds of the collapse were contained in the forces, including even traces of hubris, which fuelled the soaring rise. The purpose of the present paper is to sketch the scale and nature of these movements, and to comment upon some of their characteristics which are of particular relevance to a gathering of labour historians.

The tables (pp. 40-1) serve to summarise the nature of the Welsh experience. Effectively they show a rapid increase in nearly all the critical indicators up to the first world war; a more varied experience during the war itself and into the immediate post-war years; and a sharp decline for the rest of the 1920s and beyond. Population, together with output and employment in the main industries, rose sharply and then fell away. The figures can be left to speak for themselves but in some significant respects they speak too softly and justify some amplification. In particular their message becomes almost deafening when attention is concentrated on their locational and structural aspects.

The population increase before 1914, for example, is quite substantial. But it was very unevenly spread. Six of the (then) thirteen counties actually experienced an absolute decline in population: these constituted the rural heartland of, especially, mid-Wales. There were small gains in three of the northern counties (Caernarvonshire, Denbigh and Flint) mostly associated with the North Wales coalfield. But overwhelmingly the population trend was dominated by the few counties (Glamorgan, Monmouth and—to a lesser extent—Carmarthen) which were most directly affected by developments in the coalfield of South Wales. Indeed, of the total population increase for Wales of nearly 850,000 between 1881 and 1911, 610,000 (or 70 per cent) was accounted for by the single county of Glamorgan (Table 1). Whether such a widely spread and heterogeneous geographical experience can be usefully described as the pre-1914 expansion of the economy of Wales must be open to some doubt.

The imbalance largely reflects a similar skewness in the industrial structure. Indeed the broad occupational groups used in the census seem in some respects hardly to be appropriate to describe the Welsh economic structure—except in a negative sense. In Wales the numbers falling into most of these occupational groups were insignificant. In 1911 ten of the 22 occupational groups each accounted for less than 1 per cent of the total occupied male population.[1] This was a persistent feature of the nineteenth century Welsh economy; with minor variations the same occupational groups had been similarly insignificant at the time of the first comprehensive and comparable occupational census in 1851.[2] At the other end of the scale nearly all the (233,000) growth in the male occupied population between 1891 and 1911 could be accounted for by just six groups. And even within this leading half dozen growing sectors there was a huge imbalance: five of them (Transport; Metals, machines; Food, tobacco etc.; Building; and Commercial) accounted between them for just under half (105,000) the increase, the other half (112,000) was entirely accounted for by the single sector of Mines and Quarries (Table 2). As a result, by 1911 out of the entire male occupied population in Wales one in every three (31.6 per cent) was a miner or quarryman. Few industrial *countries* can have had so markedly concentrated an occupational structure. But if we add to those in Mining the slowly dwindling numbers engaged in Agriculture, an even more remarkable fact emerges: in what is generally considered to be one of the most industrialised sectors of the most industrialised pre-1914 nation (Britain) almost half (43.5 per cent) of the occupied male population was engaged in primary production.

The dominant sector in the Welsh economy was clearly that of Mines and Quarries, but as the nineteenth century progressed Mines and Quarries came increasingly to mean coal. By 1911 the number employed in lead mining was tiny whilst those in the slate industry numbered less than twenty thousand (Table 5). The increasing dominance of coal, and especially of South Wales coal, is thus the final point to be emphasised in this brief survey of the Welsh economy in the generation before the first world war. It is a dominance which can be economically and effectively established and demonstrated.

By 1911 30 per cent of the occupied males were in the one industry of coal-mining: an extraordinary percentage when it is recalled that most Welsh counties contained no coal deposits. In the 30 years before 1914, employment in the industry grew from about 80,000 to 242,000 (Table 4). And of this increase of 162,000 nearly all (157,000) took place in the South Wales coalfield. In a little over a decade at the beginning of the twentieth century the South Wales coal industry absorbed an *additional* 100,000 miners.[3] At a more impressionistic level the thrusting, restless activity can be conveyed by two brief illustrations, one direct and one indirect. In 1891 in the immediate hinterland of Cardiff alone it was reported that '*at the present time* the new Clydach pit was being developed (and it is rumoured that

Table 1. Population. Wales and Selected Counties, 1881-1931. (000s)

Year	Wales			Glamorgan			Caerns.			Cards.		
	M	F	T	M	F	T	M	F	T	M	F	T
1881	786	785	1,572	263	249	511	59	61	119	32	39	70
1891	892	879	1,771	360	327	687	56	61	117	27	35	63
1901	1,011	1,001	2,013	444	416	860	60	65	126	27	34	61
1911	1,232	1,189	2,421	582	539	1,121	59	66	125	27	33	60
1921	1,330	1,326	2,656	638	615	1,252	60	71	131	28	33	61
1931	1,294	1,300	2,593	617	609	1,226	57	64	121	25	30	55
1939[1]	1,228	1,259	2,487	—	—	1,158	—	—	119	—	—	52

[1] Mid-year estimate

Table 2. Occupations. Wales, 1881-1931. (000s)

	Mines & Quarries		Agric.		Metal Manuf. & Engineering		Transport & Communic.		Total	
Year	M	F	M	F	M	F	M	F	M	F
1881	102	1	100	11	56	4	37	—	490	155
1891	145	1	99	9	62	5	52	—	576	192
1901	189	—	92	12	68	2	70	1	656	180
1911	256	—	96	20	91	3	85	1	809	216
1921	278	—	95	11	99	5	87	3	880	213
1931	235	—	93	9	81	2	95	3	873	206

Table 3. Iron, Steel and Tinplate

	Iron and Steel									Tinplate	
	South Wales					North Wales					
Average of:	No. of Works	Furnaces Built	Furnaces In blast	Production Pig Iron	Production Steel Ingots	No. of Works	Built	In blast	Pig Iron	No. of mills Working	Output (00s of boxes)
1879-81	28	142	63	824	416	4	10	6	41	241[3]	5,236
1911-13	9	32	12	787	1,807[1]	2	3	3	76[2]	534	16,574
1930-32	6	20	3	392	1,375	n.a.			n.a.	403	15,194

[1] 1913 figure [2] 1909-11 to keep comparable basis. [3] Ave. 1878-80

Table 4. Coal

Year Average of:	South Wales Output (000s tons)	of which Anthracite	Shipments Foreign & Coastal	No. Employed	North Wales Output (000s tons)	No. Employed
1879-81	20,406	906[1]	9,330	69,515	2,442	10,175
1911-13	52,383	4,359	37,098	226,519	3,400	15,690
1930-32	39,022	5,435	24,811	159,024	3,104	13,813

[1]1888

Table 5. Lead[1] and Slate, Wales

Year Average Of:	Lead No. of Mincs	Output (tons)	No. Employed	Slate Output (000s tons)	No. Employed
1879-81	98	20,118	6,363	443[4]	14,019[5]
1911-13	26	7,042	1,867	312	18,764
1930-32	”	192[2]	[3]	201	18,435[6]

[1]Covers lead, zinc and copper. [2]From 1933 there was revival from Flints. Ave. 1934-6, 18,387. [3]1925-6 (last years available) less than 500. [4]1882-4 Earliest available. [5]Figs. deficient before 1895 Quarries Act made them compulsory. [6]1924-6 Last years available.

Table 6. Unemployment. Wales, number and per cent. Males, Annual Averages, 1923-32.

Year	Number	Per cent.	Year	Number	Per cent.
1923	34,209	6.4	1928	127,030	24.4
1924	49,995	8.6	1929	105,294	19.2
1925	96,557	16.5	1930	142,758	27.5
1926	104,001	18.0	1931	177,146	34.3
1927	117,108	20.9	1932	207,292	39.1

[1]Ave. percentage only available for all unemployed (males, females and juveniles). This figure normally a little over 1 per cent below figure for males only.

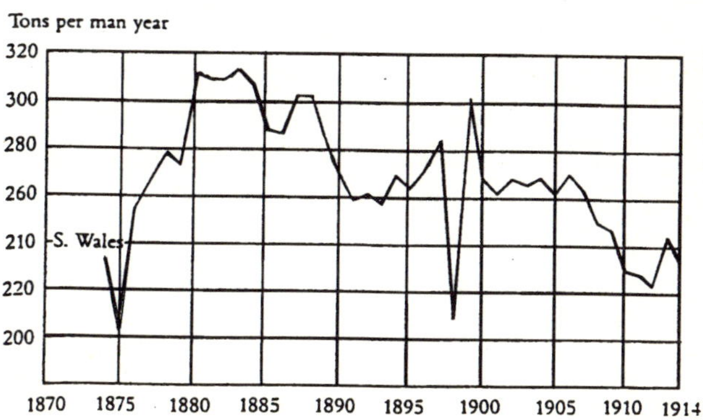

Figure 1 Annual labour productivity of coal-mining, 1874-1914

another was to be sunk); Naval Colliery Co. is going to sink a new pit; Lewis Merthyr Co. to do the same; Tylor and Co. now well on with new Cefn-nant-ddu colliery; Mardy Co. had started new shaft; Dowlais Co. is sinking two new shafts; Universal Colliery Co. to sink new pits north of Pontypridd. In Rhymney Valley, Llanbradach Co. had found fresh coal; Rhymney Co. is sinking two new shafts at Pengam; Powell Duffryn Co. contemplated sinking in the same area. Universal Co. had started two pits at the top of Aber valley, a new pit is being sunk at Llanhilleth; Ebbw Vale Co. is sinking at Cwm and at Abertillery.'[4]

The indirect effects, especially in the provision of the transportation infrastructure, were equally dramatic. By 1890 South Wales already possessed what was certainly one of the most densely-developed rail networks of the entire world. Even so, the years before 1914 saw a few minor extensions—another 32 miles for the Barry Railway, 23 miles for the Cardiff Railway, 17 miles for the Rhondda and Swansea Bay line, and 21 additional miles for the Port Talbot Railway. But the real post-1890 outburst took the form of the provision of extra port facilities. Between 1890 and 1910 more investment was made to build more dock accommodation than ever before. 'The Barry No. 2 Dock covering 34 acres was opened in 1898. At Cardiff the Queen Alexandra Dock was opened in 1907 at a cost of £1.3 million. Its 52 acres increased the Bute Docks system by almost one-third. At Newport a dock extension of 20 acres was opened in 1893 whilst the South Dock extension of 48 acres was finally completed in 1914. At Port Talbot a new dock was opened in 1898, the same year as a 28 acre extension to the Prince of Wales dock in Swansea. A decade later, in 1909, the King's Dock of 70 acres was also opened in Swansea . . .'[5]

Much of this extra dock accommodation was soon to be rendered redundant. That should not, however, be allowed to disguise the essential message arising from the energetic activity of the quarter-century following 1890: it proclaimed not only that the economy was expanding very rapidly but that contemporaries were confident that the still-growing coal industry justified capital expenditure on the infrastructure on a scale which anticipated a much greater future demand. The boosters were wrong, as they usually are sooner or later, but it would be equally mistaken to use hindsight simply to write all this off as hysteria. At the very end of this period a shrewd, sober and knowledgeable judge of the industry—Professor Stanley Jevons—was still calling for additional dock accommodation for Cardiff: 'The South Wales coalfield is now producing at the rate of nearly 60 million tons per annum, and the rate of production is pretty sure to increase within 30 or 40 years to about 100 million tons per annum.'[6]

In the event, 1913 turned out to be the peak year for coal output (56.8m. tons) in South Wales. It is impossible to know whether this would have still been the case if the first world war had not broken out in August, 1914 but it is unlikely that a downturn could have been long delayed. It is tolerably certain that the needs of war, after a great deal of initial disruption, soon called for as much output as a reduced and (because of an early patriotic exodus of skilled colliers) less efficient workforce could produce from mines which were not getting enough capital for their effective maintenance. War thus—eventually—sustained output: the post-war boom with high prices greatly stimulated output. But the wartime capital neglect, and the post-war profit incentive brought into production thinner seams and pits which had previously been closed down as too small or inefficient. Employment thus peaked in 1920 at 271,516 (over 38,000 more than in 1913) but the 1920 output at 45.3m. tons was 11.5m. tons *less* than that of 1913.

The post-war boom died at the end of 1920. The ensuing decline of the Welsh economy can again be summarised in the broad statistical indicators (Tables 1-6). But again these under-state what was happening: the Welsh fall, like the Welsh rise, is not fully captured in these figures. Thus the fact (Table 1) of an absolute decline in population (from 2.656m. in 1921 to 2.593m. in 1931) is itself significant, especially when contrasted with the still-rising U.K. trend (from 44.07 on to 46.07m.). But it obscures three facts: that Wales had suffered a dramatic reversal from having an above-average rate of population growth before 1914; that the fall was unevenly distributed—the Rhondda lost 13 per cent of its population in the decade before 1931; and the overall loss of population under-states the extent to which people were moving out of the country, and particularly from the southern coalfield. In the decade before 1931, for example the actual loss of population from the four counties containing the coalfield was 70,000. But the region had long had, and continued to have, an exceptionally high birth rate. There would thus have been a continued substantial natural rate of increase by 1931 if this had not been offset by out-migration. It was estimated that 242,000 left the coalfield during the 1920s.[7]

The decline, moreover, was not spread over the entire decade so that, when it came, it was sharper than the overall figures might suggest. In the immediate post-war boom the price of coal for export had risen exceptionally strongly. That demand came to an end in late 1920 and, together with the coincident shift of government policy to deflationary measures, hit South Wales badly. But after the disruption of the national three month coal dispute of 1921, support was lent for the view that the downturn would soon be over by the return to high levels of output and exports in 1922. 1923 was still better (because the French invasion of the Ruhr disrupted a major competitor) and the generally good trading conditions of 1924 sustained a high level of activity. In 1923 output at 54.3m. tons was almost back to its 1913 peak (56.8m. tons), and coal exports from South Wales in 1923 were actually slightly higher (30.0m. tons) than in 1913 (29.8m. tons).[8] Unemployment in coal-mining in South Wales was in 1923 and 1924—as it had been before 1914—well below the U.K. average. With national figures already above 10 per cent an overwhelmingly coal district like the Rhondda registered less than 2 per cent in 1923 and was still only 7 per cent by the end of 1924, and—partly reflecting the dominance of coal—the average for Wales (Table 6) in each of these years was below 10 per cent (6.4 and 8.6 respectively).[9]

When the bubble burst the pace and scale of the fall were devastating. Most of the reasons for the collapse of the Welsh coal economy were secular but their malign effects were hugely aggravated by a series of short-run, *ad hoc*, influences: the war; the feverish post-war boom; the invasion of the Ruhr; and, above all, by Britain's return to the gold standard in 1925 at an over-valued pound which hit directly at exporting areas like Wales. Before the war 70 per cent of the commercially disposable coal of South Wales was exported as cargo or bunkers. Compared with just two years earlier in 1923 the output of the southern coalfield had fallen by 10m. tons by 1925, fluctuated around that level (44-48m. tons) until the end of the decade before plummeting by a further 10m. tons (to 34.9m. tons) in 1932. In the decade from 1923 to 1932 the number employed in the industry fell by over 100,000. Neither output nor employment revived in the years of the British economic recovery of the 1930s. Moreover, despite the steady fall (through migration, natural wastage, etc.) in the total number of insured miners, both the number and the percentage of miners unemployed increased to over 80,000 and 42 per cent in 1932.

The experience of the South Wales coal industry was the most dramatic, but it was echoed in the other major industrial sectors of Wales (Tables 3-5). But the more important feature was the fewness of these other major industrial sectors. The Welsh economy remained throughout these years one which was narrowly based to a quite extraordinary degree. The 1921 occupational census showed that 43 per cent of the occupied male population were engaged in just 2 (out of 26) occupational groups: Mining and quarrying; and Metal manufacturing and engineering. If those engaged in transportation (largely dependent on these two industries and the fourth largest sector after Agriculture) are added over one-half the male occupied population is accounted for. The precariousness of such an economic structure was greatly compounded by the fact that each of these sectors was heavily reliant on its ability to export. The South Wales coal industry still exported about two-thirds of its (dwindling) output in the early 1930s; Welsh steel production was overwhelmingly destined for local tinplate[10] and sheetworks which in the early 1930s still exported two-thirds of their output; and in the late 1920s over 80 per cent of the more than 800,000 tons of galvanised sheets were sent abroad.[11]

Explanations are more elusive and cannot be managed in the same preemptory way. They are thus not here attempted. Instead some general comments are offered on a few selective aspects of the developments in the Welsh economy which have been briefly depicted. One of the most significant is the effect and influence of technical change.

The customary story was that there was before 1914 a long-run decline in the level of labour productivity in coal mining stemming largely from the natural operation of diminishing returns in an extractive industry. The charge was that this secular trend was not countered by the adoption of technical innovation, and the responsibility for this was variously attached to entrepreneurial failure or labour resistance to the new methods of work. It was considered that this was sufficiently demonstrated by the fact that in 1913 only just over one per cent of output in South Wales was mechanically cut, a much lower proportion than in other coalfields.[12]

More recently this has been challenged on two main grounds. It is questioned whether there was the long-run decline in productivity before 1914 (Figure 1). Instead by 1914 there seems simply to have been a return to the levels of the early 1870s; the aberration seems rather to have been the very high productivity levels of 1880-88; and the fall from these levels was concentrated in two brief bursts (from 1888-90, and after 1908) each of which could be explained by *ad hoc* factors. More specifically, the geological conditions in South Wales were unsuitable to the cutting machines which were then available. The machines required smooth and continuous working conditions if they were to be economically viable, but the seams of the South Wales coalfield were notoriously unstable. Indeed, the over-riding geological characteristic of the coalfield was that it was much more disturbed and much less stable than other coalfields. Thus the seams tended to dip quite sharply; they were heavily faulted; and the floor and the roof showed high propensities to buckle and to fall, to 'work' or move. One result of this was to make the actual process of cutting the coal a less urgent problem. Welsh colliers customarily ended their shift by under-cutting the seam, confident that by the next morning much of the overhanging coal would have been brought down by the pressure operating from the roof. Improved, more robust and adaptable, machinery together with some changes in the economics of the industry, led to a more widespread adoption of mechanical mining methods in the inter-war years though the same factors still meant that South Wales tended for good reasons to lag behind other coalfields. But for the period up to 1914 the significance is rather that alleged labour intransigence over the adoption of machinery was never a very live issue. And, more generally, it meant that the vast expansion in output could only be achieved by an equivalent increase in the labour force.

The more important technical change was probably taking place not on the production (supply) side but on the side of consumption (demand). It took the best part of the nineteenth century for steam to oust sail as the main source of propulsion for ocean shipping. In Scotland the *Charlotte Dundas* had operated on steam as early as 1802, whilst in 1833 the Canadian *Royal William* had crossed from Nova Scotia to Portsmouth using steam as an auxiliary to sail. But as late as 1870 the still-growing number of sailing vessels of the U.K. merchant fleet constituted four times the tonnage of the steam fleet (4.6 against 1.1m. tons). Thereafter the change-over was rapid: by 1890 the steam fleet (5m. tons) was approaching double the tonnage of sail (2.9m. tons); by 1910 it was ten times as great (10.4 against 1.2m. tons). In the crucial four decades from c.1870 South Wales, with its huge supplies of coal especially suited for steam-raising and with the added boon for naval vessels and passenger lines of being (relatively) smokeless, was a prime beneficiary of this process. It provided the major driving force behind the dramatic increase in output which more than trebled between the late 1870s and the first world war. That conflict was, with the possible exception of the Russio-Japanese war of 1904-5, to be the only one in which a significant war at sea was mainly fought with coal-fired ships. And unfortunately for Wales the pace of the downswing was much more rapid than the upswing had been. The Admiralty only initiated sea trials using oil at the beginning of the twentieth century but twenty years later had ceased commissioning coal-fired vessels of war. The prestigious Admiralty demand for Welsh coal had plummeted from 1.75m. tons in the last peace-time year of 1913 to one-fifth of this level in 1925 when it was still falling. In 1913, about 90 per cent of shipping generally was coal-driven; by the end of our period this had fallen to about one-half. Still more ominously, less than one-third of new shipping in 1930 was designed to use coal; oil fired boilers and internal combustion engines which had been fitted to an insignificant proportion of the world's tonnage in 1913 had within two decades already become the norm.[13]

In part this was simply one of a series of factors making for a decline in the demand for Welsh coal in the 1920s. It was, in this respect, reinforced for example by the developments being made in fuel economy. More efficient domestic appliances were supplemented by the use of powdered fuel and small coals in factories and in steel works. There was also the more particular factor of the return to the gold standard which exerted an especially baleful influence on an overwhelmingly exporting district like South Wales. These discouraging developments coincided with the more general influences of the exhaustion of some of the more accessible coal reserves, and the development of new (and often subsidised) sources of competition in countries like Poland and Germany. But what needs to be emphasised is that the significance of the decline in the use of coal for steam-raising, especially for shipping, extended far beyond the simple loss of a market.

Before 1913 Welsh coal always commanded a price premium. This was generally regarded as a reflection of the higher quality of Welsh coal and hence looked upon as a permanent source of prosperity for the region. To some degree, of course, that was so: the high price did reflect the peculiar qualities of Welsh steam coal. But the higher price also reflected the greater cost of producing Welsh coal. Even before, and apart from, the retarding effects on the introduction of coal-cutting machinery, the exceptionally difficult geological conditions made the coalfield a relatively high-cost producer. During the boom years some of the implications of this fact eluded those on all sides of the industry whose pride in the high quality of the coal led them to believe that they were thus ensured that it would stay in high demand. Causation and causal directions in history are always tricky. None the less, when taken in conjunction with the high cost characteristics, it can be asserted with some confidence that in the Welsh coal industry the causation ran (and continued to run) the other way. The nineteenth century saw the emergence of new demands for coal—especially for steam raising, and especially for steam ships—for which Welsh coal happened to be well suited. The smokeless and steam raising qualities of Welsh coal were sufficiently marked to ensure a surging demand despite the fact that it necessarily cost more to produce. The higher costs were inescapable. Once the special demand for Welsh coal declined much of the industry was doomed: its higher quality would not then be able to offset the greater cost of getting it. On this reading, therefore, the connection between cost, price, demand and quality pointed not to the security given to the Welsh coal industry by the high quality of its product, but to the precariousness which came from its high cost production.

The point has been presented here with an exaggerated starkness. The justification stems from a conviction that it is not possible to comprehend the shifts in the Welsh economy over this period without an appreciation of the basic economics of the dominant industry. It is a useful background which helps to illuminate such other characteristics of the industry as the especial vehemence with which the Welsh coalowners attempted in the inter-war years to reduce these costs by cutting wages. The high cost disadvantage in a competitive industry could only be overcome if, as in the 1950s, there was a general acute fuel shortage or if there was a particular demand for the particular qualities of the product. The latter aspect was demonstrated in the 1920s by the experience of the anthracite industry. For most of the nineteenth century the anthracite coalfield of West Wales had experienced very slow growth. The seams here were generally even more faulty and costly to work; as a result sale was confined to a few specialised uses—like horticulture and brewing—where its exceptional purity was important enough to command a high price. Towards the end of the century a new wider demand opened with the spread of coal-burning closed stoves on the continent. Output rose from 1.2m. tons in 1890 to 4.0m. tons by 1910. After the war, this demand continued so that, hugely against the general trend, output rose to 5.6m. tons in 1930 and over-rode even the handicap of an over-valued pound after 1925 by continuing to export nearly 70 per cent of total output. (In the early 1930s, and especially after the Ottawa agreements, Canada became a major market taking over 1m. tons a year).

More pertinent to the purposes and interests of the present conference of labour historians is another feature which flows directly from the economic structure of Wales and the way it developed over this period. Both before 1914 and during the 1920s there was a natural prominence, perhaps even dominance, of essentially labour questions. This was natural because of two broad features of the economy which have already been mentioned: the occupational structure and the pace and scale of the rise and fall of the economy. The occupational structure was throughout overwhelmingly geared towards manual workers. It was also heavily concentrated in industries which were strongly labour-intensive: coal, slate, lead, tinplate, railways, docks. Given these features a period which saw sharp changes in the economy was bound to create labour difficulties and tensions.

In the absence of the time and space necessary to explore the specific aspects of this pervasive influence, the immediate intention is simply to offer a few very broad comments on the implications of the Welsh economic structure for labour historians. Once again this can be most economically effected by concentrating on the coal industry. Something has already been said to counter the common charge of technological backwardness, especially before 1914. But even if it can be demonstrated that diminishing returns were just about kept at bay, and even if the apparently slow adoption of coal-cutting machines can be plausibly rationalised, some basic facts still remain. There was no sustained increase in productivity. There was no significant break-through in the fundamental process of coal-getting itself: the actual cutting of the coal was unmechanized, obtained by human muscle assisted only by a few primitive tools (mostly mandrils and shovels) and a little gunpowder. There was a huge increase in output between 1890 and 1914. The unavoidable consequence of all this was that more and more colliers were required to produce the coal, and the resultant influx of labour impinged upon all aspects of its social development.

Simply to ask where these extra bodies came from, is already to raise a number of crucial and contentious issues. At one level the answers are straightforward enough. A population increase of this sort can only come from natural increase or by migration, and the census figures—unsatisfactory as they are in many respects—clearly show that both these influences were at work. It can thus be observed that, strongly against the national trend, a high birth rate was maintained in the colliery districts up to 1914. We have the fact, but the explanation eludes us. Some commentators point to the operation of social factors: the enclosed nature of mining communities retarding the spread of outside influences, or the lack of alternative leisure facilities. Others stress economic factors: the absence of employment opportunities for women or, still more directly, the strong demand inducing the workforce to (more than) reproduce itself. But there are weighty objections to each of these approaches. Similarly, the fact of substantial net immigration into the coalfield in the two decades before the first world war is not in doubt. Where they came from, and why, are much more problematic. The Brinley Thomas thesis that emigrants from rural Wales were absorbed into the industrial south, with its accompanying implications for Welsh language and culture has more recently been challenged by Dudley Baines.[14] Even if it were possible, the aim here is not to resolve the issue but merely to point out that the answer is relevant to a wide range of social and industrial issues.

Amongst these would be the progress of labour organisations. In the case of the United States it is often asserted that much of the slow growth of trade union organisation through the nineteenth century can be attributed to the particular problems of unionising a rapidly growing, significantly immigrant workforce from different cultural backgrounds. It is not intended to press a false analogy between Wales and the United States. But it is pertinent to point out that against this background, there seems to be a perversity in the Welsh experience: in the period before the major human flood-tide, trade unions in Wales were seen to be weak; it is in the, apparently, unfavourable conditions of the early twentieth century that the first secure foundations are laid. Right into the 1890s informed observers like the Webbs were dismissive of miners' unions in Wales: by 1914—after Tonypandy, after the leading part played in the national strike for a minimum wage, after *The Miners' Next Step*—such a stance was inconceivable.

The rapid expansion of an economy whose structure emphasised labour-intensive sectors thus raises major puzzles for labour historians. These have been illustrated: they could be multiplied by looking at such features as the provision of social capital or political affiliations. The more important point is that when the decline comes in the inter-war years it necessarily makes for a similar dominance of labour problems. The industrial structure is still much the same (indeed, that is a large part of the problem), and the industries are still labour-intensive. The process was reversed, but the issues were not simply reversible. Thus immigration gave way to emigration, but it was certainly not a straightforward case of the arrivals of the 1900s returning from whence they came. Similarly trade unions under attack and in retreat were faced with a quite different set of problems. Hywel Frances and David Smith have, for example, lucidly told how 'The Fed' partly met this challenge by becoming, in significant respects, the universal providers for the community.[15] There were more subtle changes. Before 1914 franchise changes had secured the election of many workers as Poor Law Guardians, but this had not led to any significant loosening of the application of the Poor Law. Outdoor relief for adult males continued to be stringently withheld. Miners acted mostly as ratepayers since there was very little unemployment for them at this time. In the 1920s, as mass unemployment becomes a common experience, there are persistent attempts to bend or break the regulations.[16]

The Welsh economy, especially before 1914, has recently been portrayed by some writers as occupying a central role in the development of an Atlantic Economy which is seen as a major manifestation of late nineteenth and early twentieth century capitalism. Wales played a vibrant part because its world-wide network of exports led to investment and migration which in some cases—the Dowlais influence on Bilbao in Spain and the Swansea and North Wales dominance of Chile—was significant for a whole economy.[17] Others portrayed Wales as merely constituting part of England's internal colonisation and being thus persistently and consciously exploited.[18] But perhaps these dramatic scenarios, in their quite different ways, exaggerate our significance. Wales may be best depicted as an integral but peripheral part of a general United Kingdom economy. The problem would then be simply that for a crucial period the Welsh role in that economy was so obviously best suited to primary production that no sizeable, stable manufacturing was established. It is more dubious whether this crucial omission can be attributed to the malevolence, or even the unconcern, of capitalist hyenas in London or New York, or just to Welsh donkeys in Cardiff and Caernarvon.

(The Tables are taken from, or calculated from, J. Williams, *Digest of Welsh Historical statistics*, 2 vols., Cardiff, Welsh Office, 1985. The essay was first delivered as a lecture to a group of Welsh and Canadian historians at a conference in Gregynog in April 1987 and published in Hopkin D.R. and Kealey, G. S. (eds), 'Class Community and the Labour Movement: Wales and Canada, 1850-1930', *Llafur*, 1989.)

Notes

[1]Defence; Fishing; Precious metals, jewels, watches, instruments and games; Chemicals, oil, grease, soap and resin; Skins, leather, hair and feathers; Gas, water, electricity, sanitary work; Wood, furniture, fittings, decoration; Brick, cement, pottery and glass; Paper, print, books, stationary; Textile fabrics.

[2]L.J. Williams and T. Boyns, 'Occupations in Wales, 1851-1971'. *Bulletin of Economic Research*, 29, 1977.

[3]In 1899 the coal industry in South Wales employed 132,682 men: by 1913 this reached 233,134. *Welsh Historical Statistics*, vol. 1, p. 300.

[4]*South Wales Daily News*, 2 July 1891, cited in the essay on 'The Climacteric of the 1890s' which is reprinted as Chapter 12 below.

[5]Baber and Williams (eds.), *op.cit.*, p. 203.

[6]H.S. Jevons, *The British Coal Trade*, 1915, pp. 109, 111.

[7]*Second Industrial Survey of South Wales*, Cardiff, 1937, vol. 1, p. 16.

[8]When bunker fuel and the coal equivalent of coke and patent fuel exported are added the 1913 exports were 36.8m. tons compared to 35.8m. tons in 1923.

[9]*Second Industrial Survey*, *op.cit.*, p. 426, and *Welsh Historical Statistics*, vol. 1, p. 142.

[10]In the mid-1930s 15 of the 18 steelworks in South Wales were mostly engaged in supplying for tinplate manufacture. *Second Industrial Survey, op.cit.*, p. 90.

[11]*Ibid.*, pp. 103, 108.

[12]A.J. Taylor, 'Labour Productivity and Technological Innovation in the British Coal Industry, 1850-1914', *Economic History Review*, XIV (August 1961); Rhodri Walters, 'Labour Productivity in the South Wales Steam Coal Industry, 1870-1914', *Economic History Review*, XXVIII (May 1975); Trevor Boyns, *Labour Productivity in the British Coal Industry, 1874-1913*. Univ. of Wales, Ph.D. thesis, 1982. There is a brief discussion in J. Williams, 'Climacteric of the 1890s', *op.cit.*

[13]Board of Trade, [First] *Industrial Survey of South Wales*, London, H.M.S.O., 1932, p. 26; *Second Industrial Survey of South Wales*, Cardiff, Univ. of Wales

Press, 1937, vol. 1, p. 48; H. Marquand, *South Wales Needs a Plan*, London, Allen and Unwin, 1936, pp.28-9.

[14]B. Thomas, *The Welsh Economy*, Cardiff, Univ. of Wales, 1962 (especially Chapter I, 'Wales and the Welsh Economy', and for a more recent restatement, B. Thomas, 'The Industrial Revolution and the Welsh Economy' in C. Baber and J. Williams, (eds), *Modern South Wales,* pp.6-21; D. Baines, *Migration in a Mature Country*, Cambridge, C.U.P., 1985, Ch. 10.

[15]H. Francis and D. Smith, *The Fed*, London, Lawrence and Wishart, 1980.

[16]D.M. Lloyd, 'Some Aspects of the Poor Law in South Wales, 1870-1930', Unpublished M.Sc. (Econ) thesis, Univ. of Wales, 1978.

[17]See, e.g., G.A. Williams, *When Was Wales?*, Harmondsworth, Penguin, 1985, Ch. 10.

[18]M. Hechter, *Internal Colonialism,* London, 1975.

3. WOMEN AT WORK IN NINETEENTH-CENTURY WALES

Most of the work on the history of women in Britain before 1914 still remains to be done: in Wales it has hardly started. When—if—a reasonable portrayal of women as economic, social, political and cultural agents is written, it will have to draw upon a wide range of sources—government documents, newspapers, the records of a wide range of institutions personal reminiscences and contemporary accounts. And even that would still only be preliminary to the essential task of integrating such knowledge as was gained about the history of women into the general history of Wales. Against such a daunting prospectus what the present article attempts to offer seems puny indeed. The intention is to use the census material to secure some impression of women's employment in nineteenth century Wales by offering three different comparative perspectives, embodied in three separate snap-shots taken at different ranges. First, it is intended to look briefly at Wales as a whole and to make some comparisons with the broad pattern of women's employment in England. Secondly—by looking at one industrial (Glamorgan) and one rural (Cardigan) county—some general comments are offered about the way in which the pattern of employment differed in different parts of Wales. Finally four different urban areas within Glamorgan are examined to see if there are significant structural variations within the industrial region. For each of these regions or areas the aim is to cast some light on one aspect of the way in which women related to the economy by asking how many of them were engaged in paid labour and in what kinds of labour they were involved.

Even these limited questions cannot be answered with any certainty. The main obstacles lie in the deficiencies of the data. The first of these arises from the limited chronological span. In the period before the first world war a census was taken at ten-yearly intervals from 1801 onwards. Unfortunately, however, the material which was collected on employment and occupations in the first four censuses (up to and including 1831) is inadequate for our (and most other) purposes. It mostly classifies families rather than individuals, and categorises them into a very small number of very broad groups. It was not, indeed, until 1831 that an occupation that specifically related to women appeared when, alongside nine occupation groups for men, there was listed 'Female Servants'. The census of 1841 gives much more detail but it suffers from two crucial defects: low reliability and the impracticality of putting its data in a form comparable to that of later years. These considerations have limited the present study to the seven census years between 1851 and 1911.

Even when the more serious short-comings of the census material up to 1841 have been drastically resolved by eliminating it altogether from consideration, substantial caution is still necessary. The compilation of occupation tables was, and is, an extremely difficult and complicated operation. An occupation like 'washery slurry bed labourer' might be precise in itself and useful for television panel games, but presents problems for those trying to produce a classification which is both meaningful and manageable. With the accumulation of experience, the census information on occupations tended to improve over time: none the less every census report during these years refers to the particular difficulties involved in compiling the occupation tables and the tables themselves are hedged with notes which need to be read with care. Because the present exercise is mostly concerned with general trends and is thus mostly looking at very broad occupational groups, it has been possible to avoid many of the worst difficulties.

The improvements in the successive censuses were primarily aimed at securing greater precision and uniformity. In this respect it was 1851 which saw the crucial breakthrough in the provision of seventeen classes and 91 sub-classes into which the raw census material was to be fitted. And from 1861 onwards the census office provided the clerks, who performed this crucial task of classification, with detailed instruction books which by 1901 listed 10,000 separate occupations. In addition the classification system was itself continuously adjusted. These changes naturally complicate one essential feature of the present study, that of making comparisons over time. But again a study dealing mostly with broad occupational groupings can assimilate most of this. And fortunately the largest revision of the classification during this period—in 1881—does not cause substantial difficulty in dealing with the occupation of women. The major change was to remove the 'retired' from their occupational groups and to classify them as 'unoccupied'.

If a concentration on women's employment makes it possible to evade some problems, however, it also raises acute difficulties of its own. These are largely inherent in women's work and in the attitudes of contemporaries towards it. Thus women, even single women, were more likely than men to be engaged in occupations which were seasonal, part-time or unpaid. Such characteristics were difficult to contain within the format of census classifications. That general problem was, however, compounded in the case of women: men, whether employed or not, would probably give or be given an occupational label, whereas many women whose employment was on an irregular basis would pass right through the occupational net.

The problem emerges in a particularly acute form in the case of unpaid female relatives who were at home 'assisting' heads of households in their occupations. It is acute here both because the numbers involved are significant and because the practice varied from census to census. To meet the latter point, the figures for the three years (1851, 1861 and 1871) where 'assisting' wives were enumerated have been adjusted by placing all these in the unoccupied category. In this way the greatest degree of consistency is obtained. However, the category involved is substantial. It covers, especially, the wives (or those among them who directly assisted their husbands) of innkeepers, shoemakers, shopkeepers, farmers, graziers, butchers, and lodging-house keepers. Where they were separately returned they amount to over ten per cent of the total number of occupied women in England and rather more than this in Wales. Thus, although formally excluded from the figure of occupied women, specific reference will be made to this category and its significance for the extent and pattern of work performed by women in Wales.

The other large category is that of wives, daughters and other female, relatives engaged in unpaid domestic duties at home. In 1851, 1861 and 1871, wives and others engaged in household duties formed a specific class or order but subsequent censuses excluded them from the occupied categories altogether. The wording was not, however, always clear and householders, enumerators and census clerks must sometimes have been uncertain. Only in 1911 did the instruction seem decisive ('No entry should be made in the case of wives, daughters or other female relatives wholly engaged in domestic duties at home'), and even then the 'wholly' was not entirely free from ambiguity. Any identifiable women in this category who were placed amongst occupied groups have been excluded from the present exercise. Fortunately, one of the categories within which they were most likely to be included—'wives assisting husbands with their businesses'—has already been excluded.

The other category most likely to be affected is that of Domestic Service. Indeed, this was the main source of what seems to have been a definite distortion of the figures for those in the Domestic Service class in 1891. In that year there was a new instruction (rescinded for the next census in 1901) to classify under Domestic Service those female relatives who described themselves as assisting in household duties. As a result the number of women returned in 1891 as engaged in Domestic Offices or Services is inflated in comparison with other censuses, and in consequence the proportion of women who were returned as occupied is also slightly increased. Any distortion in such a major category for female employment is, of course, regrettable and there is no way in which the figures can be confidently adjusted. As a consolation, however, the kinds of comparison (between England and Wales, Glamorgan and Cardigan, etc.) which are central to the present article are much less affected because the distortion applied to all areas even though the new instruction was unlikely to be uniformly interpreted.

The effect of Victorian attitudes to the employment of women on the way in which census forms were filled in by householders and enumerators, and then interpreted by census clerks is impossible to measure and is not even an easy topic on which to offer reasonable impressionistic judgements. The language of the census reports is ambiguous. In 1841, for example, the large number of domestic servants is welcomed because in that occupation 'habits of steady industry, of economy, and of attention to the maintenance of good character are so necessary.' But in

1851 the eulogy is directed towards the wife, mother and mistress (sic!) of the British Family and attention drawn to the danger that 'where the women are much employed from home, the children and parents perish in great numbers.' In 1871, however, the report emphasises that 'it is only in a few cases that the whole of a wife's lifetime is filled up with childbearing, nursing and housekeeping', and goes so far as to suggest that the rigid exclusion of women from the church, law and medicine conflicts with the (by implication, desirable) principle of free trade. In attempting to assess the effects of attitudes to women's work not much weight can be attached to such comments: they are inconsistent, rare (the above constitute almost all the explicit judgements contained in the reports) and, in any case the reports only appeared after the census and would not necessarily influence the way in which it was conducted. In this respect the instructions to enumerators were more important but these reveal little about attitudes.

One of the basic concepts in what follows is that of the participation rate which measures the proportion of a given population which is engaged in paid employment. Any attempt to secure a reasonably dependable measure of the participation rate obviously needs to know the size of the appropriate total population, and also to have an accurate computation of the number of those who were actually gainfully occupied. These seemingly simple requirements always raise problems. In the present case, where we are concerned with the female participation rate over a span of sixty years, the problems are especially pressing. Some of the difficulties of determining from the material available the number of women who were in the paid labour force have already been indicated. It is, however, also necessary to make some decision about what should be the appropriate total population—which women should be considered as forming the total potential occupied group. In what follows the female participation rate is expressed as the proportion of all females over the age of ten who were in paid occupations. The age of ten is taken because the figures are available on that basis and because it is reasonably near to the age at which many girls would have started work. By the end of the period ten is certainly too young and it would be more accurate to remove from the potential workforce all girls up to the age of twelve or fourteen. To this extent the participation rate is understated, but it seemed more important to maintain a basis of comparability between the different census returns.

In England (Table 1) the female participate rate rose from 35.7 per cent in 1851 to 38.3 per cent in 1871 and then fell to 32.8 per cent by 1911. In Wales the comparable shift was from 26.0 per cent in 1851 to 28.9 per cent in 1871 to 22.2 per cent in 1911. In each case neither the upward nor the downward movement was necessarily consistent and regular. It is clear, therefore, that England and Wales both shared the same general pattern for women's employment: an increase in the proportion of women working up to 1871 followed by a declining trend up to about the first world war. The more striking comparison is the considerable and persistent difference in the levels: the participation rate for women in Wales was consistently significantly lower in Wales than in England.

The distribution of the occupied female population also suggests several interesting comparisons and contrasts between England and Wales. There is a strong similarity in that in both countries women's employment was concentrated into a narrow range of occupations. For Wales, seven occupational groups (out of 22) account for about 90 per cent of all employed women, and the proportion would only be very marginally reduced if only five occupational

TABLE 1: FEMALE OCCUPATIONS: ENGLAND, WALES, GLAMORGAN AND CARDIGAN, 1851-1911

		NUMBER OF FEMALES IN OCCUPATION CLASSES(1) AS A PERCENTAGE OF TOTAL OCCUPIED(2)								Occupied(2) as a % total females aged 10 years & over	Total number of occupied females(2)
		Professional Occupations	Domestic Offices or Services	Food, Drink, Lodging, etc.	Dress	Mines & Quarries	Metals, Machines, etc.	Agriculture	Total Cols (i) - (vii)		
		(i)	(ii)	(iii)	(iv)	(v)	(vi)	(vii)	(viii)	(ix)	(x)
	(England	4.2	34.4	3.0	24.2	0.4	1.3	6.4	73.9	35.7	2,319,316
	(Wales	2.1	34.9	4.8	18.5	1.6	1.8	29.3	93.0	26.0	115,195
1851	(Glamorgan	2.3	41.2	5.5	22.1	3.3	4.3	14.6	93.3	24.5	20,705
	(Cards.	0.7	23.2	4.8	15.4	0.1	2.4	2.4	91.9	26.7	10,744
	(England	4.3	36.1	6.0	25.7	0.1	1.3	4.2	77.7	37.3	2,713,159
	(Wales	2.6	49.0	5.1	21.2	1.1	2.0	13.4	94.4	27.2	134,240
1861	(Glamorgan	3.1	46.8	6.0	26.4	2.0	4.5	5.2	94.0	24.6	28,289
	(Cards.	1.0	47.3	4.9	18.1	0.0	2.8	21.8	95.9	30.0	12,339
	(England	6.9	38.8	3.5	22.2	0.3	1.1	2.6	75.4	38.3	3,156,016
	(Wales	2.1	54.3	4.1	19.5	1.3	2.0	8.9	92.2	28.9	152,880
1871	(Glamorgan	3.8	51.5	5.4	23.0	2.1	4.5	3.0	93.3	26.6	37,619
	Cards.	0.9	50.8	4.8	19.1	0.5	1.7	18.4	96.2	33.7	14,012
	(England	5.6	44.8	3.9	18.2	0.2	1.1	1.7	75.5	34.5	3,249,161
	(Wales	4.2	57.0	6.2	17.0	0.9	2.4	6.9	94.6	26.5	154,757
1881	(Glamorgan	5.6	55.1	5.9	19.4	1.3	4.8	2.2	94.3	24.0	43,545
	(Cards	1.5	50.5	6.1	19.5	1.1	0.1	17.2	96.0	33.2	13,656
	(England	7.0	40.3	7.1	17.1	0.1	1.5	0.8	73.9	32.0	3,977,927
	Wales	8.2	50.7	9.4	18.3	0.2	1.4	4.1	92.3	22.9	175,206
1901	(Glamorgan	10.2	46.6	8.9	21.5	0.2	2.4	0.9	90.7	20.4	62,859
	(Cards.	4.3	54.0	54.0	16.6	0.1	0.1	8.9	94.2	29.9	8,468
	(England	7.2	36.0	9.8	15.8	0.1	2.1	0.7	71.7	32.8	4,571,163
	(Wales	9.1	44.6	14.0	16.5	0.1	1.7	3.6	89.6	22.2	202,715
1911	(Glamorgan	10.3	41.2	13.6	19.1	0.1	2.7	0.7	87.7	20.2	80,378
	Cards.	5.6	44.6	10.5	15.5	0.0	0.2	11.0	87.4	29.6	8,251

NOTES

1. Classes based on 1901, 1911 censuses.
2. The censuses for 1851 to 1881 include children 'occupied' under ten years of age, but this makes little difference to the comparability of the figures. At the peak in 1851 only 0.6 of total occupied females in England and Wales were under ten, and for Wales alone the proportion was even lower.

   The figures exclude: the wives of Innkeepers, Shoemakers, Shopkeepers, Farmers and Graziers, Butchers, Licensed Victuallers and Beershop Keepers, Lodging and Boarding Housekeepers, the daughters, grand-daughters, sisters and nieces of Farmers and Graziers.

groups were considered.[1] The same seven groups account for about three-quarters of all female employment in England.[2] A further similarity is that even within this restricted range of occupations there was a strong dominance by two groups, the same two groups in each country. These were Domestic Service and Dress which between them never accounted for less than half of all female employment from 1851 to 1911.

Perhaps the most significant contrast arises from the *extent* of the dominance of these two groups. In Wales it was normally higher and this resulted entirely from the importance of Domestic Service. From 1871 to 1901, covering four of the seven census years considered, Domestic Service alone accounted for over half the total number of women employed in Wales. Moreover, at every census except that of 1851 the proportion in Domestic Service in Wales was at least ten per cent higher than in England, which perhaps raises some interesting questions about just who employed them since it seems plausible that Wales should have had proportionately fewer institutions such as hotels and hospitals to act as a source of demand. The other main area of contrast is that the proportion of employed women engaged in Agriculture was consistently higher in Wales than in England. Initially, both the difference and its significance were substantial (in 1851 7.5 per cent of employed women in England were in Agriculture compared to 29.3 per cent in Wales) but they dwindled with the dwindling importance of Agriculture (in 1911 the comparable figures were 0.8 per cent and 3.6 per cent). For Wales the shift of Agriculture from being the second largest source of female employment in 1851 to a weak fifth position by 1911 was the only significant change in the relative importance of the different occupational groups during this period.

For Wales in general the other main points to notice concern the rising importance of Food, Drink, Lodgings etc. and Professional Occupations, and the decline of Mines and Quarries. In 1851 Food, Drink and Lodging accounted for 4.8 per cent of female employment in Wales; by 1911 this had risen to 14.0 per cent. Similarly, Professional Occupations rose from 2.1 to 9.1 per cent, reflecting mostly the growing army of teachers and nurses. Moreover, women's employment in this sector was increasing at a much faster rate than for England. These were the bonanza years for Welsh mining, but the proportion of employed women engaged in Mines and Quarries fell consistently from a low starting point in 1851 (1.6 per cent) to total insignificance in 1911 (0.1 per cent).

Naturally, the Welsh experience was itself far from homogeneous as can perhaps be briefly illustrated by comparing industrial Glamorgan with rural Cardigan. The first, and perhaps most striking point is that the overall participation rate was (except in 1851) much higher in Cardigan than in Glamorgan. From 1861 to 1911 from six to ten per cent more of the total female population over the age of ten was in paid employment in Cardigan than in Glamorgan[3] and this gap tended to widen towards the end of this period. In each county the participation rate tended to rise from 1851 to 1871, fall in 1881, rise to a peak in 1891 and then fall to 1911. By 1911 only about one in five of the female population over ten years old was in paid occupation in Glamorgan, compared to just under one in three in Cardigan. If some allowance were made for the excluded group of wives assisting in their husbands' occupation the result would be two-fold: it would greatly increase the gap between the female participation in Cardigan and Glamorgan as the latter would be little affected by such an adjustment; and it would perceptibly—perhaps even

TABLE 2: FEMALE OCCUPATIONS, CARDIFF, SWANSEA, MERTHYR TYDFIL AND RHONDDA, 1851-1911

		NUMBER OF FEMALES IN OCCUPATION CLASSES[1] AS A PERCENTAGE OF TOTAL OCCUPIED[2]								Occupied[2] as a % total females aged 10 years & over	Total number of occupied females[2]
		Professional Occupations	Domestic Offices or Services	Food, Drink, Lodging, etc.	Dress	Mines & Quarries	Metals, Machines, etc.	Agriculture	Total Cols (i) - (vii)		
		(i)	(ii)	(iii)	(iv)	(v)	(vi)	(vii)	(viii)	(ix)	(x)
1851	(Cardiff	2.7	51.7	5.3	33.4	0.1	0.1	1.4	94.7	29.3	1,834
	(Swansea	3.6	47.1	8.7	31.1	0.2	0.1	1.9	92.7	27.6	3,402
	(Merthyr (Tydfil[3]	1.7	39.6	5.5	23.5	9.7	8.7	90.8	90.8	23.3	4,894
1861	(Cardiff	4.2	48.4	6.0	35.8	0.1	0.0	0.7	95.2	28.4	3,281
	(Swansea	4.0	44.2	9.4	31.8	0.3	1.9	1.4	93.0	29.5	4,628
	(Merthyr (Tydfil[3]	2.6	37.6	5.9	27.4	6.2	9.6	1.6	90.9	22.3	6,391
1871[4]											
1881	(Cardiff	5.9	59.3	5.6	20.4	0.0	0.1	0.2	91.5	26.6	7,923
	(Swansea	6.1	56.2	7.4	21.2	0.1	3.4	0.2	94.6	28.2	6,913
	(Merthyr (Tydfil	n.a.	n.a.	n.a.	n.a.	n.a.	n.a.	n.a.	n.a.	n.a.	n.a.
	(Rhondda	5.6	59.9	4.5	23.0	3.7	0.1	0.2	97.0	16.8	2,846
1891	(Cardiff	7.6	52.0	9.9	20.3	0.0	0.2	0.2	90.2	26.6	12,488
	(Swansea	6.7	47.8	9.3	21.0	0.1	7.8	0.1	92.8	29.8	10,167
	(Merthyr (Tydfil	6.0	46.5	16.5	19.3	2.1	0.8	0.3	91.5	28.3	5,714
	(Rhondda	5.8	44.6	22.1	23.4	0.8	0.0	0.1	96.8	23.6	6,359
1901	(Cardiff	9.4	46.2	10.9	19.3	0.1	0.2	0.1	86.2	24.2	15,160
	(Swansea	9.1	44.9	10.1	21.3	0.0	4.1	0.1	89.6	24.0	8,999
	(Merthyr (Tydfil	11.3	44.2	10.3	22.0	0.8	0.4	0.2	89.2	18.4	4,351
	(Rhondda	11.4	43.6	7.5	30.2	0.1	0.1	0.1	93.0	14.4	5,259
1911	(Cardiff	9.5	39.3	15.5	17.7	0.2	0.3	0.1	82.6	26.9	19,481
	(Swansea	9.3	37.3	14.5	19.0	0.2	4.8	0.1	85.2	24.1	10,676
	(Merthyr (Tydfil	12.0	40.5	13.9	19.3	0.3	0.2	0.7	86.9	18.0	5,032
	(Rhondda	12.4	40.6	14.2	23.0	0.0	0.1	0.2	90.5	14.4	7,105

NOTES:

1 and 2. See Table 1, f.n. 1 - 2.

3. Parliamentary Borough - a much larger area than the administrative areas used in subsequent censuses.

4. Census tables for 1871 only give occupations at local level for age twenty and over.

substantially—increase the overall participation rate for Cardigan.

The similarities and differences in the distribution of this occupied population are also interesting. In both the industrial and the rural county most women were employed in Domestic Service and in Dress. In Glamorgan, however, this was true of each census year, whereas in Cardigan Agriculture was the biggest single source of female employment in 1851 and the second biggest (to Domestic Service) in 1861. But perhaps the more surprising fact about the Cardigan pattern was not the early discrepancies but that from 1871 onwards Agriculture has slipped to the third largest group. In each county, too, the proportion of women occupied in Agriculture (again the reminder is necessary that unpaid farmers' relatives are not included) tended to decline. But there was still a crucial difference between them: by 1911 the proportion in Glamorgan (0.7 per cent) had become negligible, but in Cardigan Agriculture still accounts for a significant (11.0 per cent) part of female employment.

The other significant shift in the relative importance of the different occupational groups was the upward march of Professional Occupations. This was a feature common to both counties, but much more pronounced in Glamorgan. In 1851 Professional Occupations was the smallest of the seven selected groups (2.3 per cent); by 1911 it occupied the mid-position with 10.3 per cent. In Cardigan the comparable figures were 0.7 per cent in 1851 and 5.6 per cent in 1911. On a smaller scale there was also in Glamorgan the decline (from what was already an initially low level) of women's employment in Mines and Quarries and in Metals and Machines. In Cardigan these two groups were always insignificant.

Women's work in these two counties followed the apparently general nineteenth century pattern of being concentrated into a narrow range of occupational groups. But whereas, in Glamorgan, the dominance was exercised simply by the two groups of Domestic Service and Dress, in Cardigan there was rather more spread in that the population of women occupied in Agriculture (even without including farmers' relatives) was always as, or nearly as, large as the population in Dress. Thus instead of the two dominating groups as in Glamorgan, there were really three such groups in Cardigan. This, and the fact that the overall participation rate was substantially higher in the rural county constitute the major points of comparison.

Within Glamorgan an attempt was made to pin-point more particular differences by examining the corresponding material on women's occupations for four urban areas—Cardiff, Swansea, Merthyr Tydfil and Rhondda. The first two of these were major ports and commercial centres servicing their industrial hinter-lands (although Swansea was actually in the coalfield and had a long tradition of non-ferrous metal manufacturing); the others were heavily engaged in the direct exploitation of the coalfield—Merthyr as a (declining) iron and coal producer, the Rhondda as the most vigorous coal-producing region.

There were problems specific to this part of the exercise. For example, the census provides no separate occupational figures for the Rhondda before 1881, in which year Merthyr is excluded. For 1871 there are no comparable figures for any of these towns as the census only gave a sub-county break-down for those aged twenty and over. These constraints are, however, annoying rather than crippling. They certainly do not obscure the basic fact that the female participation rate in all these towns was consistently low, nor do they disguise the clear downward trend in this ratio.

The last point to emerge at this overall level is that the participation rate in the valley towns was persistently lower than in the commercial centres. Thus the picture which emerges is one in which the employment opportunities for women in these four urban centres of industrial Glamorgan were relatively low; that these limited opportunities were, moreover, tending to decline over time; and that the chances of female employment in the valleys were even more restricted.

For those women who were employed the occupational distribution follows the same general pattern that has already been noted—most women were engaged in one of the two groups Domestic Service or Dress and of these the former was normally much the more important (from 1881 on there were more than twice as many engaged in Domestic Service as in Dress). Moreover there is not much likelihood of any serious distortions being introduced in these cases by the exclusion of unpaid farmers' relatives and assisting wives: Agriculture was, even in 1851, a very small source of employment. The more notable feature was the growth in the relative importance of the next two groups—Food, Drink and Lodgings; and Professional Occupations. In 1851 these had been relatively insignificant in these towns (in Cardiff, for example, 85 per cent of all occupied women were in the two dominant occupational groups); but by 1911 Food etc. and Professions had grown sufficiently to make it plausible to talk of women's employment being now spread over four groups instead of being concentrated in two. The rise of these two additional groups was a development common to all four centres: indeed, it is initially surprising to find that by 1911 the proportion of women engaged in Professional occupations was higher in Merthyr Tydfil (12.0) and Rhondda (12.4) than in Cardiff (9.5) and Swansea (9.3).

The only other significant distribution changes relate to Mines and Metals. In 1851 these provided respectively 9.7 and 8.7 per cent of total women's employment in Merthyr where they clearly constituted an important source of work. But by 1911 these two occupational groups between them only account for half of one per cent of total women's employment. No figures are available for the Rhondda until 1881 when although Metals etc. were insignificant Mines and Quarries provided 3.7 per cent of women's employment but this fell rapidly to zero in 1911. Neither group attained any significance at all in Cardiff (it is mildly surprising that the shifting of the Dowlais iron works to Cardiff in the 1890s seemed to have no perceptible impact on the employment of women in Metals, etc.); whilst Swansea, despite its long tradition, only employed noticeable numbers in Metals from 1881 onwards, peaking in 1891, falling and then levelling out in 1901 and 1911—a brief activity which seems to have been associated with the development of tinplate.

It would be informative to be able to distinguish the marital status of working women. Unfortunately there are severe constraints on the extent to which this can be done. The census for 1911 is the only one which breaks down the occupational data on women into the three separate groups of single, married and widowed (the absence of a divorced category is—statistically at least—of no significance in this context before 1914). The broad results are indicated in Table 3. As would be expected (Table 3A) in each of the areas considered most of the women who were working were single, the range being from three-quarters (in Cardigan) to four-fifths (in Glamorgan and Swansea). There is much more variation in the way the remainder of the occupied women were divided between those who were married and those who were widowed. The main contrast

TABLE 3

	A. Marital Status as a % Total Occupied, (1) 1911			B. Occupied(1) as % in Marital Group, 1911			
	Unmarried	Married	Widowed	Total Occupied	Unmarried	Married	Widowed
England	77.1	[1]14.4	8.5	32.8	54.6	10.6	30.2
Wales	78.8	10.4	10.8	22.2	39.0	5.0	27.7
Glamorgan	80.3	10.9	8.7	20.2	37.6	4.4	22.8
Cardigan	75.4	8.8	15.8	29.6	41.8	7.5	38.9
Cardiff	80.3	10.8	8.9	26.9	47.3	6.3	27.9
Swansea	80.8	9.3	9.9	24.1	43.9	4.8	25.4
Merthyr Tydfil	79.1	11.2	9.7	18.0	34.4	4.0	20.8
Rhondda	77.9	15.2	6.9	14.4	28.8	4.0	15.2

1. Excludes assisting relatives of Farmers and Graziers.

here is between Cardigan (8.8 per cent married and 15.8 per cent widowed) and Rhondda (15.2 per cent married and 6.9 per cent widowed). More generally these two categories were proportionately of equal importance for Wales as a whole, whereas in England married women formed a substantially larger part of the total female labour than did widows (14.4 per cent to 8.5 per cent).

Table 3A shows what proportion, of the total number of occupied women, were single, married and widowed. Table 3B shows what percentage of each group (total, single, married, widowed) were working: it gives a separate participation rate for each marital group. Several striking features emerge. First, in none of the various geographical groupings used for Wales does the participation rate for single women approach the average ratio for England as a whole. So not only were the chances of single women getting work less in Wales than in England, but this was true in industrial Wales and rural Wales, at the heart of the coalfield and in the commercial ports and cities. The same was not true for widows: the proportion of widows gainfully occupied was much higher in Cardigan (38.9 per cent) than for England (30.2 per cent), Wales (27.7 per cent) or any other of the parts of Wales used in this study. The striking aspect here was the exceptionally low participation rates for widows in the two coalfield districts of Merthyr (20.8) and Rhondda (15.2). Perhaps this simply reflected the demographic peculiarity of the coalfield where, in contrast to England and Wales, generally, there was a heavy preponderance of males (130 to every 100 women in the Rhondda) so that widows were so to speak short-lived. The final point is that the chances of married women working in Wales were markedly less than in England: in England one in ten was gainfully employed, in Wales one in twenty. For Merthyr and the Rhondda this fell still further to one in twenty-five which was, as the Census report pointed out, the lowest participation rate for married women in the whole of Britain. Thus the Rhondda provided a curious case where married women formed an unusually high proportion of the total occupied female workforce, but where the participation rate amongst married women was exceptionally low.

Finally, we should perhaps bring together a few of the main findings and—although it is not the intention to offer explanations—make a few tentative suggestions about the causes of the occupational patterns revealed. The fact that the female participation rate was persistently lower in Wales than in England is clearly important for any attempt to understand or comment upon women's work in Wales during this period. The fact of the lower participation rate is important in itself, even apart from the reasons for the lower rate. Part of the reason may, in any event, be connected to cultural differences beyond the scope of the present article. However, in so far as the explanation lies within the different occupational structures, the most likely candidate would seem to be that Wales had a lower participation rate because it was more rural than England, implying that industrialisation increased the opportunities for part employment for women.

Such an explanation and such an implication would however, have to confront another of the broad findings: namely, that the participation rate for Glamorgan was always less than in Cardigan and, moreover, that this discrepancy tended to increase over time. Here the implication would seem to be—in direct contradiction to the comparison between Wales and England—that employment opportunities were greater in agricultural areas than in industrial districts. It may be that the apparent contradiction is resolved by the peculiar nature of the industrial process in Glamorgan. The industrial structure of Glamorgan was, as an examination of the occupational structure for men starkly reveals,[4] to an extraordinary extent dominated by coal-mining. As a result there were untypically few industrial employment opportunities for women: the employment of women below ground was statutorily prohibited, coal villages offered little demand for other occupation, and the household demands on women—with different shifts and no pit-head baths—in any event restricted their ability to take up paid employment outside the home. It may, therefore, be the peculiar industrial structure of Glamorgan which accounts for its lower female participation rate than rural Cardigan. Some confirmation of this is, moreover, contained in a further finding of the study: within Glamorgan the participation rate in the coalmining valleys (Merthyr and, especially, Rhondda) was lower than in the commercial ports of Cardiff and Swansea. Indeed, one of the most striking findings is that by the beginning of the twentieth century only 14 per cent of females over the age of ten were working in the Rhondda district. That is, whilst in England one woman in every three was gainfully occupied, in the Rhondda only one woman in every seven was so employed.

The fact of fewer opportunities for women's employment perhaps also helps to explain why the occupational distribution of this employment was more concentrated in Wales than in England. It needs, of course, to be borne in mind that the concentration of women's employment into a small number of occupational groups was a general phenomenon. In England as well as in Wales, in Cardigan as well as in Glamorgan, in Rhondda as well as in Cardiff, the overwhelming majority of working women were concentrated into just two or three of the 22 occupational groups used in the census. Thus consideration of greater concentration in Wales has to be related to that broad background. None the less it is important to notice that the proportion of the total occupied women who were employed in Domestic Service (everywhere the largest single group) was always at least ten per cent higher in Wales than in England. It seems at least plausible that this mostly reflected fewer alternative occupational possibilities in Wales as already suggested by a lower overall participation rate.

Explanations are clearly elusive even at the aggregate level: it is perhaps even more difficult to account for changes between the particular occupational groups. There are exceptions. No doubt the consistently higher proportion of women in Agriculture in Wales as compared to England (and in Cardigan as compared to Glamorgan) is obvious enough—or, at least, is expected, and so is the very large decline in that proportion (from 29.3 per cent in Wales in 1851 to 3.6 per cent in 1911). It is not so obvious why the (normally increasing) proportion engaged in the Food, Drink and Lodgings group should be higher in Wales than in England. Nor is it immediately clear why the proportion of the total occupied women who were engaged in Professional services should have risen much faster in Wales than in England (in 1851 this proportion was twice as high in England as in Wales, by 1911 the proportion in Wales was a little higher than in England). Moreover, by 1911 the proportion of women in Professional Services was twice as high in Glamorgan as in Cardigan, and, within Glamorgan, was significantly higher in the valleys than in the commercial centres. There is clearly much still to investigate.

(This paper was originally written with Dot Jones and published in *Llafur*, 3,3,1982, pp.20-33. Since that time the growth in interest in women's history has led to a large number of publications: the best over-view and starting-point is provided by the series of essays collected in John, A. (ed.), *Our Mother's Land: chapters in Welsh Women's History, 1830-1939*, University of Wales, 1991. The counties are throughout referred to in their pre-1974 form.)

Notes

[1]The seven groups are: Domestic Offices or Services: Dress; Agriculture; Food, Drink and Lodging; Professional; Metals, Machines, etc.; and Mines and Quarries. The last two have been included because, although they are of minor significance for Wales as a whole, they are of some interest for Glamorgan.

[2]It would, however, be misleading to conclude from this that the concentration of female employment was necessarily lower in England: the particular seven groups were chosen because they are most pertinent to the Welsh experience, but if the two groups of Metals, and Mines and Quarries were excluded and replaced by Textiles, the English concentration in the resultant six groups would be nearly as high as in Wales.

[3]If anything this under-states the difference because our exclusion of farmers' relatives and wives at home assisting their husbands in their employment tends to affect a greater proportion of the total female population in rural areas than in industrial districts. On the other hand the gap between the higher English participation rate and the lower Welsh rate would be partly closed if this factor were taken into account.

[4]L.J. Williams and T. Boyns, 'Occupations in Wales, 1851-1971', *Bull. of Econ. Res.*, 1977.

4. FIGURES IN WELSH HISTORY[1]

The aim of the paper is to plead a case for a wider use of statistics in the study of Welsh history, to ask that there should be more figures, and that they should be given a more prominent place, in Welsh history. To do so it will be necessary, in part, to make a discourse on method: but the sortie into methodology will be low-level and low-key. Perhaps this simply reflects a widespread reluctance amongst historians to ask themselves at all closely or precisely just what it is that they do in case such introspection might lead them to doubt the value of what might be contained in the answers.

First, in order to be sure that the exercise is more than one of tilting at windmills, it has to be asked: is there a problem? Do we suffer from a lack of quantification in Welsh history? On this issue, an affirmative answer can be given with some confidence since the evidence fills and continues to fill our book-shelves. Of course, this is not meant to stand as a major criticism of recent writings on the history of Wales. On the contrary one gratefully accepts the continued flow of major authoritative works from Dr. (now Professor and Principal) K.O. Morgan and rejoices in the group of brilliant young scholars who have recently been casting bright shafts of insight along the dim tunnels of our past. It is none the less possible to notice and to regret that in one aspect of their craft (the use of figures) many of our most respected and glittering practitioners are, relatively, under-developed. Thus K.O. Morgan's towering and otherwise awesomely comprehensive work, *Rebirth of a Nation, Wales 1880-1980*, contains no tables and no graphs; there is just one graph in Merfyn Jones' brilliant, innovative book on *The North Wales Quarrymen, 1874-1922*; the exciting, evocative and substantial history of *The Fed* by David Smith and Hywel Francis has only one table in the text (relating to post-1949) and one in the appendix (usefully giving coal-mining output and manpower since 1890, but no one place gives a chronological record of the membership of the union); and the two leading historical journals—*Llafur* and *Welsh History Review*—contain only rare excursions into quantification.

If it is conceded that there has been some quantitative neglect, the more difficult question then arises of why this should be so. Why has the recent outburst of historical talent in Wales developed this one collective blind-spot? The suggestion is that a substantial part of the explanation can be found under two broad headings: availability and attitudes.

By the first it is meant to imply that statistics have been neglected because of their relative lack of availability. Except for very recent times there are no easily-accessible official sources that the hard-pressed historian can run to whenever he wants a statistical series. In general it is simply not possible to get any particular series by a quick visit to the nearest reference library. And since, quite reasonably, the statistics are not the central concern of most historians inaccessibility makes for inattention. The publication of a collection of the presently widely-scattered material (which it is hoped will soon be provided[2]) would ease the problem, but it would be a delusion to think that such a collection could provide a complete cure. Some of the reasons for this relate to the particular problems and limitations attached to such a compilation for Wales and will be glanced at later. More generally, however, any such collection can only provide a partial solution because it would necessarily be selective. The recurring basic needs can be met, but beyond that each generation of historians has its own questions and until these are formulated it is impossible to know precisely what statistical material will be useful for resolving them. A case in point would be provided by the recent upsurge of interest in the part played by women in history.

The part played by attitudes may be even more fundamental. Suppose, for example, that the figures were reasonably available, can we be sure that the thrusting young historians would swoop down on them like starlings on winter crumbs? Any answer to this would have to take note of the existence of a hesitancy, a suspicion, a reluctance on the part of many Welsh historians to give a positive response to any proposal that quantifications should be given more weight. Such attitudes seem, perhaps strangely, to be especially prevalent amongst Welsh social historians apparently reflecting a fear that fiddling with figures will somehow neuter the human values and passions with which they are rightly concerned. It is a mistaken attitude. It would be difficult, for example, to imagine passion, outrage, injustice being more economically conveyed than in the *Rhondda Leader* headline after the courts had imposed their derisory fines on the colliery company and officials after 439 miners had been killed in the Senghenydd disaster of 1913: 'Miners lives at 1s. 1.1/4d.(5.1/2p.) each!' But, mistaken or not, there is no doubt that the attitude exists. It is an attitude which partly arises out of the kind of training received by most Welsh historians. The complaint is not that this is basically literary: the problem is that the training is often anti-numerical. The resultant tendency to parade a supposed inability to manipulate figures as a positive virtue is, of course, simply reflecting more general social values.

A very conscious effort will be required if such attitudes are to be shifted. It should be emphasised, however, that it is not a vast shift which is required, or even which is desirable. The aim should not be to produce a new breed who would want to busy themselves counting the trees in order to avoid seeing the wood. At present such a possibility seems to be remote: at present it could be more plausibly argued that the greater danger is of an intoxication with words. This too can be a distraction from the main business: coining phrases can debase the currency.

Attitudes may well be the major problem, but availability is the prior problem. That is to say, it is a pre-requisite for any shift in attitudes that the statistics should be available. What problems are there in the way of providing statistics for Wales? The question needs to be asked because there are difficulties which are peculiar to Wales, difficulties which help to account for the undoubted fact that the statistics which are available for Wales are fewer (and less accessible) than those available for Great Britain (or the United Kingdom) or Scotland or Ireland.

Much of the reason for this can be conveyed by asking the simple question: does Wales exist? or, more precisely for our purposes, did Wales exist? In the context of explaining a paucity of statistics the existence of Wales becomes a serious question. Most figures relevant to an economy and a society relate to a particular time and a particular place. For some of these purposes—like the collection of population figures—Wales forms as natural a geographical unit as England or Scotland. There are, however, many other categories for which Wales does not (or did not) form the obvious basis for the collection of statistics. The implication and significance of this can perhaps be made plainer by giving brief consideration to two further questions: why are statistics collected? and what use is to be made of them?

An exhaustive answer to the first of these queries would have to range over a variety of factors, including individual eccentricity and official inertia. But most figures are collected because some person or institution wishes to extend knowledge of the empirical situation as an aid to understanding; or as a basis for taking decisions; or as a means of advocating a particular policy or belief. Again, the description is far from exhaustive but the essential, simple point is clear enough: most statistics are not collected for their own sake but to meet a separate need or problem. And—in the past, at least—these problems were often not perceived as Welsh problems or as having an explicit Welsh dimension. The absence of such a concern was quite general but it was probably less marked in demographic and social issues (where the cultural differences separating Wales and the Welsh from the rest of Britain was a matter of more or less significance) than it was in economic issues. If no-one was being asked or required to answer questions, or make decisions, about the railways of *Wales*, or the *Welsh* iron industry or the *Welsh* coal industry then it was unlikely that figures would be collected under these heads. In some cases, this does not prevent us from now constructing figures relating to the past and on a basis of Wales. Figures were, for example, collected at the time about the iron (or the coal) industry of South Wales, and of the iron (or the coal) industry of North Wales. And it is obviously a relatively simple task now to add these together to give a total for Wales.

Aggregation of that sort, however, raises the second issue of the use to be made of the statistics. In some cases the total reached in this indirect way is useful and significant. Thus several of the Welsh totals for religious denominations can only be obtained by aggregating the figures for county associations or those for each separate diocese. And it is obviously helpful and historically meaningful to know, say, the number of members of the established Church in Wales at any given period. But there are also dangers, especially in dealing with some of the economic sectors. To be able to add up the separate figures for South Wales and North Wales does not necessarily provide—except in the most literal and superficial sense—a Welsh figure. It is easy to convince oneself, for example, that the result of an aggregation process of this type for the iron industry (or the coal industry) creates a Welsh iron industry (or a Welsh coal industry). And no doubt this aggregate is pertinent for some purposes: if, for example, the occupational structure of Wales is being investigated then knowledge of the total number of miners in Wales becomes vital. For many other purposes, however, it is necessary to keep in mind the economic realities of the time. There was very little contact between the nineteenth century coal industries of North and South Wales. They produced for different markets. North Wales found its natural links with the inland Midland districts of the English federation; South Wales had more in common with Northumberland and Durham, areas which also looked abroad for a substantial part of their market. Neither saw Wales as the relevant economic unit: but it is easy to forget this when faced by a table giving totals for 'the Welsh coal industry'. Of course, the industries, or sectional interests within them, worked in association from time to time but usually only as part of a body wider than Wales. Indeed, it is difficult to think of any occasion on which the coal industries of North and South Wales acted together and without any other areas being involved. In large measure, of course, this reflected political as well as economic realities. The object of association was often to influence government legislation or policy and the operational unit for such purposes was Britain. Industrial organisations and associations tended to reflect this. Moreover, the regional organisation of such bodies rarely saw Wales as a natural unit—either North and South Wales appeared separately or they were each (separately) included with a region which spilled over into England ('the South-West', for example, or 'the North-West').

Most of the other issues arising under the first general heading—problems encountered in attempting to collect figures relating to Wales—are more mundane and can be dealt with more summarily. Three categories can be singled out for brief comment: the problems of tracing the sources; the problems of ensuring consistency; and the problem of ensuring that the figures do relate to Wales.

Government publications are the major single source for any compilation. Often, however, such publications followed the deeply-entrenched tendency for administrators (and others) to lump Wales in with England. There are figures for the United Kingdom; and Scotland and Ireland are usually separately designated. But the historical investigator for Wales is perpetually balked by the irritating phenomenon of 'England and Wales'. Thus in many cases a figure for Wales had to be sought elsewhere or reconstructed for each year from detailed county figures (a tiresome process but one which normally solved the Monmouthshire problem which in general turns out to be much less troublesome than might be expected).

The frequent necessity to construct a series year by year makes the consistency problem—a general difficulty with any exercise of this kind—especially acute for Wales. For example, government statistics for the U.K. frequently appear not just in the publication for that particular year, but each annual publication gives the U.K. total over a series of years allowing later revisions and improvements to be consistently incorporated. Such revisions were, however, rarely given at the level of detail from which the figures for Wales were constructed. In some cases the figures are not given on a basis, such as counties, which could be readily (if laboriously) built up to a total for Wales. The areas of transport and public utilities were especially prone to this difficulty which can be quickly illustrated by the example of railways. The railways were required by statute to provide extensive statistical information which is incorporated into the weighty annual publication, *Railway Returns*. These give a total for 'England and Wales'. Beyond this, however, the only disaggregation is by company arranged in alphabetical order. Thus any attempt to compile figures for Wales involves, *for each year*, going through a complicated and time-consuming process. First, the companies which provided rail facilities wholly or partially within Wales have to be identified; then, for those companies whose lines were not confined to Wales, some decision has to be made about the proportion of their mileage, traffic, revenues and costs which was attributable to Wales; and, finally, summing up the computed totals for the relevant companies. Each step is labour-intensive, error-prone and—above all—subject to much conceptual ambiguity.

The limitations of the statistics are both general and specific. The general limitations (beyond those which have already been mentioned) mostly take the form of various gaps and omissions. The specific limitations relate mostly to the reliability of a particular set of figures. We can begin with some examples of omissions.

The most serious category of omissions relates to entire topics which have to be left out. For some of these the information is not available, and is not going to be available. The volume and make-up of Welsh trade with England is not a topic for which we can hope to find any reasonably exact, securely-based quantitative evidence. Statistics on many important issues, however, cannot readily be provided even though the information is (notionally) available. A comprehensive index of prices would, for example, fall into this category. There is a substantial amount of information on prices scattered about in estate and business records together with the detailed reports of local markets contained in many nineteenth century newspapers. The systematic collection and processing of this material would, however, constitute a major research project. The possibilities are indicated by the excellent work of Dr. David Howell on agricultural prices. A similar situation exists over wages in that any kind of comprehensive index running over a substantial period of time awaits some gruelling quarrying at the basic sources. Nonetheless the position over wages is a little easier in that there is already available quite good material on wage-rates (though not earnings) in coal-mining, and some weaker, but long-run data for agriculture. And these were the two sectors of overwhelming dominance in pre-1914 Wales.

A comparable limitation in terms of omission derives from the comparatively late starting date for many of the series. Even where figures were collected on a county basis, which makes possible the construction of a figure for Wales, the mid-nineteenth century is the earliest at which most Welsh series can be started. But many others had to wait still longer before there was any collection of information for Wales. Which, to echo an earlier point, meant that there had to be some functional or administrative or political reason for treating Wales as a unit. Regional policy, which provides one such reason, only begins to emerge in the 1930s. And the awareness of a separate Welsh national consciousness has waxed and waned, even within Wales, and mostly failed until recently to percolate through to Whitehall on any reasonably persistent basis. Where and when it did, as with the setting up of the separate Welsh department in the Board of Education in 1906, there were substantial statistical gains.

A second group of limitations relates to reliability and needs to be judged case by case. The problems are, therefore, best illustrated by looking at them as they relate to a particular sector. The statistics on religion have been selected for this purpose because they raise such issues most persistently and starkly.

If it is natural to associate religion with doubt, it is inescapable to surround any figures on religion with substantial doubts about their meaning and accuracy. These represent serious limitations but, more encouragingly, there is a considerable—and surprising—bulk of information which is available. Nor are its shortcomings necessarily more marked than those of other sources which have been used to comment on the religious history of Wales. The shortcomings are possibly more obvious, but that may be a positive advantage if it alerts scholars to the due caution needed in using such material.

Most of the difficulties are inherent in the subject and need no lengthy elaboration. It is not possible to reduce the depth of religious conviction or enthusiasm to a statistical measure—and certainly not to cover the population at large over any lengthy period of the past. And even indirect and imperfect proxies—like the membership of organised religious bodies—run into major conceptual and definitional problems. The intractable, but fundamental, issue of why people belonged to a particular church or chapel is—statistically—beyond redemption, and most of the question of measuring exactly who belonged (in terms of sex, age, social class, location, etc.) is beyond even faith, and has to be similarly abandoned. But even the simpler issues of how many belonged and to which organisation, bristle with difficulties. What does it mean to belong?

For example in the case of the established Church (from 1920 the Church in Wales) there is a variety of possible indicators: the number of baptisms or confirmations or communicants. Baptisms, however, is obviously inappropriate since there is no way of knowing how many of these (mainly) infants were later involved in the Church at all: for many their penetration of the Church ended after this one involuntary excursion to the font. Moreover, since (given its parochial, rather than the congregational, basis) the Church always acted in a residual capacity, baptisms would be more closely correlated with changes in the birth rate than with religious beliefs. Confirmations are a much better indicator in that they eliminate this residual element: candidates for confirmation necessarily attended church and received some instruction in its beliefs. Confirmation, however, shares one basic disability with baptism as a measure of membership: they each relate to a single act (mostly performed in infancy or childhood) which has no necessary connection with later religious beliefs or actions. The use of the number of Easter communicants is undoubtedly the best of these three indicators. It relates to a number of people, mostly adults, who are actually present at a particular occasion in each year. None the less—even apart from the problems of getting the number right—it both under-states and over-states Church membership. It under-states the number because not all communicants, not even all reasonably regular communicants will be present on the particular day (and, of course, not all the congregation actually present will necessarily choose, or be eligible, to take communion). It over-states the membership because it is reasonably certain that many more attend communion at Easter than on any other occasion, and for many who are then present it will be their only (or nearly their only) attendance for the year. But does membership depend on attendance?

Similar conceptual problems arise when trying to determine the numbers who belonged to the various nonconformist denominations. Indeed, the concept of a denomination is itself open to difficulties. There were, for example, various kinds of Baptist and it is not always easy to determine the exact sense in which the term is being used in any particular context. Fortunately, the definition of denominations is not intractable mainly because of two basic considerations. In the first place the denominational pattern of nonconformity in Wales has been relatively simple and has avoided the sectarian profusion which flourished in parts of England. Secondly, most of the figures on denominations can be obtained from the handbooks or yearbooks of the denominations themselves and it seems reasonable to assume that the denominations would know well enough which particular congregations would properly fall within their aegis. In any event, only the major bodies were considered.

But if the concept of a denomination might become blurred, especially around the edges, that of membership was—on the face of it, at least—much more straightforward. The congregation was the basis of the chapel and the congregation could reasonably be expected to know its own members, especially as membership universally involved payment. There were still areas of uncertainty. No doubt, for example, there was variation in the promptitude with which lapsed members were crossed off. Normally, too, the membership payment (which, of course, was not a uniform amount and often took the form of a pew rent) covered the member's immediate family, but this too was an obvious source for a lack of homogeneity in treatment. The major difficulty, however, related to the 'hearers' or 'adherents'. These were the people who, whilst not formally becoming members, attended a chapel (or chapels)—often very regularly. Although they raise statistical problems of various kinds (they could, for example, in some cases be wrongly returned as members) the over-riding one is simply that most congregations and denominations did not regularly record them. But for some purposes—like judging the extent of nonconformist influence—it is vital to know their numbers. The treatment of this substantial outer fringe of dissent, moreover, accounts for much of the apparent discrepancy between the numbers of members returned by the denominations and the number of worshippers returned at the religious census of 1851, where attendance not membership was being counted. 'Adherents' cannot lightly be ignored, especially as their numbers were large, probably as large as the number of members; but the Royal Commission of 1910 was defeated in its attempt to get any reasonable uniformity into the collection of statistics about adherents.[3]

Almost every attempt to classify religious statistics involves similar definitional problems. The distinction between a church and a chapel is, for example, not easy to maintain. Essentially a chapel might be defined as a place of worship and a church as a body of people. But even if—where it was necessary—reporters were instructed, and were able, to keep this in mind, problems still arise over branch churches, mission stations and schoolrooms. In addition to the various conceptual problems, the methods by which the statistics were collected form an obvious possible source of error. In the case of the Church the figures originated with the parish priest and were sent to the diocesan authorities: in the case of the nonconformist denominations the minister of a particular congregation provided the figures for the county association or equivalent body. The aggregation process clearly provides a source of possible errors. On the other hand, as far as one can judge the response-rate of ministers and priests to these enquiries seems to have been very high. The diocesan figures, for example, include the number of parishes from which returns were obtained and the absentees could only have been a handful out of several hundreds, and for the small number of non-responders the practice was simply to include their figures for the previous year. A more likely source of uncertainty was that—given the possible conceptual confusions which have already been briefly indicated—some differences in the interpretation of what was needed was likely. At all events, it is clear that figures based on such sources and compiled in such ways need to be used with care.

What uses can be made of such figures as can be collected? At one level, of course, statistics are simply a form of information about the past. In this respect they are much like other forms of historical information—like letters or memoirs or building plans or blue books—and need to be subjected to the normal kinds of tests used by historians to establish their dependability as evidence. But so straightforward a statement, though true enough as far as it goes, ignores some more or less inherent aspects of statistics which give them a more explosive potential.

The mere process of quantification, on anything more systematic than just the random scattering of a few figures, adds an extra dimension of summary and precision. A single graph or table can occasionally encapsulate a process which might otherwise require a long descriptive narrative. Figures can give exactitude to accounts which otherwise seem only impressionistic and may be misleading. The common historical practice of quoting a couple of (presumably typical) examples and then moving on to assert that 'many' or 'a lot' or 'most' follow this pattern which is thus asserted to be 'typical' or 'characteristic' or 'not infrequent' or 'common', conveys a blurred and—possibly—inconsistent picture (since a single historian describing a single situation may use all of these terms—or most of them, or more than them). If, instead it can be asserted that, say, 23 per cent conformed to the particular pattern under discussion this conveys a greater degree of precision to the reader whose response to and perception of the information is likely to be less ambiguous.

There is yet another consideration which lends additional power to the process of quantification. Scientific progress is properly—though sometimes excessively—associated with quantification. Many scientific concepts are as abstract and arbitrary as those used in other disciplines: but scientists have succeeded in making them operational largely by producing agreed means of measurement. There is a natural desire for workers in other fields, including history, to emulate the successes of science. And, so far as they attribute part of this success to an ability to measure and compute and calculate, workers in other fields are perhaps led to over-estimate the uses of quantification. Thus figures can acquire a cultural compulsion beyond their real advantages.

They can, but often they do not. This is partly for bad, but inescapable, reasons of cultural attitudes amongst historians. But it is also partly because of the very good reason that one of the most fundamental of the constraints on the use which can be made of statistics in historical studies is the simple fact that the statistics may not mean what they purport to mean. Part of the earlier discussion of the problems raised by religious statistics related to this issue, but the basic difficulty can be more explicitly stated. Any use of statistics carries with it a presupposition that it is possible and legitimate to categorise: that people and things and institutions can be grouped together in meaningful ways. For historical studies, however, it is often asserted that this presupposition runs into (at least) two formidable obstacles. Firstly, that the nature of the material (often its human nature), and of the concepts involved, defy useful categorisation: that the people (and things and institutions) fit into the boxes to which they are allocated only with varying degrees of discomfort. Secondly, that this more or less forcible categorisation is unnecessary because history is not about generalisations but has to maintain the emphasis on the uniqueness of events. Whilst each of these objections has some force they cannot in the end be sustained if only because neither categorisation nor generalisation is being introduced into history to suit the convenience of those who wish to make some use of statistics: both processes are already being widely practiced by historians.

Indeed, some of the most fruitful historical work of the last generation has depended on combining statistical analysis and manipulation with specific theories (mostly drawn from economics and sociology). This is a controversial development which is not dwelt upon here except to make the crucial point that without the figures Welsh historians do not even have the choice of whether or not to join in this game. Some consider that to be a desirable outcome, but even they must recognise that our statistical starvation cuts us off from saying anything useful and interesting about many basic bread-and-butter problems of Welsh history. For example, it has already been indicated that we know next to nothing about the course taken by wages and earnings or by prices in nineteenth century Wales. A consequence of this is that we cannot say what happened to real wages and hence to the standard of living. These matters are essential in themselves and an indispensable pre-requisite for tackling such questions as: at what stage did the general living standards of most of the people begin to improve? Of course, the statement that we know 'next to nothing' is an exaggeration, but what we do know is mostly dependant on information relating to England or to Britain as a whole. And that is of limited usefulness if one of the major concerns is to identify what, if anything, was distinctive about the Welsh experience.

Instances could be multiplied of problems which are presently beyond our grasp. In addition, however, it is often the case that lack of attention to the figures which are available can mean that historical problems are, in important respects, mis-specified or inadequately interpreted. For example, the history of the South Wales miners is usually (and rightly) seen as taking a great leap forward with the formation of the S.W.M.F. after the trauma of the six-month stoppage of 1898. The story of the decade or so up to 1914 is then generally seen as the conversion of this great body to militancy—how faint-hearted leaders (the Mabons and, soon, the Braces) were thrust forward or aside, and how the combines were confronted and concessions wrested from them. In all this, however, some other central features of the period are perhaps given less attention than they deserve. For example, the S.W.M.F. made enormous, sometimes desperate, efforts to win and hold members through such means as show-card days and the exertion of colourful, and often cruel and crude, community pressures on non-members. The available figures, however, both of union membership (less than half the total workforce in some of these years) and of the scale and pace of growth (an extra 100,000 miners were recruited into the South Wales industry during these years) make the pre-occupation with membership problems not merely understandable but an essential pre-requisite for any advances —industrial, social or political—that were made by the union.

The intention has been not to preach a gospel of quantification. It is well-recognised that much that is most significant in history will always elude the arithmetic, not just because the records are incomplete or deficient but because much is quite simply conceptually beyond quantification. But there is a message and it is hoped that Welsh historians for some small part of their time will go forth and multiply—and add, and subtract, and divide, and perhaps even correlate.

Notes

[1]This talk was given after the author had attempted to compile a series of Welsh historical statistics and its main aim was probably to justify so eccentric an activity. The title reflects such defensiveness: probably most people who heard it did so by accident having been misled into expecting something quite different.

[2]Since been provided as: John Williams, *Digest of Welsh Historical Statistics*, 2 vols., Welsh Office, 1985.

[3]*R.C. on the Church of England in Wales and Other Religious Bodies in Wales and Monmouthshire*, 1910, p. 137.

5. THE COALOWNERS

The concept of labour history has changed substantially over the last decade or two. In particular it has been opened out from a central concern with (at its widest) the development of the labour movement and, more usually, a concentration upon a small range of institutions dominated by the trade unions. The change has been very evident in Welsh labour history where *Llafur* (both the journal and the society) has been an innovating influence. The nature of the shift is too broad to be easily itemised and catalogued. However, perhaps something of its flavour can be indicated by suggesting that labour historians now take as their province the general social history of the (widely-defined) working class. It may be that the result has been to make the subject too amorphous for coherence, that in breaking out from the earlier tight institutional constraints it has overflowed into excessively broad pastures. Time will tell whether this intellectual imperialism can or should be maintained. But at present the subject seems comfortably able to span the elucidation of movements in the patterns of popular culture and recreation; the search into the particular processes and rhythm of work; and the effects of education (or religion or whatever) on the working class or—more usually perhaps—some particular group of workers or the working community. All this and much else is, of course, in addition to a continuing commitment to the traditional interest in strikes and unions and political activity.

Despite all this current permissiveness an essay on the coalowners may seem incongruous, seem to be stretching matters too far. Even in the present atmosphere the elasticity of the subject is not infinite. There are still topics, even in the mainstream concern with industrial strife, which are not tackled—perhaps because of some inherent feeling for the rightness of things. It might seem, for example, that the tendency to want to look at the full range of labour response and thus to reduce the emphasis on the history of union leaders and the sacrifices of the rank and file, would have given rise to some sympathetic accounts of blackleg labour. Sympathy, after all, need not imply approval. It is a matter of fact that most strikes of any consequence threw up a rash of blacklegs. And it is a demonstrably inadequate and false response to imply that these were only the dregs of the community, that they were all motivated by only the most sordid of considerations. It needs little imagination to see that, in some situations and at some times, the role of blackleg demanded substantial courage; nor to see that this courage could as well be fuelled by religious belief or moral principle or individualistic ideology as by simple greed. But it remains a theme without a literature.

At all events, it is concluded here that coalowners are a fit subject for labour history, and that the time is right at least to begin a reassessment. We are now into the second generation in South Wales which is growing up with only the N.C.B (or British Coal) as coalowner, more anonymous even than Amalgamated Anthracite but perhaps—though perhaps inadvertently—no less lethal. Of course, not even a contemporary child of the valleys—even of valleys where the soft-shoed and civil assassins of the N.C.B. have killed off all the pits—can escape the myth which surrounds the old coalowners and be unaware of their pride of place in the demonology of the region. Nor is it intended to dislodge them from the high depths of this position or to tear aside the myth—whatever the 'objective' findings there will remain a sense in which the myth incorporates the essential truth.

The possibilities for upward social mobility within South Wales before 1914 were generally constrained. They were constrained everywhere, of course. But—although the assertion at present rests only on impressionistic grounds and could not be convincingly substantiated—it seems reasonable to state that the difficulty of workers moving up the social ladder were greater in South Wales than in Britain as a whole. Indeed, it is likely that this was one of the contributory factors making for the extraordinarily strong development of working-class consciousness in the region: the more able and gifted amongst the workers were not siphoned off.

In part the limited opportunities for social mobility simply reflected the occupational structure of the region. In 1911, 40 per cent of the occupied males in Glamorgan were engaged in mines and quarries. The dominance of mining meant the dominance of a heavily labour-intensive industry with over 150,000 workers in this single county before 1914 and it also meant that, proportionately, the outlets for a shift of social class were meagre: in 1911 less than three per cent of the occupied male population of Glamorgan was classed as professional. It would be a mistake, however, to suggest too rigid a framework. There was bound to be substantial fluidity in a region as buoyant and expansive as was South Wales in the decades before the first world war. It is not difficult to find examples of Nonconformist ministers who started life as working miners or the sons of working miners—S.O. Davies would have fallen into this category if his basic radicalism had not been so pugnacious: Nonconformity demanded a high degree of conformity. But although the celebration of such social shifts serves as eloquent testimony of the values of the society, they were statistically insignificant. The recruitment of teachers from working-class backgrounds took place on a larger scale but it was still relatively unusual and, in 1914, still a relatively recent phenomenon. A more general experience was to become one of the clerks servicing the growing labour-intensive commercial sector of the region. And a still more natural progression was for a worker to move upwards within his own industry. In mining some few made the eventual jump to become managers, but the more normal progression was towards the positions of the lesser officials in the pit, the deputies and overmen who were generally recruited from the rank and file. It was this sector which, in terms of talent at least, perhaps most directly competed with the unions looking for their lodge secretaries, checkweighers, agents and delegates—and perhaps this element of competition has been too easily passed over in labour histories.

Thus although there was a fair degree of mobility most of it was severely constrained in social terms. In particular, it was overwhelmingly occupational mobility rather than social mobility, a shift of job rather than of class. Given the status and prestige which they carried with the general community a miner who became a preacher or a teacher had certainly altered his social standing, and if he became a manager his economic standing also shifted. But the more characteristic change was much more ambiguous. To become a low-level clerk represented a definite occupational shift but—though it might (and was often meant to) distance a man from manual work—it was hardly a decisive class change: and those who joined the ranks of the minor colliery officials often found themselves uncomfortably straddled across the social fence.

An even more constricted channel for social progress was that offered by becoming a coalowner. It was *not* the case that every miner carried in his jack-tin the keys of the board room any more than field marshal's batons realistically resided in knapsacks. There were cases, of course, and enthusiastic Victorian propagandists made an enormous mileage out of them. David Williams of Ynyscynon, who played an important part in the early development of the Aberdare valley, probably best fitted this mould. He had certainly been a working collier at one stage, as had William Thomas of Brynawel who had been a child working underground at the time of the 1842 report on the employment of women and children in mines. George Elliot would be a similar case, although his days as a pit-laddie were already well behind him before he came to South Wales in the early 1860s. Naturally none of them made a direct leap from collier to coalowner: they followed some variation on a progression up the colliery hierarchy—colliery clerk, surveyor, manager was the particular path of William Thomas, for example. Two broad features stand out: the cases which occurred were rare and they were early. Not many could thrust themselves along this path and those who did so successfully seem mostly to be confined to the pioneering days of the industry.

It needs to be noted that these comments about social mobility really refer only to a conception of coalowners as being confined to the leading group of men in the industry. If the definition was widened, some—indeterminate—modification would be required. By the end of the nineteenth century when most of the larger enterprises had become public companies it would probably be the case that amongst the list of shareholders—now occasionally numbering several hundred—would be found men holding five or ten pounds who were, or had been, working colliers. The point is of some importance simply because it highlights the basic problem of knowing who, at any time, were the coalowners. At the one extreme it could be plausibly argued that every shareholder in a coal-mining company was a coalowner. But this seems too wide. At the other extreme the term can denote just the handful of the most dominant—the David Davieses and the D.A. Thomases. But this seems too restrictive. In general this essay relates more nearly to the second group. That is, it has in mind the major proprietors in the various firms—not necessarily just one for each firm, but certainly not including all shareholders. The imprecision of this approach needs to be constantly borne in mind. It has a number of obvious immediate consequences. Thus it would be difficult—even for a particular moment of time—to attach a precise number to the group, still less to list their names. It makes even more difficult any effort to indicate the changing composition of the owners as a group. Moreover, it rests on an embarrassing dearth of detail about most aspects even of this limited group. On some of their personal characteristics—social and religious backgrounds —there is tolerable information; on others—their education—there is very little. On some aspects of their public activities—like involvement in politics—there is sporadic knowledge: but on others—particularly on the vital issue of how they conducted their businesses—these are still the dark ages.

The remainder of this essay aims to consider two aspects of the functions and activities of the coalowners. The first concerns the coalowners as economic actors: what economic function did they perform and how did they and others perceive their role? The second concerns their relation to the society around them.

In general views about coalowners have not been given anything more than ritualistic airings for over a generation, at which time they were rigidly and simplisticly polarised. On the one hand, the owners were viewed as men of vision, energy and enterprise. This was the broad line taken by such books as Elizabeth Phillip's *Pioneers of the Welsh*

Coalfield, a work first published in 1925 and which had, tellingly, previously appeared as a series of articles in the *Western Mail* then still looked upon as the organ of the South Wales coalowners. It was written in a generally eulogistic vein the overall flavour of which can be conveyed by a brief and reasonably typical quotation: 'one who had spent a life full of work and good deeds, and was well beloved as only a good and kind master could be'. On the other hand, the owners were portrayed as greedy and grasping individuals who appropriated an excessive proportion of the wealth created by the labour of the miners. What these conflicting judgements have in common is a tendency to concentrate upon the personal characters, the moral traits, of the coalowners. It is an approach which is unfruitful, unpromising and unsatisfactory: not just—or even mainly—because it is necessarily subjective, but because it is uninformative on the functions and relationships of the coalowners as a social group.

The economic characteristics and attitudes of the coalowners reflected and were conditioned by—amongst other things—two broad factors, the one relating to industry in general the other to a particular feature of the coal industry. Most businessmen right up to 1914 simply accepted the broad economic orthodoxies of the age. They accepted the inherent superiority of an economic system based on competitive private enterprise operating through a general market system which fixed the 'proper' price for all commodities (including labour) and which provided the signals on which owners of capital could base their decisions. It is true, of course, that few businessmen interpreted this model in too literal a sense: none the less, in so far as they consciously thought of general economic principles as opposed to the pragmatic problems of running their own concern, most businessmen from the mid-nineteenth century to the first world war subscribed to the liberal competitive model. Indeed, so dominant was this view of the way in which the economy did and should operate that it is difficult to imagine what else nineteenth century businessmen could turn to. It is, therefore, reasonable to presume that this view of the economy was part of the more or less unconscious attitudes of the South Wales coalowners—and, indeed, of most other groups in the region. (D.A. Thomas was certainly exceptional in his more explicit acceptance of the theory acquired by some reading of economics, and especially J.S. Mill, during his Cambridge days in the late 1870s.) All of which is obvious enough, but if it is kept in mind as a background factor it helps towards an understanding of the actions and policies of coalowners over such fundamental aspects as wages, prices and output. The attachment to the presumed inherently beneficial nature of the competitive market economy, however, went deeper than this: it provided the material basis and justification for the bourgeois social order based on property. We'll return to this point in a less generalised way later.

The second broad factor arose from the extent to which luck was an essential feature determining the degree of success obtained by any particular firm in the industry. The element of fortune does, of course, enter into all business enterprise but the contention here is that it was, for reasons inherent in the industry, likely to be a more marked and more significant factor in coal mining (and, indeed, most extractive industry) than it was for industrial and manufacturing undertakings in general. As time passed and the coalfield became more comprehensively worked the accumulation of detailed geological knowledge did, of course, reduce the area of uncertainty. None the less large doubts still remained, especially in a coalfield as geologically disturbed and varied as that of South Wales. It is in this sense that coal mining was to some degree a 'bingo' industry.

Against these two general conditioning factors—the operation of the competitive private enterprise system and the heightened significance of good fortune in the industry—what did the coalowners contribute as providers of capital, managers, entrepreneurs and potential monopolists?

They certainly provided the capital: that was, indeed, the only function which defined them as a group. It was fortunate (or was it?) that in the early years the amounts of capital required were not vast and could often be raised by local men such as the more successful of the shopocracy spawned by the growing iron industry. Thus the Merthyr and Aberdare draper David Davis was able to embark first on the tiny Rhigos level, which led eventually to the vast Ferndale taking; whilst the Cambrian Combine's foundations were laid when the Merthyr grocer, Samuel Thomas, opened a pit at Ysguborwen with his brother-in-law Thomas Joseph. Few undertakings were financed by a single man, although one man might come to dominate or symbolise the firm. David Davies of Llandinam bestrode the Ocean Coal company in this way but the capital for sinking the initial pits at Parc and Maendy in 1865-66 was also provided by Thomas Webb, John Riches, Morgan Joseph, Abraham Howell and Ezra Roberts. The smallness of the group was typical. In most companies throughout the pre-1914 period the majority of shares were held by about half a dozen main owners and often several of these belonged to the same family.

The process of capital formation need not be pursued in detail: in general there was little that was particularly distinctive about the experience of the South Wales coal industry in the second half of the nineteenth century. The banks played a relatively modest role, the expansion of the limited liability principle helped to widen the sources from which capital could be mobilised (though there were very few cases where money was raised by direct public subscription), and existing firms grew largely by ploughing back profits. There are, however, two aspects—related to what we have called the 'bingo' principle—which perhaps merit mention and would repay investigation. The first relates to the rate of return on capital. Recent work suggests that the level of profits before 1914 was relatively modest at around ten per cent. Given the nature of the evidence it would be easy enough to quibble about this finding, but its general validity seems well-founded. But it blurs the extent to which some companies fared much better than others. The differences seem unlikely to be explained simply by better management. More favourable conditions also played a part. Moreover, it was this possibility of much higher earnings which served to attract capital. On the whole people did not enter a high-risk industry like coal mining on the basis of earning a steady five per cent or so on their capital: they were lured by the possibility of much higher gains. The fluctuations were reinforced by wide variations over time. In the years of very high activity—the early 1870s, 1889-91, 1900-01—it was impossible rapidly to increase supply to meet the greater demand. As a result prices and profits soared. For the well placed firms this was a lucrative bonus, but for many of the more marginal undertakings it was their life-blood. This, too, was in the nature of the industry. If a pit was sunk and did not turn out well, abandonment entailed the more or less total loss of the capital. Thus a firm might rationally carry on even if, in normal years, it barely covered costs in the expectation of making high returns in the occasional boom years. The second aspect is that many of the firms which expanded most vigorously—like the Ocean, Ferndale and Cambrian undertakings—were those whose coal take was recognised to be unusually good.

The situation was in some respects like the eighteenth century slave trade. The new economic historians may indicate that the average rate of return was relatively modest: but most contemporaries (and historians) were more aware that some adventurers extracted substantial fortunes from the business. Similarly in South Wales before 1914 the ghostly ranks of failed or faded capitalists were barely perceived. The million pounds left by John Nixon seemed more substantial (and perhaps also raises some reservations about how far distributed profits were a reliable indicator: in 1893 Nixon had stated—as a boast so it was unlikely to be an underestimate—that the total amount distributed by the company over the previous thirty years had been £1.8m). Nixon was, at his own wish, buried at Mountain Ash despite his North Country origins, and despite the fact that he had, at the time of his death, hardly visited South Wales for a quarter of a century. In his case, the withdrawal was largely a function of age (he was 60 in 1875), but it underlined the fact that being a coalowner did not necessarily carry with it active participation in management.

None the less, the characteristic pattern before 1914 was for one or more of the major shareholders to be involved in management. Partly for reasons indicated below, the trend was away from the proprietor directly managing the process of coal production. He was more likely to be found in the Cardiff or Swansea or Newport office and be concerned with general administration and coal sales. Did they, as owners, bring any special features—apart from self-interest—to the tasks of management, and was it an especially crucial function in the coal industry? In the present state of the game any answers to such questions are bound to be both tentative and subjective: my judgement would be to give a qualified negative to each.

Of course, skills in management were essential and important but there is no reason to suppose that these skills were necessarily best provided by the owners. Indeed there are some good reasons for considering that the significance of the owners' contribution to management was severely constrained by the nature of the industry. The obviously dangerous nature of the industry produced pressure for legislation on matters of safety. The slow accumulation of such legislation in itself encouraged the emergence of a profession of colliery managers. The Act of 1872 gave this trend a more explicit push by requiring, in all but the smaller collieries, that managers needed to be certified. Such a development necessarily meant that at the production end control was increasingly in the hands of salaried professional managers. Of course, managers could be made partners, and proprietors—like W.W. Hood of the Glamorgan collieries or John Nixon's nephews (H.E. Gray at Merthyr Vale and C.J. Gray at Navigation)—could acquire the necessary quantifications, but the general drift was clear enough.

As a result, control over the most crucial aspect of coal production—dealing with labour and restraining wage costs on a day to day basis—was not normally in the immediate hands of the owners. The nature of colliery working made the day to day aspect particularly important and also imposed its own constraints on the normal processes of management. In the often narrow, often dimly-lit, often shifting underground passages supervision as it was understood in workshops and factories was hardly possible. A mine could not, for example, be laid out as were many factories so a foreman could instantly and constantly view the workers. And yet a colliery because of its peculiar hazards demanded a more disciplined work-force—Mackworth, the pioneer mines inspector in South Wales, was fond of remarking that mines safety required the miners to observe discipline as scrupulously as a good regiment. The basic instrument of control was the piece-rate method of payment to the coal-cutters since it was their output and rhythm of work which dominated the entire pit.

Moreover, the range of management decisions was, in several crucial respects, restricted. Once a mine was sunk or acquired, the location of the enterprise was fixed with a rigidity greater than in most other industries. The basic product was also determined: coal mines produced coal. Nor could managerial decisions do much to alter or affect the particular product of a particular mine. It could be washed or sized or double-screened at the point of shipment but these were all minor adjustments compared to the range of choices normally facing managers in manufacturing industry. The basic point being made here was, moreover, reinforced by lack of significant technical change before 1914 in the basic process of coal-getting in South Wales.

There is a tendency to see in the lack of change in the basic system of coal-getting a proof of the coalowners' failure to innovate, and more particularly to treat the substantially lower proportion of coal which was machine-mined in South Wales before 1914 as substantive proof of the especial backwardness of the owners of South Wales. And it may be so. But an impressionistic and unsystematic survey of the evidence suggests that much if not all the difference can be accounted for by the peculiar geological conditions of South Wales. It is at least uncertain that a lack of technological initiative has to be added to the coal-owners' sins.

Their significant entrepreneurial failure lay elsewhere. The possible sources of industrial capital in and around the coalfield were still limited in the second half of the nineteenth century. The coalowners were a major group amongst these limited sources. A vast labour force had been attracted to South Wales to meet their needs. It was in the nature of the industry that its size would eventually diminish. Yet the coalowners as a whole contributed very little towards diversification by investing to establish subsidiary, ancillary or alternative industries in the region.

Some commentators have seen further shortcomings (or virtues) in the inability of the coalowners to combine together to form a selling cartel. The argument, used at the time, rested on the special qualities of South Wales steam coal which could only be obtained from a relatively small area worked by a relatively small number of producers. The obvious course, instead of driving down the price by competing amongst each other, was to work together to raise prices by restricting output. Yet none of the schemes which were proposed was implemented. The most common explanation suggests that the coalowners as a group were too individualistic to be contained within such combines, an explanation which again places great emphasis on the personal characteristics of the owners. A subsidiary explanation stresses that their belief in the virtues of competition made such monopolistic proposals unattractive. Both these possibilities can be used to show the coalowners in a relatively favourable light: the first depicting them as a bunch of amiable eccentrics unwilling, for mere material gain, to subdue their individualistic traits; the second suggesting a positive philosophical commitment to full competition as an ideological system. Neither seems more than superficially plausible. Of course, personalities played some part: the 1896 scheme, for example, partly foundered on the personal antagonism between W.T. Lewis and D.A. Thomas. And, of course, once it had been decided not to adopt a scheme the decision was imbued with virtue by the rhetoric of free competition. It seems more likely, however, that the supposed advantages of such schemes were less overwhelming than was suggested. And there are good reasons for doubting whether the main, much less the only, constraint on the price of South Wales steam coal was the intensity of the competition amongst producers. Cardiff steam coal did have special qualities which did enable it to command a higher price, but before these facts could be easily transformed into a secure basis for cartelisation there were several major qualifications to be added. South Wales was, and always had been, a high cost producer so some ability to command a higher price was necessary before it could compete at all. The special qualities, moreover, only conferred a limited price advantage. In addition the market for South Wales steam coal was overwhelmingly overseas: there was not a large home demand where a degree of natural protection from outside competition might exist in the form of high transport costs. And the coalowners were acutely aware that the price they could obtain overseas was—whatever the degree of internal competition—largely determined by the price of alternative coals from whatever source. They had to accept the prices at the given markets and these prices were only partially determined by the amounts of Welsh coal available. The possibility of monopoly gains was thus likely to be generally limited.

In any event, the stress on individualism and the attachment to the abstract concept of price competition is given some perspective by observing the behaviour of coalowners in another sphere, that of their relations with the miners. Labour costs normally represented about 70 per cent of total production costs so the control of these costs was a matter of crucial concern for all coalowners. In this area, where their interest was clearly and directly involved, they could and did work together: the Coalowners' Association from its early beginnings in the 1860s was overwhelmingly concerned with matters of industrial relations. There was a fierce resistance to wage claims, safety legislation, reduction in hours, union organisation—anything that was likely to add to the labour cost whether at a general level or at the level of the individual colliery. The resultant antagonism between owners and men was not the product of the personal characteristics on either side—though these could exacerbate any particular situation: it was embedded in the economic realities which made labour-cost the most important consideration for everybody and thus continually underlined the inherent conflict of interest between owners and miners. But even for those who do not attribute everything to the wickedness of the coalowners but acknowledge a degree of objective reality making for a clash between labour and capital, the intensity of the pressure exerted by the owners on wage-levels is still surprising. They are, even in the generally expansionary market before 1914, continually trying to curtail or abolish established customs, cut back on allowances and press legal rights to an astonishing degree. Between the wars, in a less favourable economic climate, all these pressures on the miners, their wages and their working conditions were sharply intensified into a naked antagonism.

The nature, extent and significance of the contribution made by the coalowners to the wider life of the coalfield was full of ambiguities. Did they, for example, provide some justification for their incomes by using the money for further development rather than for personal consumption? At the impressionistic level, which is all that is currently available, the evidence suggests a cautious affirmative. On investment, for example, it has already been suggested that a significant proportion of the capital for coal mining was obtained by ploughing back profits, and parts of the essential infrastructure—the building of the Barry railway and docks would be the outstanding example—was largely financed by coalowners: but it was also noted that they provided little capital for the industrial diversification of the region. Similarly, they moved into or built substantial houses, often in or around Cardiff or Swansea, they sent their sons away to school, they bought land (some like the Davies family of the Ocean Coal Company or D.A. Thomas of the Cambrian Combine, deliberately buying up land near their ancestral origins at Llandinam and Llanwern); but the overall impression is not one of ostentatious living. Holidays seem to have been more characteristically spent at Tenby than at Nice; they were more likely to cultivate flowers than to breed racehorses; and there is an extraordinary, almost unnatural, absence of scandal. These impressions chime in with the deeply-held Nonconformity of many of them.

More positively, there is considerable evidence that the coalowners (not necessarily all of them, of course) made financial contributions towards the social capital and institutions of the coalfield communities. Chapels and churches seem to have been the commonest beneficiaries, but assistance was also given to schools, libraries, hospitals and workmen's institutes. Porth Intermediate School was provided by the County Council, but it charged weekly fees. At the ceremony to lay the foundation stone it was revealed that Edward Davies of Llandinam had given £2,000 towards a fund for scholarships and amongst several others—mostly landowners—who had each given £100 were F.L. Davis, Ferndale and Cory Bros. Councillor

Clifford J. Cory had provided Ystrad-Rhondda with a library costing over £2.000. Sir W.T. Lewis presented Merthyr hospital with an accident-receiving ward which was then equipped by the Dowlais and Cyfarthfa companies. Workmen's Institutes, although mostly dependent on deductions from the pay of the miners, were often given a lump sum assistance from the local colliery owner—as in the case of T.W. Powell's contribution at Abertillery or that of Thomas Griffiths at Cymmer.

An even more direct form of activity was that of sitting on public bodies. Until somewhere around the 1880s this type of involvement by the owners was very frequent both for representative bodies like the Boards of Guardians and for nominated functions like the Justices of the Peace. There was, indeed, almost a prescriptive right about the process epitomised perhaps by the youthful D.A. Thomas who in 1881 at the age of 25, just down from Cambridge and learning the trade at the family's collieries in Clydach Vale was elected top of the poll from a score of candidates for the Ystradyfodwg Local Board of Health and also appointed as Justice of the Peace (at a time, before the Local Government Act of 1888, when the counties were governed by the JPs sitting at Quarter Sessions). The close participation of the coalowners in local administration and government declined both relatively and absolutely from the 1880s. This was partly because many moved away from the collieries to the ports (or beyond); partly because the 'natural right' to such positions was being challenged (although the extent of this challenge before 1914 should not be exaggerated); and partly because the legislative changes substantially increased the democratic nature of local government (although again it is important to remember the limitations of this process—the effective franchise, for example, was still severely restricted). Part of the decline was, in any case, deceptive. The owners simply delegated this representative function to their professional managerial staff at the collieries.

It is not at all clear that the involvement of the coalowners in community affairs amounted to a conscious attempt to exercise social control. Other considerations apart, such deliberate manipulation of the community was frequently otiose. Many colliery villages were essentially one-company communities. They were established in areas which had previously been relatively empty and barren so that there was little in the way of an established, traditional authority structure: they were frontier settlements in an almost American sense. They were economically dependent on a single enterprise to a degree which was rarer in most urban industrial areas. In such a situation it was clear enough where the ultimate power lay. Indeed, the basic power relationships (who could do what to whom) were so clearly defined in the South Wales coalfield before 1914 that a plausible case could be made for turning the whole 'social control' thesis on its head: the financial assistance given by coalowners to community activities were intended to disguise the degree of control they already possessed.

In addition emphasis upon concepts like social control fail to do justice to the complexity of the motivation which was involved. Given the nature of the time and place, and given what we know of the character and beliefs of some of the coalowners, an act of some historical violence is required to stress that they were only, and consciously, concerned with the manipulation of their workforce. Some gave funds and joined in community activities because they were aware of, and wished to maintain, cultural values and links; many more were doubtless moved by a variety of religious considerations (the need to do 'good works'; missionary zeal; to glorify God; to undermine the established church);

others were concerned with moral elevation—and were more likely to be concerned with deflecting workmen from drink than from revolutionary thoughts; and there was some simple benevolence as well as the provision of conscience money.

Such moral justifications were certainly important to the coalowners themselves. They naturally saw their riches as a reasonable reward for their own individual virtues: they were not likely to consider that they were merely active as the agents of abstract forces like capitalism when they were—like all the other actors on the historical stage—all too conscious of their own personal feelings and thoughts. In one of his novels (*A Time to Laugh*) set in South Wales around the beginning of the twentieth century, Rhys Davies presents three contrasting coalowners. There was the self-made C.P. Meredith, who had:

> an intrinsic sympathy with the men. He was one of them. And even now he wanted to be a democratic employer, knit into the same texture of thought as his men . . . [But] . . . they had struck in violation of their agreements . . . They had burnt down his house, though last year he had built for them a meeting-hall complete with library and billiard-room. Something had gone seriously wrong with the bond that existed between him and his men; *they* had soured. He blamed the secret trading of a pernicious doctrine brought to the valley by elusive outsiders. A respectable trade unionism, kept by temperate men, was to be welcomed . . .

In contrast Sir Rufus Morgan ' would not recognise a Trade Union, except to fight it with bitter and intolerant wrath'. Sir Rufus 'tried to imitate God' and the novel also contains independent, pragmatic John Johns:

> He was solid as a bank safe, as impregnable and full of riches. People never knew whether to admire and like

> him or to roundly abuse his apparent soullessness. He paid his men a better average than other employers—remaining outside the Association of Owners, whose men he had encouraged to fight for the abolition of the Sliding Scale. In fact, he had inflamed them to strike once, declaring that the Scale ought to be abolished. When this strike had happened five years ago, his own pits at Nant Vale did very well indeed: a fortune had been made. For this he had been attacked and reviled at the time: he remained unaffected.

In the novel, when John Johns' own men struck he considered himself to have been deserted and betrayed. 'I shall cease to think of you as men in my care and honest men with respect for their word . . . we will fight to the bitter end, the last ditch. You need not send your Federation to us with offers. *We* will dictate terms, when *we* think fit . . .' Such a situation could be depicted as a fictional illustration of the breaking down of the methods of social control developed by the coalowners. And the actual parallels are obvious enough (they have to be there because the novel is modelled on them). Compare, for example, the statement of D.A. Thomas to The Times (5 September, 1909) at outset of the Cambrian stoppage: 'Since the Cambrian men have taken matters into their own hands I am off for a holiday . . . I am certainly not going to beg the men to return to work I shall certainly not go out of my way on the present occasion to secure a peace which seems impossible of any permanency . . .' The six month stoppage of 1898 and the nearly year-long Cambrian Combine confrontation of 1910-11 can be interpreted as major breakdowns in social control with the inference that such control had previously been successfully implemented. There would certainly be grounds for such an inference. For at least a generation before 1898 the miners seemed to have adopted attitudes that mostly embodied the values of the coalowners. In particular, they accepted the sliding-scale system of wage regulation which in its apparent automaticity emphasised the mutuality of interests between owners and miners, and played down strife and conflict. It is, however, still not established that such action by the men mostly reflected manipulation by the owners. It could as easily be explained by the extent to which the incipient unions were effectively crushed in the long stoppage of 1875.

The discussion of the nature or existence of social control should not, however, be allowed to get out of perspective. There is a prior point. So far as most people were concerned, in most places, for most of the time, the relationship with the owners was one of (not necessarily malevolent) neglect. In looking at the evidence of the coalfield before 1914 it is difficult to view it as an area with a high provision of social needs. And much of what did exist stemmed not directly from the owners but from the new local government structure set up around 1890. In areas like education, for example, there is no doubting the acceleration of the pace of development about this time, though again caution is needed. The local government bodies were mostly very wary spenders and not just because the effectively limited franchise helped to sustain a significant representation of owner interest: even where miners were in a clear majority (despite a restricted franchise) those who were voters were as interested in keeping down the level of rates as were the colliery owners.

There is much, therefore, to suggest that the coalowners' constructive impact on the social institutions and infrastructure was relatively muted. There is even more to suggest that their direct social influence in any functional sense was waning before 1914. By then most of the largest coalowners had moved away from the actual collieries, they were much more likely to be found in the Vale than in the valleys. Cultural leadership or involvement, especially in terms of Welsh cultural activities, had not disappeared but had become a less prominent characteristic of the coal-owners. Political leadership, especially at the parliamentary level, was still a reality. D.A. Thomas persistently polled more votes in Merthyr than did Keir Hardie who was arguably only carried in as the second member for the constituency on the Liberal coalowner's coat-tails. The hold was, however, becoming more tenuous. The nature of the tensions was, for example, clearly indicated in the Gower campaign in 1900 won—just—by the coalowner Aeron Thomas standing as a Liberal against John Hodge the secretary of the Steel Smelters' union standing as a Labour candidate. The resultant splits and ambiguities pointed up the difficulties of the Liberals hanging on to the labour vote. The men of Bwllfa colliery roundly condemned the miners' leaders, Mabon and John Williams, 'for supporting the candidature of Mr. J. Aeron Thomas, a capitalist . . . against Mr. John Hodge, a Trade Unionist candidate..' But Aeron Thomas's own workmen gave him a dinner at the Mackworth Hotel in Swansea at which Thomas declared himself totally unrepentant about being a capitalist, but more defensively said he would have stood down if the miners had had a candidate and even thought about stepping aside for a Labour candidate but felt the district should be represented by a Welsh-speaker who 'knew and sympathised with Welsh aspirations.'

After 1898 there is a shift of emphasis in the relations between owners and miners, a shift which is no less decisive for being intangible, gradual and difficult to pin down. Previously the necessary co-operation between capital and labour in the productive process had been predominant and had encouraged a notion of an inherent mutuality of interest. After the crucial conflict of 1898 it was the equally necessary distribution of the proceeds of production which was stressed carrying with it the notion of an inherent antagonism of interest. It was a change which gave force and impetus to the other developments tending to constrain the social influence of the owners. In the atmosphere of gathering suspicion and conflict the functional possibilities of owners' exerting any substantial social influence based on consent receded.

All these trends increased in the inter-war years. Up to 1914 the positive role of the coalowners was, implicitly or explicitly, generally accepted. The acceptance was partly based on very general considerations affecting society as a whole—the nature of the dominant (liberal) economic and political ideas, and the general atmosphere of deference in social relationships. But, in the South Wales coalfield, the acceptance was difficult to combat and withhold in a region which was so obviously expansionary and buoyant. The growth depended upon capital investment which involved very real risks (there were many examples of failed colliery enterprises). The coalowners were the risk-takers. They were men of some enterprise and much energy, energy perhaps being the characteristic which the most successful had in common. The acceptance, moreover, was essential if they were to play any positive social role. None the less even before 1914 there were important qualifications to be attached to the functional significance of the coalowners. The nature of the industry severely constrained the range of decision making; success—especially big success—was likely to owe more to fortune than to skill; and social control was less a matter of winning the consent of the community by manipulation than a simple reflection of the power realities in single-enterprise communities. And once the cushion of growth was removed the limited function of the owners was more exposed. Their one undisputed role as providers of capital was vastly demoted in significance. Managerial skills became more important in the face of falling markets and ageing collieries, but even if the skill was provided it was not likely to command much admiration or acceptance when its exercise required—or, at any rate, received—much ruthlessness. The end of growth also saw the clash between owners and men emerging stark and strong. Any social role by the owners would have been difficult: but in general there is little evidence that they sought one.

It is now the 1980s. A whole generation, more than a generation, has grown up without there being coalowners. There are still capitalists: like the poor they are always with us, though nowadays they are more likely to come from Japan or represent a minor activity of some multinational company wooed by the Welsh Development Agency's financial blandishment. But no coalowners: and it is as if they had never been. It is difficult to find many permanent legacies. There is no great architecture, no school of literature or art. The Misses Davies of Gregynog seem to have been alone in using their money from Ocean coal to build a significant art collection (now at the National Museum), and unique in their direct patronage of music and of the Gregynog Press. There were no model colliery villages, no hopeful experiments in industrial or social relations. There are a few undistinguished statues of themselves. When the coalowners went in 1947 there was—and perhaps this is the most damning indictment—no sense of anything missing. They left the slag heaps, of course, and on 21 October 1966 at least one of these demonstrated that they could still exact death and destruction over the generations. But if most of the coal tips—indeed most of the collieries—now have a decent covering of grass, the coalowners still live on in the bitter, sour angry memories of miners and their descendants:

> 'You should forget all that. Banish hatred,' said Willie zealously. 'You cannot forget things that have been your entire life for many years. The insult of a moment, Willie, is hard enough to forget but when men have to endure the insult of being idle, degraded and useless for years on end, not only is it impossible to forget that, it becomes an act of faith to cherish the memory of it every moment one lives, because one's duty as a human being from that time on is to fight against the possibility of that insult being levied against oneself or against others again. You're young, Willie. You only caught a glimpse of the knife that went right through our bodies.' (Gwyn Thomas, *The Sky of Our Lives: The Dark Philosophers*)

(This essay was originally written as a chapter in D. Smith (ed), *A People and a Proletariat,* Pluto, 1980, pp. 94-113. It is pleasing that there is now more, and more reliable, information available on at least the most prominent figures. For example, several are included in Jeremy, D. (ed), *Dictionary of Business Biography*, Butterworth, 5 vols., 1984-6; there is an illuminating account of one coalowner in Williams, H., *Davies the Ocean: railway king and coal tycoon*, Univ. of Wales, 1991, and a few articles, such as K.O. Morgan, 'D.A. Thomas: the industrialist as politician' in Williams, S. (ed), *Glamorgan Historian, vol., 1966*. My chapter on 'Caitalists and Coalowners' in Prys Morgan (ed), *Glamorgan County History*, vol. VI, 1988, slightly widens the discussion.)

6. THE COALOWNERS OF SOUTH WALES, 1873-80: PROBLEMS OF UNITY

Although there is still much to be done, work in recent years has gone far to fill out the story of the development of miners' unions in South Wales.[1] However, we still know comparatively little about their counter-part, the Owners' Association. The history of the efforts of the owners to act in concert necessarily carries with it less appeal and less dramatic impact than does the story of the attempts to obtain concerted action amongst the colliers. There is, for example, no equivalent of the basic nature of the sacrifice and sufferings borne, not only by a few outstanding leaders, but by a large number of union lodge officials and by the countless anonymous members of the rank-and-file and their families. Nonetheless, it is a mistake to assume that the formation of an owners' association was painless and that its continuance was a matter of smooth inevitability.

It is, however, easy to see how such a view has developed. An initial overall glance at the history of the Coal Owners' Association immediately suggests both permanence and a persistent development. The Association enjoyed an unbroken and active existence from its formation—which would certainly date from the founding of the Monmouthshire and South Wales Collieries Association on 19 December 1873, and might very reasonably be dated from the setting up of the Aberdare Steam Collieries Association on 14 March 1864—until and beyond the nationalisation of the industry in 1947. Such stability suggests a strong common purpose amongst coalowners which provokes the assumption that the creation of an association was a straight-forward affair. Similarly, the rise from the Aberdare association of 1864, whose members controlled about 15 per cent of total output of the coalfield, to the situation in which, by the time of nationalisation, virtually all the output of the coalfield came from the members of the owners' association, naturally suggests a steady progression and encourages the assumption that its growth was continuous and assured. The present article is an attempt to temper these assumptions by singling out two particular aspects—the relatively slow evolution of an association of owners, and the highly precarious nature of the early years of that association. In the process, it is hoped that some small shifts in the entrenched perspectives on industrial relations in the coalfield will emerge.

Attempts to set up formal or informal associations of the coal owners of South Wales have a long history. It is enough to mention the combination of Monmouthshire owners who, after the Monmouthshire Canal Act of 1797, attempted to use the statutory advantage which this gave them in the important Bridgwater trade to regulate prices amongst themselves.[2] Moreover, the efforts to develop joint action in order to escape from, or reduce, the pressures of competition tended to increase as the sale-coal trade became more important. In particular, the emergence—from about 1840 onwards—of a rapidly growing export trade in steam coal did much to drag the sale-coal industry out from under the shadow of the coal produced as a purely subsidiary activity by the iron and copper companies. Nonetheless, no stable or successful association was established until at least the last third (1864), and possibly the last quarter (1873) of the nineteenth century.

The movements towards joint action were all prompted by one or more of three broad impulses. The first of these tended to be largely *ad hoc* in character, representing occasions on which owners might come together to dispute with a railway (or canal) company over freight rates, or act as a lobby to press upon parliament and the public the needs and claims of the coal industry of South Wales, or of some particular section of it. The other two influences were both more homogeneous and more permanent: the desire to exert some form of control over prices, and the need to present a common front in dealings with the miners.

There are many examples of coal owners uniting for some specific objective. Often the issue concerned transport. There need be no surprise at this, since transport constituted a significant part of the total cost of production. Between 1840 and 1870, for example, railway charges accounted, on average, for between one-fifth and one-quarter of the price of steam coal at Cardiff.[3] Thus, in Monmouthshire the freighters were engaged in a running battle with the Monmouthshire Canal Company for a full decade after 1840, forcing the company both to lower its rates and to supplement its canal and tramway system by the provision of railway facilities. In the following decade, the Monmouthshire coal owners transferred their attention to the high charges exacted by the Newport Dock Company.[4] At Cardiff there were periodic outbursts against the Taff Vale Railway Company, the fiercest being in 1858 over an attempt by the company to extort charges for 'extra and special' services after a parliamentary committee had imposed a reduction in the company's maximum freight rates when the company had applied for an extension of its powers.[5] At Swansea, the freighters united to infuse some urgency into the attitude of the Great Western Railway Company towards the carriage of coal.[6] Everywhere, applications to parliament to build new, or to extend existing, transport undertakings in the district received the close scrutiny of the freighters, who often raised a common fund to secure the hearing of their viewpoint and the protection of their interests.[7]

Other *ad hoc* occasions on which the coal owners acted together for a time covered a wide variety of objectives. There was, for example, the short-lived South Wales Anthracite Association of 1839, formed to extend the use of anthracite by publicity and experiment;[8] while coal owners also acted together to urge the acceptance of the Severn Tunnel scheme in 1869[9] or to press the claims of Welsh steam coals upon the Admiralty.

On their own, however, issues of this sort were too disjointed, disconnected and discontinuous to form the basis for any stable and permanent association. They were important; indeed, they were vigorously pursued, as is demonstrated by the history of the Coal Owners' Association when it was eventually formed. But they were pursued as a useful supplement to what were considered to be the basic activities of an association; they were not a sufficient condition for the formation of such an association. They gave an added flavour once an association had—for other reasons—been bound together. They were the sauce and not the cement.

On the face of it, the desire to exert some control over prices offered a wider, sounder and more permanent basis for combination. There were, indeed, several initiatives taken on this basis. It has already been seen that the coal shippers of Newport joined together in the first decade of the nineteenth century to regulate prices. There are indications, too, that, at least as far as government contracts were concerned, the west Wales owners acted together in the 1830s.[10] It was quite common for informal meetings to take place amongst the shippers at a particular port to try to secure agreements over the timing and amount of significant price changes.[11] During the nineteenth century, however, the most persistent attempt to control prices in a major part of the Welsh coal trade was that made amongst the Monmouthshire house coal owners during the 1830s and 1840s.[12] But even this was, at best, only intermittently successful and it was eventually overwhelmed by the competition from Cardiff acting as the outlet for the development of the house coal seams in the lower Rhondda valley during the 1840s.

The fact was that, for all its attractions, any scheme of price control faced fierce practical difficulties. Any effective scheme to maintain prices above their market level would, for example, necessarily have involved a systematic control of output. A major constraint on this would necessarily have been that a significant part of the relevant output would be produced by those who would be beyond the control of an association—owners in other coalfields or Welsh owners who refused to participate. Even apart from this, however, the problems of allocating, and securing the observance of, output quotas were vastly complicated by the fact that for most of the century the industry included a very large number of relatively small individual producers. The problems were still further compounded by two other considerations. It was relatively easy, and not prohibitively expensive, for new firms to enter the industry. Secondly, there was a strong long-term tendency for the demand for coal to increase. The first of these considerations threatened any association based on price control, because the price would be under-cut by new firms which could and would enter the industry. The second meant that output quotas, with their troublesome and potentially acrimonious bargaining between the members, would have to be frequently adjusted. It also meant (since a strong upward trend in demand tended to cushion the impact of recurrent periods of depression) that owners were less strongly attracted towards price control.

For all these reasons, the Coal Owners' Association was not founded in South Wales on the basis of regulating prices. Indeed, for as long as these conditions applied—which would be at least up to 1914—the Association did not even include price control amongst its objectives. There was a brief period in the 1890s when the Association seemed to be tempted. At the time, the Association was subjected to the triple pressures of a long period of falling prices; the publicity given to plans for price control suggested by Sir George Elliot in 1893 and by D.A. Thomas in 1896;[13] and the growing reluctance of the colliers to have their wages governed by a sliding scale based on prices, especially when these prices remained low for long periods. Nonetheless, it is difficult to escape the conclusion that the examination of schemes of control conducted by the association in 1897 was less than wholehearted. The fruits of such schemes seemed uncertain, whilst attempts to operate them carried substantial dangers of disrupting the Association because of the potential divergences between members.

The effective impulse towards association amongst the coal owners of South Wales derived from a quite difference source: the need to present a united front in dealings with their workers. In this the region was broadly in tune with most of British industry at this time. By 1914 most industries in Britain had adopted some form of trade association. Nearly all of these attempted to devise and implement policies for dealing with labour; but most of them did not interfere directly with prices.[14]

There were particularly strong reasons which drove the Welsh coal trade towards action over labour problems. Increasingly the main sources of demand were exports and such producer-goods industries as iron and copper smelting. These were sectors which were subject to quite wide and sharp fluctuations in demand, unlike the much steadier demand for household consumption, where the main variation was a regular seasonal fluctuation. The effects of the changes in demand were exacerbated because in the short run it was difficult to adjust output. In a period of booming demand, supply could be increased to some extent by opening new working places or working longer hours. Once the limits of such adjustments had been reached, however, supply could only be increased by the time-consuming process of opening new pits. The reduction of supply was subject to similar constraints. It was often better to work a colliery—even at a loss—rather than to stop production altogether. The shaft and workings deteriorated rapidly if all work was discontinued. If the pit was not constantly pumped and the headings and roadways kept in repair—especially in South Wales, where the roof and floor were subject to constant 'squeeze'—the whole mine, together with the capital invested in it, might have to be abandoned or could only be re-opened at a considerable cost. Thus, as long as the coal could be sold at a price which covered the variable costs such as cutting and transport, and also made some contribution to the essential cost of keeping the mine in order, operations were likely to be continued. Thomas Brown, the Welsh coal owner and mining engineer, was only giving a slightly dramatic expression to the essential truth of this when he told a parliamentary select committee that 'you cannot shut up a colliery'.[15]

The combination of a volatile demand and a relatively inelastic supply resulted in sharp variations in coal prices. Wages were always either formally or informally, closely geared to price changes. Thus in the Aberdare valley the basic wage unit (the price paid for cutting each ton of large coal) was altered on twenty-two occasions between 1848 and 1875, even though there was no formal mechanism such as a sliding scale to link wages to prices. The changes were, moreover, fierce as well as frequent: most increases in the rate were of the order of ten per cent; most reductions were between ten and twenty per cent.[16]

Wage changes of this magnitude were usually only won or conceded after some sort of struggle. Thus, the whole market situation facing the industry necessarily tended to produce situations making for industrial conflict. Such a tendency was significantly intensified because wages formed a high proportion of total costs—probably between one-half and three-quarters of the total pit-head cost of production of steam coal in South Wales in the second half of the nineteenth century. Any decline in price, therefore found owners pressing rapidly and promptly for wage-reductions: equally, to delay wage increases in times of price rises could contribute enormously to profits. Such circumstances made for labour unrest.

These broad influences were supplemented by the constant variation in working conditions, variations which were largely beyond the control of owners and men. The particularly difficult geological conditions in South Wales made for frequent variations in the thickness of seams, the quality of the coal, the stability of roof and floor, and the amount of water. All these provided additional sources for wage disputes, not only at the general level of the coalfield or valley, but at the individual pits and, indeed, the individual working places.

The existence of these numerous potential sources of labour conflict necessarily encouraged some form of association amongst the coal owners, and any tendency for the miners to combine into unions could only enhance this encouragement. Nonetheless, even over dealings with their workmen, even over wage issues, there was no simple identity of interest between the various owners. There were particular difficulties arising out of the differences in the personalities and philosophies of individual owners, but these were not of over-riding significance. More generally, wide variations in the size and financial resources of colliery undertakings could produce differences in outlook. There were, in addition, two further considerations operative in South Wales at this time, each of which acted as a formidable obstacle to common action. Firstly, the coal produced in the region was far from homogeneous. South Wales, unlike the other British coalfields, contained virtually the whole range of coals—bituminous, steam and anthracite. Each of these faced quite different markets and hence could not be assumed to be ready for action over wages at exactly the same time and to exactly the same extent—or even in the same direction. This problem was also one which tended to become rather less acute because of the tendency for the industry to be more and more dominated by the steam-coal trade. A second division which was especially marked in the 1860s and 1870s, was between producers whose main business was selling coal and those—often with a very large coal output—whose main business was producing iron or copper. Such divisions of interest did much to complicate relations between different groups of owners.

From this brief survey it should be clear that the area of labour relations offered the most permanent basis for the formation of an owners' association in the South Wales coal trade. Other possible bases were either too discontinuous like common action against transport companies, or potentially too disruptive like price control. It should also be clear, however, that common action even on labour issues was by no means straightforward. After many gropings, however, the basic form emerged in the mid-1860s and the initial negotiations to accommodate the major groups were successfully conducted in the mid-1870s.

The form was taken over from the Aberdare Steam Collieries Association, which was established at a meeting held at the Windsor Hotel, Cardiff, on 14 March 1864.[17] There were three essential ingredients. Members were required to sign a formal, detailed and binding Deed of Association, which clearly set out their various rights and obligations. Although the preamble naturally put the objects of the Association in very broad terms ('for the protection and benefit of the trade generally'), the detailed clauses made clear that the central aim was to present a united front over labour issues. Finally, the essential financial position was secured by the requirement that members should enter into a financial commitment in advance of actual need by depositing a promissory note, payable on demand, for an amount equivalent to 3d. (just over 1p.) per ton of their output. Actual funds were raised by levies whenever money was needed for general expenses and to compensate any member for loss of profit that resulted from any stoppage which he suffered through resisting, with the prior approval of the association, the demands of his workmen. If a member failed to pay his share of any levy, his promissory note would be cashed and used instead.[18]

The Aberdare association had a clear, coherent and viable form of organisation. It was vulnerable, however, because its members controlled only a small proportion (fifteen per cent) of the total trade of the coalfield. Even in the more particular market for steam coal, the Aberdare valley was already in 1864 beginning to lose its dominant position as the Rhondda valleys began to be exploited and as the iron masters gave more and more attention to the sale of their steam-coal output. It was essential that the basis of the association should be widened. A first step was made in 1870, when some Rhondda owners were included and the association reconstructed as The South Wales Steam Collieries Association. But although the controlled output thus went up from 1.6m. tons to 2.1m. tons, this still only represented fifteen per cent of the total output of the coalfield. The reorganisation had barely enabled the association to keep pace with the general growth of the coalfield.[19]

The fundamental change came in 1873 when a new organisation, The Monmouthshire and South Wales Collieries Association, was founded.[20] This was on an altogether wider basis. It included owners in the hinterlands of Newport and Swansea as well as Cardiff, and in particular it included the iron masters. The possibility of such an amalgamation had emerged largely from the experience of two major strikes in the coalfield in 1871 and 1873. On each of these occasions the workmen had achieved success. The most important explanation for this was the general buoyancy of the markets for coal and iron. Two other factors, however, had clearly been of some significance. The first was the mushroom growth in South Wales of Thomas Halliday's Amalgamated Association of Miners, founded in Lancashire in 1869. The second was the extent to which there was a split between the coal owners and the iron masters: the 1871 stoppage was confined to the coal owners and the iron masters continued to work their pits and sell their coal; in 1873 the positions were reversed.[21] These considerations led to intensive negotiations at the close of the 1873 stoppage, negotiations which led to the formation of the new association on 19 December 1873.

It must have seemed to the architects of this organisation that, at long last, a powerful, stable and widely-based owners' association had finally been established. The members controlled about seventy per cent of the total production of South Wales and they represented all sections of the industry of the region, but especially the steam coal owners and the iron masters. Moreover, the favourable portents soon received resounding confirmation when the owners defeated, and substantially destroyed, the miners' new union in the long strike and lock-out of 1875, the third major stoppage in the coalfield in four years. But in the next few years the whole edifice came close to total collapse.

Why was this? The explanation is to be found in the final settlement of the 1875 strike. The owners secured an immediate reduction in wage-rates, a reduction which faithfully and starkly reflected the victory of the newly-formed Association. But they also agreed, in an attempt to avoid every change of trade leading to a strike or lock-out, to set up a sliding-scale system whereby future changes in wage-rates would be determined by reference to changes in the selling price of coal.[22]

The idea of a sliding scale seemed well-designed to strengthen the Association. Members would have the wage-rates they paid regulated automatically, avoiding the bitter and disruptive conflicts which had characterised the early 1870s. There would also be a Board for settling particular disputes and, where this failed, a member who was in dispute with his workmen would have the full support of the Association. These advantages seemed likely to attract additional members, which would further increase the bargaining power of the Association.

All that was needed was to ensure that the terms of the initial agreement were such as to secure these advantages to the Association. There seemed little reason to doubt that this would be the case. After the 1875 strike the owners were united and victorious; the falling market favoured them; and the men were defeated, dispirited and disunited. Yet the terms on which the first sliding scale was negotiated totally failed to serve as a rallying ground for the Association and, indeed, greatly undermined its strength. To understand this, it is necessary first to sketch the terms and how they were arrived at, and then to indicate why they worked so badly for the owners.

The owners' negotiating committee started from the assumption that the final terms of the scale were unlikely to be decided without reference to the independent umpire. They were confident, however, that they had a strong case to present. This case involved a fairly sophisticated formula for determining profit trends; to provide the evidence, the committee called for a substantial degree of information on prices and costs from their members. The response was meagre in the extreme. Most owners were simply not prepared to risk confidential information falling into the hands of their commercial rivals on the Association's committee.[23]

The rebuff was important. It indicated how sharp were the limits of unity of interest and action amongst the owners. But it did not alter any of the fundamentals in the bargaining with the men. The Association's negotiators managed quite graciously to abandon their sophisticated approach and accepted—apparently as a concession—the more rough-and-ready procedures proposed by the miners. The men had simply suggested a minimum cutting-price, proposed a selling price to which this would be equivalent, and also the amounts by which the cutting price would vary for each shilling change in the selling price. Indeed, direct negotiations with the men over a few straightforward issues began to seem attractive. The possibility of any reference to an umpire had come to seem both embarrassing and dangerous—embarrassing because of their own lack of hard evidence and dangerous because many owners felt that the dominant principle behind most decisions by umpires was that of 'splitting the difference'. More positively, the owners felt that in direct and final negotiations, the Association would be free to make the best use of its superior bargaining power in a falling market and against men's leaders whose utmost struggles were doing little more than keep the ideas of unionism alive.[24]

The negotiations were thus basically concerned with the minimum piece-wage, its equivalent selling price and the ratio by which the wage-rate was to increase as the selling price increased. Both sides tacitly accepted that the relationship between wages and prices which had existed immediately before the boom of the early 1870s should be regarded as 'normal'. The men, however, argued that the wage-rate of that time was too low to be accepted as a minimum in 1875 because of the increased prices of food and rent; the employers argued that the prices of 1869 were too low to be taken as equivalent to the minimum wage-rate because of the extra cost of production that the 1872 Act had involved.[25]

Some recognition was afforded to both these claims in the final agreement, which was signed on 11 December 1875.[26] The minimum wage-rate was to be five per cent more than the 1869 rate, this being taken as covering the increased cost of living since that date. The equivalent selling price was 12s. (60p.) per ton, this price being taken as covering the claims of the owners arising from the extra costs resulting from the 1872 Act. If prices increased beyond this level, wage-rates were to be advanced by 7.1/2 per cent for each complete shilling (5p.) rise in the average selling price, until wages reached their maximum when the average selling price was 21s. (£1.05p.). The prices were to be obtained from half-yearly audits, the average selling price of one half-year governing wage-rates for the next, whilst either side could end the scale by giving six months' notice in either December or June.[27]

It is important to realise that, at the time, the scale that had emerged in December 1875 seemed eminently satisfactory to the owners. This much is clear from a letter explaining the mechanics of the scale written to John Nixon by Alexander Dalziel, the manager of Nixon's Navigation Company.[28] Dalziel considered that the selling price that was equivalent to the minimum wage-rate had been established sufficiently high to ensure that the results of the first audit would put the wage-rate at the minimum and thereby involve a substantial reduction. The immediate needs of the Association would thus be met. He also pointed to its advantages for the future. Under the scale no advance in wages was applicable until the average selling price had increased by a full shilling over minimum prices. Such advances spread over the sales of all firms for six months would, he considered, only slowly be achieved. If, for example, an audit revealed that the selling price of steam coal was 13s. 11.1/2d. (nearly 70p.) a ton (1s. 11.1/2d.(nearly 10p.) above the standard), this would involve only an advance of 7.1/2 per cent over the minimum wage-rate. For the Navigation Company, such an advance meant an increase of only 4d.(about 1.1/2 p.) a ton in labour costs for a rise in price of nearly 2s. (10p.). Moreover, companies like Navigation, whose reputation stood high in the market, generally commanded prices higher than the average. Dalziel thought that when the average price was a little over 13s. (65p.), Navigation coal would be selling at nearer 16s. (80p.) and yet still only be paying an extra 4d. (1.1/2p.) per ton in labour costs. 'My impressions of the scheme,' Dalziel concluded, 'is that it is a good one and will work well for you.'

Nevertheless it was this scale that nearly brought the Association to grief. The benefits for the owners that Dalziel had predicted mostly failed to materialise. It is true that the first audit (based upon sales made in the last three months of 1875) showed prices that in each group placed the wage-rate at its agreed minimum. This meant that rates were reduced from 1 January 1875 by some 7 per cent in the steam-coal collieries and 21.1/2 per cent in the bituminous collieries. It was the men, therefore, and particularly the house-coal colliers, who first expressed dissatisfaction with the scale.[29] The very fact that there were minimum rates, however, meant that the scale would give no further gains to employers by way of extra reductions; any further advantages that the owners could derive would have to result from the lagging of wage increases behind rising prices. These were the long-term benefits that Dalziel had claimed for the scale. In the event, the owners were never allowed to taste these fruits, for throughout the duration of this particular scale prices failed to rise above the minimum and, indeed, showed a disastrous tendency to fall. The owners in brief had sadly misread the trend of trade at the time the scale was negotiated. This, given the short time horizons of most businessmen, was not altogether surprising. For over four years they had enjoyed high prices and had come to regard a price of 10s. (50p.) a ton for steam coal as abnormally low. Yet only in years of high activity had the annual average selling price exceeded 10s. (50p.) per ton before 1870 and the productivity of mining was rising rather than falling during the 1870s.[30] To the coal-owners, the fall in prices from an annual average of 23s. 3d. (£1.16p.) a ton in 1873 to 10s. 7d. (53p.) a ton at the end of 1875 must have appeared catastrophic. In thinking the nadir had then been reached, they under-estimated the general downward trend in activity. More particularly, however, they under-estimated the impact upon coal output of the substantial investment which had been stimulated by the exceptionally high prices and profits of 1872-73. Between 1874 and 1880, coal output in South Wales rose by 4,675,000 tons, an increase of twenty-eight per cent at a time when industrial output (after 1877 at least) was falling.[31] The impact of this on coal prices was severe, the annual average price of steam coal, f.o.b., at Cardiff falling from 14s. 3d. (71p.) in 1875 to 8s. 6d. (42.1/2p.) in 1879.[32]

It is against this background that the operation of the first sliding scale needs to be studied. The persistent fall in prices which, under the strict terms of the scale, could not be matched by wage reductions directly threatened the unity of the Association. It did so in three broad ways. Firstly, it meant that members were tempted to leave the Association altogether if they felt they could secure more favourable wage-terms for themselves; secondly, it tempted the Association as a whole to seek remedies which were not strictly in accord with the spirit of the agreement; and, finally, it tempted individual members to act in ways which contravened the terms of the scale to a greater or less degree.

The first trend is easily demonstrated. The number of members in 1875 was 84; by 1880 this had declined to 47. Many of those who withdrew were relatively small firms, but there were also some very significant losses, such as David Davis and Sons of Ferndale, and the Ocean Coal Company. The proportion of the total output of the district controlled by the members of the Association fell spectacularly from seventy per cent to less than half.[33]

The operation of the second trend is best illustrated by the action taken by the Association in 1877 to increase working hours. The need for some such action is indicated in the comment of W.T. Lewis (later Lord Merthyr), one of the leading architects of the Association and of the sliding scale, to the secretary of the Association, that 'the Association is in a most critical condition arising from the increasing dissatisfaction among large owners with the sliding scale basis and the desire to reduce wages below it'.[34] To secure some relief, the Association first turned its attention to the hours of work. The men were informed of the intention of the owners to return to the hours for adults that had been general before the Act of 1872, namely, sixty-nine hours a week instead of the current fifty-four. The men's representatives reasonably claimed that the sliding scale had settled hours as well as wages because, in fixing the selling price equivalent to the minimum cutting-price, an allowance for the costs of the 1872 Act had been added. Some of the working colliers put this view more bluntly: 'We have paid for the Nine Hours! they are ours and not yours as they are paid for dearly! If you wanted to make any alteration at all, why not do it in a straightforward manner and give us six months' Notice according to the Award?'[35] Despite the protests of the men, however, many members—with Powell Duffryn giving the lead—imposed longer working hours or double-shift working on their men. By August 1877 the 'system of lengthened hours had . . . really become general in the Aberdare valley'.[36] The action was, however, divisive. Several important members, like David Davies of the Ocean Company, refused to follow or followed only reluctantly. In any event, the extent of the relief that could be gained by increasing hours was limited. Many collieries were already unable to secure enough orders to work their pits full-time and idle days were numerous.

Inevitably, some of the members turned their attention to negotiating reductions of wages with their own workmen outside the scale, a process that had already made some headway amongst those firms outside the Association. This, the last of the three broad trends mentioned above, clearly constituted a threat both to the operation of the scale and to the existence of the Association which was pledged to maintain it. The most dramatic illustration was precipitated by the sudden announcement in May 1877 that the colliers at the Plymouth and Aberdare ironworks had voluntarily accepted a reduction of ten per cent below the minimum wage-rates provided by the scale.[37] Although a few small firms had already left the Association in order to be free to obtain a similar advantage, this new case was much more serious. The pits at these works were responsible for an output of some 600,000 tons a year; they were still members of the Association when the reduction was determined upon; and closely concerned with their management was W.T. Lewis, a prominent member of the J.S.S.C.[38] The action caused a decisive rift in the Association. W.T. Lewis sharply and vigorously defended the reduction. Rule 70 of the Deed of Association, he pointed out, warned only against advances being made without the consent of the Council. 'The spirit of the Deed', he said, 'is to prevent the men making encroachments, but it does not prevent owners making favourable terms with their men, otherwise the incentive to good management would be removed.' But the existence of the sliding scale Agreement, which had not been in operation when the Deed was drawn up, blunted the force of this argument. More pertinently, Lewis also pointed out that the owners' side of the J.S.S.C. had already considered longer hours to be within the scope of the award, while many members had also introduced Billy Fair-play[39] and reduced the wages of carpenters, smiths, fitters and enginemen. All these were private arrangements with the men at individual collieries to secure economy of working and had been tacitly approved by the Association. He refused to see any difference between them and the reduction at the Aberdare and Plymouth works. Moreover, the award did not oblige any owner to continue working at a loss: each member was free to give notice to close his pits. This was the course that had been taken at the Aberdare and Plymouth collieries, but the men had asked the reason for the closure and had expressed their willingness to accept a reduction if the works continued.[40]

These arguments proved unacceptable to the bulk of the members of the Association. They strongly felt that both the company and its workmen were bound by the award and that neither side was free to come to such an arrangement. Only those members, like David Davies, M.P., of the Ocean Coal Company, who had also opposed the changes in hours, could claim full consistency of attitude. Nonetheless, the Association as a whole was deeply concerned: the public, moral ground for concern was that the Plymouth action constituted a breach of faith with the men; the private, commercial, ground was that it gave the Plymouth company an edge in the market. This indignation, too, was all the greater as W.T. Lewis had, only shortly before the reduction was negotiated at Aberdare and Plymouth, advised the Association that it would be impolitic to give notice to end the sliding-scale agreement.

There was no possibility of disguising the rift in the Association that was caused by the unilateral action of the Aberdare and Plymouth Company. At the outset of the crisis, David Davies had penned a trenchant letter to the press, wholeheartedly condemning the action of the company and their workmen as a violation of the sliding-scale agreement. He asserted that the only reason given by the company was that it had accepted contracts that it could not profitably fulfil without a reduction. More bluntly, they had undercut their competitors and sought to avoid the consequences of this by seeking special advantages from their colliers. The vigour of David Davies's opposition largely arose from his belief that the company's action merely underlined a permanent fundamental difference of opinion amongst the members of the Association. The interest of companies such as the Aberdare and Plymouth, which were largely iron-producers, was that the coal should be cheap as it was an important element in their cost of production in ironmaking, whereas the coal-selling companies proper had a greater interest in keeping up the level of prices.[41]

In the event, the colliers of the company, under pressure from their fellow-workmen, withdrew their acceptance of the reduction and the company, faced with a strike, thought it prudent not to force the issue.[42] The whole incident, however, clearly indicated the divisive possibilities of a situation in which individual members were tempted to seek gains outside those obtained through the general agreement with the men.

The lessons were largely absorbed. Prices continued downwards, so the strain on the loyalty of Association members continued. But at the end of both 1877 and 1878, the Association itself sought this relief, not through subterfuges and expedients, but by a direct approach to the men's representatives on the joint sliding-scale committee.[43] On the first occasion the men reluctantly agreed to a general five per cent reduction outside the scale. The intention was that this should be a 'loan' that would be returned to the men as prices rose. But prices continued to fall, and a year later the Association was asking for a further reduction. This time, despite their weakness, the men refused.[44] They felt they had nothing left to give, since throughout the winter which followed the reduction of December 1877 soup kitchens, largely financed by contributions from England, had operated in several parts of the coalfield.[45] The Association could only give the six months' notice to end the agreement. In the meantime, most non-associated owners secured a ten per cent reduction from their men. A few members left the Association to secure a similar freedom of action, but most remained in the conviction that unity would be essential if the end of the agreement resulted in a conflict with the men.

The Association insisted on two basic pre-conditions for any fresh sliding-scale arrangement. First, their whole experience since 1875 had convinced them that 'the bottom would have to be kicked out of the scale', or in other words they would not contemplate any idea of a minimum cutting-rate being incorporated in a new scale. And, secondly, they would have to be given—unconditionally—the ten per cent reduction which their non-associated rivals had already obtained. Weak as the men undoubtedly were—organised unionism had virtually died out in the coalfield after 1877—they refused to grant their representatives power to negotiate on this basis. At the end of June, therefore, the first general sliding-scale in the South Wales coalfield was allowed to lapse. For a week there was a complete stoppage at the 170 pits belonging to the fifty-nine members of the Association, but thereafter the colliers gradually trickled back on the owners' terms.[46] In the process, the owners' association had been vastly depleted: in 1874 the Association controlled seventy per cent of the output of the coalfield; by 1880 this had dwindled to some forty-six per cent.

From the prolonged birth-pangs and the anxieties of the early survival of a widely-based owners' association for the coal industry of South Wales, a few broad conclusions emerge. It is all too easy to think of the coal-owners as a uniform and homogeneous group having obvious and simple common interests. They were not. The actual situation was much more complex. Different owners produced markedly different types of coal which were sold in broadly distinct—but untidily over-lapping—markets. Many of them—though by the 1870s to a decreasing degree—found their major objective as ironmasters or copper-producers. As such, they were substantial consumers as well as producers of coal, and to this extent they had an interest—in direct contrast to that of the normal coal-owner—in keeping coal prices low. There were also vast differences in size. Thus, to take examples from the 1873 Association, it was not to be expected that the Powell Duffryn Company or the Ebbw Vale Steel, Iron and Coal Company, each producing one million tons, would have the same outlook, interests and policies as J.C. Hill and Company, whose output was 3,477 tons.[47] It gradually, but decisively, emerged that there was only one objective which was sufficiently important, sufficiently permanent and sufficiently acceptable as a basis for common action—dealing with the workmen.

Even here, however, the path was not easy and the experience of the first sliding-scale demonstrated at least three things. First, it emphasised how illusory it was to think that the creation of some machinery, like the sliding-scale and its joint committee, would by itself solve the problems of industrial relations. The 'automatic' nature of the scale was only apparent; or at least it lasted only as long as both sides found acceptable the underlying bases (the standard wage-rate and its equivalent selling-price, the size and frequency of adjustments, etc.). For the owners, an acceptable scale had to embody terms which would secure for the members of the Association at least as much as they could secure for themselves and as much as their competitors outside the Association were able to obtain. The 1875 scale failed this test, even though the owners were in a very strong bargaining position at the time it was negotiated. It failed because the owners' representatives in 1875 totally misread the future course of coal prices.

Secondly, the experience between 1875 and 1879 demonstrated the fragility of the unity of the owners even on the issue of wages. Most owners were simply not prepared—not even for the purpose of securing a more favourable wage-bargain—to give information about their costs of production and capital values to the officers of the Association. And many coal-owners quietly slipped away as soon as their membership of the Association seemed to come into conflict with their immediate self-interest.

The third consideration points in a different direction and provides some necessary qualification to the points just made. The fact remains that, despite the unfavourable terms of the first sliding-scale, despite the strains this put on the loyalty of members, and despite the private—and even occasional public—disagreements amongst members, the Association did survive. Its membership, although it had fallen disastrously, still represented nearly one-half of the total coal output of South Wales. All this suggests that it fulfilled a strong need, and the later history of the Association fully bears this out.

(Originally published in *Welsh History Review*, vii, 1, 1976, pp. 75-93.)

[1]See, e.g. Page Arnot, *The South Wales Miners* (1967), and E.W. Evans, *The Miners of South Wales* (Cardiff, 1961). In addition, the formation of the Society for the Study of Labour History (and the publication of its journal, *Llafur*) has naturally given impetus to work in this field. What we now urgently require is a scholarly account of the development of industrial relations in the South Wales coalfield from an explicitly right-wing stand-point.

[2]A.H. John, *The Industrial Development of South Wales* (Cardiff, 1950), pp. 117-18, 130.

[3]The average freight charge from the pit-head to the docks at Cardiff was 1s. 10d. (9p.) per ton. The f.o.b. price at Cardiff fluctuated between 8s. (40p.) and 10s. (50p.) a ton for most of this period.

[4]See, for example, *Monmouthshire Merlin*, 31 December 1842; 14 January, 14 and 28 April 1843; 10 June, 1848; 22 December 1849; 5 November 1852; 25 July and 10 November 1855.

[5]*Merthyr Guardian*, 9 and 23 January, 20 February 1858.

[6]*Western Mail*, 7 May 1869.

[7]See, for example, Dowlais MSS (Glamorgan Record Office), Cardiff Agency Letters: S. Howard to Dowlais Iron Co., 19 January 1861.

[8]N.L.W., Bute MSS, Box 141 (22 July 1839).

[9]*Merthyr Guardian*, 30 October 1869.

[10]Nevill MSS 8: R.J. Nevill to S. Rhode, 11 May 1833.

[11]See, for example, *Cambrian*, 17 January 1846; *Merthyr Guardian*, 16 October 1863; and Dowlais MSS, Cardiff Agency Letter Books: S. Howard to Dowlais Iron Company, 2 January 1861.

[12]*Monmouthshire Merlin*, 10 April 1841, 10 and 17 July 1841, 5 May 1849; *Merthyr Guardian*, 2 and 16 February 1839, 11 January 1840, 31 July 1841, 15 January 1842, 10 and 17 March 1849.

[13]*The Times*, 20 September 1893; D.A. Thomas, *Some Notes on the Present State of the Coalfield* (1896).

[14]W. Ashworth, *An Economic History of England, 1870-1939* (1960), pp. 100-1.

[15]*Select Committee on Payment of Wages Bill* (P.P., 1854 (382), XVI: evidence of Thomas Brown). A modern-day Thomas Brown would need to add a rider: 'You cannot shut up a colliery—except to prepare for its privatisation.'

[16]A recent attempt to measure fluctuations in miners' earnings confirms their cataclysmic variation. G.J. Barnsby, 'The Standard of Living in the Black Country in the Nineteenth Century', *Economic History review*, 2nd ser., XXIV (1971).

[17]*Colliery Guardian*, 19 March 1864.

[18]W.G. Dalziel, *The Monmouthshire and South Wales Coal Owners Association* (1895), pp. 3-5.

[19]W.G. Dalziel, *op.cit.*, p. 8.

[20]Ibid., pp.9-11.

[21]J.H. Morris and L.J. Williams, *The South Wales Coal Industry, 1841-1875* (1958), pp.278-81.

[22]*South Wales Daily News*, 29 May 1875; N.L.W., Coalowners MSS, Association Minutes, 21 May 1875.

[23]N.L.W., Coalowners MSS, Scrapbook 1. Notes for discussion prepared by John Nixon; Owners' Sliding Scale Committee Minutes, 18 and 25 June 1875; Circular, 29 June 1875; Report of Owners S.S.C. to Association Council, 6 August 1875.

[24]E.W. Evans, *Mabon* (1959), pp. 16-18.

[25]N.L.W., Coalowners MSS, J.S.S.C. Minutes, 17, 18 and 29 November 1875. In fixing the selling price that was to be equivalent to any given minimum wage-rate, it was in the interests of the men to have a price as low as possible and for the employers to ensure it was as high as possible. If, for example, the minimum wage-rate was equivalent to a selling price of 8s (40p.) a ton, and wage advances were given for each shilling rise in price, then when the price was 10s. (50p.) the men would have secured two advances on the minimum. If the equivalent selling price for the same minimum wage-rate was 10s. (50p.), there would be no wage increase at all until the selling price rose to at least 11s. (55p.).

[26]The collieries were divided into three groups: the steam-coal collieries; the bituminous collieries of Monmouthshire and Caerphilly; and the remaining bituminous and anthracite collieries. This arrangement, which was not repeated in later scales, has been largely ignored in the text, which concentrates on the provisions for steam-coal. The essential argument is not affected.

[27]*Ibid.*, J.S.S.C. Minutes, 2 December 1875; Sliding Scale Agreement, 11 December 1875.

[28]N.L.W., Coalowners MSS., Scrapbook 2: A. Dalziel to J. Nixon, 7 December 1875.

[29]*Western Mail*, 21 April 1876.

[30]The average price of steam coal, f.o.b., Cardiff in 1871 was 10s.6d. (52.1/2p.); 1872 19s. 3d. (96p.); 1873, 23s. 3d. (£1.16p.); 1874, 16s. 1d. (81p.); 1875, 14s. 3d. (71p.); and for the last three months of 1875 as revealed by the sliding-scale audit, 10s. 7.82d. (56p.) (W.G. Dalziel, *op.cit.*, p. 108). This source also gives average annual prices as far back as 1848. The output per head in South Wales in 1874 was 277 tons (for underground workers) and 224 tons (for all workers); in 1880 the comparable figures were 363 tons and 306 tons (F.A. Gibson, *op.cit.*).

[31]W.W. Rostow, *British Economy of the Nineteenth Century* (1948), p. 201.

[32]W.G. Dalziel, *op.cit.*, pp. 108c, 108d.

[33]*Ibid.*, pp. 9-14.

[34]N.L.W., Coalowners MSS, Scrapbook 3: W.T. Lewis to A. Dalziel, 15 May 1877.

[35] *Ibid.*, Scrapbook 10: Workmen's Committee, Aberaman, to A. Dalziel, 25 July 1877; J.S.S.C. Minutes, 8 May, 28 August 1877.

[36] *Ibid.*, Scrapbook 8, Cardiff District Board Minutes, 25 May 1877; J.S.S.C. Minutes, 28 August 1877.

[37] *Western Mail*, 26 May 1877.

[38] Until 1875, the principal partner of these ironworks had been Richard Fothergill, M.P., who was chairman of the Association for the first three years of its existence (1873-75). The firm had, however, failed in June 1875 and had since been run by a committee of creditors—chiefly the London and Westminster Bank. W.T. Lewis was the agent for the Bute Trustees, the lessors and large creditors: *Western Mail*, 16 September 1875, 1 November 1876; N.L.W., Coalowners MSS, Scrapbook 8: A. Dalziel to F. Buckle, 20 June 1877.

[39] Billy Fair-play was a machine for separating the large coal from the small before weighing. It was resented by the colliers because they considered the bars were too far apart, thus making too much small coal—for which they were not paid.

[40] N.L.W., Coalowners MSS, Scrapbook 8: Case of W.T. Lewis in support of reduction, June 1877; W.T. Lewis to A. Dalziel, 2 June 1877; W.T. Lewis to D. Davies, M.P., 31 May 1877.

[41] *South Wales Daily News*, 2 June 1877.

[42] *Western Mail*, 30 July 1877.

[43] N.L.W., Coalowners MSS., J.S.S.C. Minutes, 14 and 28 December 1877.

[44] *Western Mail*, 14 December 1878.

[45] A soup kitchen was started at Merthyr, for example, on 22 December 1878 and was not closed till the end of April 1879. See *Western Mail, passim.*

[46] *Western Mail*, 1-15 July 1879.

[47] W.G. Dalziel, *op.cit.*, pp. 10-11.

7. THE DISCHARGE NOTE IN THE SOUTH WALES COAL INDUSTRY, 1841-98

The discharge note was a certificate given to each worker who satisfactorily completed his contract of service at one colliery and which had to be produced before he could be engaged at another. It merits attention because it was an aggravating factor in industrial relations over a long period, becoming prominent whenever attempts were made to enforce it systematically. In theory its use had, from the employers' point of view, several advantages. It strengthened their position in disputes by preventing men on strike at one colliery from obtaining employment in another while the strike lasted. It aided industrial discipline by acting as a check on the collier who left at the least provocation—often without giving due notice—and sought work at another colliery. It helped the employer whenever he engaged fresh workmen, since men who possessed their discharge could be assumed to be of suitable character and competence.

The circumstances of the industry made these objectives particularly desirable to the owners. The disturbed geological conditions of the coalfield gave rise to frequent negotiations over wage rates, not only when a new pit or a new seam was started but also whenever the state of the seams altered as new areas of the colliery were exploited. In these negotiations neither side would make concessions easily; the men because the level of their earnings depended on the outcome, and the employers because wages formed a large proportion of their working costs. Often agreement was reached only after a strike had occurred, and the duration of these strikes was curtailed if the owners, by using the discharge note, could prevent men on strike from obtaining work at other collieries.

In an expanding industry, too, and particularly because collieries were often sunk in sparsely populated districts, there were recurrent general and local scarcities of labour which aggravated the difficulties of imposing industrial discipline. These labour scarcities attracted into the valleys a flow of immigrants, including large numbers of unmarried males whose mobility was unusually high. Herbert Mackworth, inspector of mines, commented that 'the collieries being large and recently commenced, a considerable but changing population has been collected round each mine. The mixed character of these people collected from all parts of South Wales and the South-west of England renders it less under the control of the masters than that near the ironworks'.[1] Yet control was essential, above all in fiery mines where safety depended on the colliers being as disciplined as a well regulated regiment. The discharge note, including the threat of withholding it, could be used to check the mobility of the worker who left without notice and to curb the intransigence of those who did not comply with the discipline of the mine. Its presentation, too, by a new worker was some guarantee that he would not endanger the lives of others by his lack of skill.

In theory the discharge note appeared to be a device well adapted to meet the needs of the owners; in practice it proved difficult to apply. Nevertheless, recurrent attempts were made to enforce it for at least sixty years. Its history dates from before 1841, as is evident from a letter written in that year by the Marquis of Bute to Sir Charles Shaw.[2] 'I am afraid', he wrote, 'that within the last five or six years, viz. since the great increase in the demand for Coal and Iron, the managers of Ironworks and Collieries have admitted men without enquiring into their characters, and without looking for the marks upon their discharges according to the former understanding'. It is not surprising that when the South Wales ironmasters met at London in 1847[3] to consider measures of mutual protection they decided that they would employ no men involved in a turn-out and employ no new men without a written discharge. The coal and iron industries were so closely intertwined at this period that the practice of the ironmasters naturally provided precedents for the coal owners. In 1860, for example, an advertisement of 100 vacancies at Nixon's Navigation colliery stipulated that 'every man must have his discharge and his character from his last employer'.[4] When the coal owners of the Aberdare valley formed an association in 1864 they applied a similar rule and it was stated that, in consequence, the Aberdare colliers had become more manageable.[5]

The evidence, indeed, suggests that these efforts of the employers were not wholly ineffective. In 1841 a Monmouthshire collier, complaining about truck, said that 'if a man gets a pound in debt he can't get his discharge, and it is useless to attempt to get work without a discharge'.[6] John Owen, a Monmouthshire solicitor, whose services as 'attorney general' for the colliers enabled him to speak with authority on industrial relations, in 1843 criticised the employers for leaving too much to their 'gaffers', saying that if any man went to law against his employer he was sacked. His discharge was not withheld, but a black mark was put against his name and his character transmitted to other 'gaffers'.[7] When Owen accompanied the men's delegates to negotiate the settlement after the Monmouthshire strike of 1843, he secured an addition to the agreement of a pledge by the coalowners that 'we will not exclude any man from vindictive feeling arising from the late turn-out, and will employ as many of the old workmen as we can find employment for, and will give every man discharged such character as he deserves'.[8] In 1854 John Lewis, a miner, related how, after he had won a truck case with Owen's help, he received his discharge, but it had a notch cut in it. He was told by an employer that he could get work 'but as soon as he saw my discharge, he said "No, we do not want you."' Lewis was unemployed for nine months, had to enter the workhouse, and succeeded in getting work only after he had, on Owen's advice, cut the notch off his discharge.[9] After the Aberdare strike of 1857 Thomas Beddoe, overman at the Lower Duffryn pit, said that 'no man going out on strike had a discharge . . . It is the practice not to give discharges in Aberdare on such occasions'.[10]

Nevertheless it is clear that men, and even men on strike, could obtain employment without a discharge note. James Darby, for example, who said that he had been sacked from Risca colliery after he had complained about gas, had not been given a discharge note yet had obtained work at Abercarn colliery.[11] When a strike occurred at Coedcae colliery in 1867 most of the strikers found work in other collieries, many of them perishing in the Ferndale explosion.[12] More generally, the attempts of the association of the owners of steam coal collieries to prevent men from finding employment at non-associated collieries and ironworks during the strike of 1871 were a complete failure.[13]

The evidence for the period before 1873 is thus somewhat sketchy and a little conflicting. No doubt the importance of the discharge note varied from time to time and from place to place but, however partial its application, the men evidently considered its possession a valuable aid in their search for work. Some owners used it as a reputable disciplinary device, while in the hands of other owners, or of their agents, it became a tyrannical weapon to be used for the victimisation of 'agitators'. In these early years no strong trade unionism had developed amongst the men and the simplest way for them to resist the discharge note was to seek work at collieries where it need not be produced rather than to make an explicit issue of it in trade disputes. Such evasion was easier because the employers, themselves lacking any strong formal association, were not able to operate the discharge note on a continual and general basis.

In 1873, however, the Monmouthshire and South Wales Collieries Association, with 86 members accounting between them for nearly three-quarters of the total output of the coalfield, was formed.[14] Since the Association indemnified members for any loss of output suffered during a stoppage it was clearly anxious that its funds, so useful in a general struggle, should not be dissipated by protracted local disputes. To strengthen their position the owners resolved on 14 August 1873 that no workman who had been employed in an associated colliery should be employed at any other colliery in the Association unless he could produce his discharge to be handed over to his new employer.[15] A few days later the owners appointed an agent to investigate complaints that men on strike in the Rhondda were gaining employment at associated pits.[16] On the complaints proving well founded, the employers concerned pleading that the strikers had been 'inadvertently engaged'; the Association insisted that the men concerned should be discharged immediately. By 23 August the committee of Rhondda owners could report that this had been done and that no other men on strike were being engaged. At the same meeting it was asserted that the men out at the Rhymney Level were returning to work because, without discharge notes, they could not obtain employment elsewhere.

The employers' policy now applied by an Association considerably more powerful than that of the Aberdare coal owners in 1864, aroused the immediate resentment of the men.[17] The discharge note was stigmatised as a 'ticket of leave' and Halliday advised the men not to accept this 'infamous' document in any circumstances. But the Amalgamated Association of Miners, while promising to defray the legal expenses of any man proceeding against his employer for improper dismissal, decided that they could not pay men who were unemployed because of the operation of the discharge note. In the event, it was not the men but some of the owners who secured a relaxation in the policy of the Association. The original proposal had been that the possession of a discharge note should be essential at all times before employment was given and that the note might, after an investigation of the facts by the Association, be withheld from men at any colliery where a strike was in progress or pending. This proposal preceded the formal establishment of the Association, but when the time came for signing the Deed of Association two potential members, Sir George Elliot and Mark Curtis, raised objections.[18] Representing the Powell Duffryn Company and the Ebbw Vale Iron and Coal Company respectively, they formed no inconsequential minority. Sir George Elliot, himself an ex-pit boy, insisted that all men who had given and served a proper notice should be entitled to a discharge note.[19] To meet this view the original proposal, despite the misgivings of a majority of the members, was amended so that discharge notes could be withheld only 'under exceptional circumstances'. Mark Curtis, unlike most of the owners in his belief that trade unions should be acknowledged, wanted the discharge note to be used only 'during the existence of a strike at any one pit in the association'. This involved the abandonment of the general disciplinary advantages of the discharge note, and to some owners it seemed dubious if the Ebbw Vale membership was worth this price. There was a general belief, however, that Monmouthshire as a whole would fall away if Ebbw Vale did not join. 'After careful deliberation the meeting seemed to prefer adopting Mr. Curtis' view (altho' most prejudicial) rather than lose the Ebbw Vale Co., and this opinion gained ground *in the hope that at a future date the discharge note will be returned to as a permanent system*'.[20]

The resulting policy of the Association was thus considerably less stringent than that originally proposed. The note was to be used by all members only when any associated colliery was stopped through a dispute and it was not to be withheld from men simply because they were strikers. To operate this policy members were informed when disputes resulting in stoppages occurred. Although the employers were putting this policy into practice in the following year, and the Amalgamated Association of Miners was countering by prohibiting union members from working in strikers' places,[21] the issue remained largely dormant for over a decade. During these years unionism more or less collapsed in South Wales and the comparative depression in the coal trade curbed the militancy of the men. Also the introduction of the Sliding Scale, which from the beginning of 1876 regulated wages on an automatic basis, reduced for some years the number of widespread strikes, whilst many disputes were settled by the Sliding Scale Joint Committee without a strike actually taking place. Moreover, as W.T. Lewis (later Lord Merthyr) scornfully observed in 1874, the discharge note, as accepted by the Association, was ineffective.

The difficulties inherent in the enforcement of the discharge note were revealed by the strike at the Albion colliery in 1888.[22] This strike had started in May, but complaints that Associated collieries were employing strikers were reiterated throughout June, ultimately leading the Association to appoint a Committee of Investigation with power to report to the owners the names of the men whom the Committee thought should be peremptorily dismissed. The main plea of the offending owners was the difficulty of identifying strikers because, apart from the problem of identifying any particular David Davies or Evan Jones in the Welsh valleys, strikers might give false names, or work for a short time at a non-associated colliery and give this as their place of last employment. But this plea also served as an excuse to cover a certain reluctance on the part of owners to apply a policy, the principle of which they approved (for who knew when they might have a strike themselves?), but which, on occasion, might prove inconvenient. In 1888, after four years of falling prices, trade was reviving and this made owners look less searchingly at any experienced colliers who applied for work. At the time of the Albion strike, for example, it was found that the Penrhiwceiber Company, after it had reluctantly permitted an examination of its registers, was employing 33 of the strikers, while Nixon's Navigation Company, which was prominent amongst those pleading the difficulty of identifying strikers, refused to allow any inspection of its registers or to send a representative before the Committee.

The experience of the Albion strike led E.M. Hann, who represented the Powell Duffryn Company, to suggest that the Association should alter its policy and 'adopt the use of the Discharge Note at all times and not merely when strikes are pending or existing.'[23] This was rejected, not on grounds of principle, but because it would have prevented the associated owners from employing colliers from most of the collieries outside the Association. The majority of the non-associated coal owners did not use the discharge note and they had an unrestricted choice of labour. For most of the members of the Association, in face of the revival of trade, the attractiveness of the stronger line over discharge notes suggested by Hann was outweighed by the disadvantage it involved in competition for labour.

The opposition of the men, however, was now becoming more vocal. They had not made the use of the discharge note a serious issue during the negotiations which preceded the Sliding Scale agreements of 1875, 1880, 1882 and 1887, nor do the minutes of the Sliding Scale Joint Committee relating to disputes give any indication of the men's dissatisfaction over this question before 1889. With the tendency towards a more militant policy the Unions now adopted a more positive attitude. The proposals put forward by the men at the end of 1889 for a revision of the Sliding Scale agreement included a clause stating 'that it shall be a violation of this agreement to victimise any workman under any circumstances whatever.'[24] The subsequent discussion left no doubt that this clause was directed against the discharge note. The demand was withdrawn in return for an improvement in the Scale itself, but the ensuing decade was to show that suspicion remained.

The principal issue in the coalfield during these years was whether or not the Sliding Scale should be retained as a regulator of wages. Most of the coal owners were anxious to retain it and they were generally supported by the trade union leaders of the Liberal tradition, personified by William Abraham, M.P. (Mabon). The opposition to the scale stemmed from the Miners' Federation of Great Britain, an importation from England, and the 1890s saw the long struggle for supremacy between this militant, unified organisation and the more cautious, disconnected native unions. The discharge note, with its potentialities as an instrument of victimisation, inevitably played some part in this issue. At the close of the hauliers' strike of 1893 (in which the men had been soundly defeated) the report of the Coal Owners' Emergency Committee, under the chairmanship of Sir W.T. Lewis, included a recommendation for 'the adoption of the Discharge Note system forthwith in order to protect the Associated Owners from the insidious actions of the M.F.G.B.'[25] It is difficult to see how the permanent use of the discharge note would have been much more effective for this purpose than its existing use whenever a strike occurred unless, implicit in the proposal, was the employment of the note as a method of victimising M.F.G.B. members. In this context the attitude towards trade unions of Sir W.T. Lewis, whose strong personality dominated the Association at this time, was significant. He had spent a life-time dealing with industrial disputes, but had never been able to reconcile himself to the need for trade unions. Discrimination against M.F.G.B. 'agitators', then, may well have been excluded from Sir William's definition of victimisation.

Following his lead the Association decided that the Emergency Committee should continue in being to take the necessary steps to secure the permanent adoption of the discharge note. This intention was thwarted, however, because the 1892 Sliding Scale agreement included a clause that made all the customs in operation at the collieries in 1879 permanent, unless both sides agreed to their alteration. The co-operation of the men for such a purpose was not to be expected and the owners, anxious to uphold the Sliding Scale, were reluctant to 'go it alone'. By the beginning of 1896, however, the misgivings of the owners had been swept aside, largely because of the demonstrated ineffectiveness of the old system during the Caerau strike. This strike, over the identification of a seam, had started in

April 1894; at the end of 1895 settlement seemed as remote as ever, virtually all the men involved having obtained employment elsewhere. After an Association enquiry had revealed that 'several hundreds' of the Caerau men were working at other Associated pits it was felt that the usual instructions that these men should be discharged were not enough.[26] As a first step it was decided to appoint paid officials who were to inspect the registers and discharge notes at all collieries. More important, however, was the decision of the Association, after twenty years of irresolution, to impose the discharge note on a permanent basis.[27] Nobody was to be employed without producing a discharge note; engagements were to be made only by the certificated manager and no worker was to be employed until it was 'absolutely certain that such person was not engaged at a Colliery immediately before a strike occurred at such Colliery'. These new regulations were effective, perhaps too effective. They led to the collapse of the Caerau strike by mid-February but they also provoked an immediate and violent reaction from the men. Not since 1875 'has any matter met with such universal condemnation at the hands of the workmen', a local newspaper commented.[28] At a meeting of miners' delegates a strong minority favoured an immediate strike, without even waiting to discuss the matter with the owners, to force the withdrawal of the discharge note.

This withdrawal was demanded by the men's representatives when the Sliding Scale Joint Committee met on 7 March 1896. William Abraham sketched out the basis of the opposition of the men: 'A number of men who believe they have a right to employment are today idle because of this system. The Discharge Note will be a vexatious system even in the hands of the best managers, but in the hands of unscrupulous or inconsiderate officials it is a demoralising instrument. In adopting this system the Owners, perhaps unintentionally, consent to victimising some of their best workmen . . . With all the evidence brought before the Royal Commission on Labour there was nothing reported that was so severe in the system of employment as the Discharge Note lately adopted.'[29] The owners repudiated any intention of using the note to victimise men and dilated on its value in promoting discipline and safety; during a strike it was a legitimate tactical weapon to offset the practice of the unions of preventing, by picketing and intimidation, the replacement of men on strike. The decisive consideration, however, was not so much the cogency of the arguments that either side could adduce as the certainty that, if the owners did not reconsider their policy, a general stoppage would ensue. The men, too, made it clear that if the owners wanted the Sliding Scale agreement to include the discharge note it would be better for the Sliding Scale to be abolished. Unwilling to risk so much, the owners agreed on 28 March to suspend the use of the discharge note.[30]

The owners, underestimating the opposition, had misjudged the situation; an even greater error of judgement was the refusal to accept this suspension as final. It was even suggested, as a way out of the impasse pending revision of the agreement, that the owners should engage no new men at all. The importance attached to the issue by some owners was indicated by this drastic suggestion, but it was withdrawn when others showed that they considered such a mammoth self-denying ordinance a cure worse than the malady. The chance to reimpose the discharge note finally appeared to come with the outbreak of the great strike of 1898, when the survival of the Sliding Scale was at stake. The owners originally made the reintroduction of the discharge note one of their terms of settlement but, although they were eventually victorious even to the extent of securing the abolition of the miners' monthly holiday, the men's much-prized 'Mabon's Day', they were unable to reintroduce the discharge note.

The owners had yielded to the opposition to the discharge note because some believed that the new Workmen's Compensation Act would enable them to secure their original aim in a different way. As soon as the strike had ended it was suggested that all collieries should keep a 'register book' containing full particulars of all new applicants for work. 'If all Owners keep the register for the purposes of the Compensation Act and at the same time find out where the applicant for work was previously employed it will be known whether or not he is a striker from any of the Associated Collieries'.[31] Despite the reluctance of some owners to obtain 'by a side wind that which we have deliberately abandoned' and the fear that 'the workmen will see thro' the attempt', the register book was introduced in May 1899. The men's leaders immediately demanded its withdrawal. They felt that the owners had violated the agreement of the previous year and that the register was simply the discharge note in a new form to be used to trace and persecute marked men.[32] At first the right of the owners to ask the questions was conceded but the men won their claim not to sign any statements made. Later the possibilities of the register as a substitute for the discharge note were killed when the men were advised by their leaders not to answer the questions of the employers. In the long battle over the discharge note the final round had gone to the men.

Despite the real potential advantages of the discharge note to the owners—as a strike weapon, as a certificate of competency and as a disciplinary instrument—the wisdom of their persistent attempts to enforce its use was questionable. Partly it was ineffectual as it could be evaded, and this still remained true even after the employers had formed a strong Association. Partly it generated friction as the men, while not denying that it had a legitimate use, believed that it lent itself too easily to abuse. Memories recalled the early years when the note had often been used frankly to victimize 'agitators'; even later, when most owners disavowed such practices, its operation was left to managers and overmen who were often less scrupulous. The failing of the coal owners was their persistent insensitivity to the deep suspicions that the discharge note aroused in the minds of the men.

Notes

[1]*Mines, Inspectors' Reports*. Mackworth's Report for July—December 1853.

[2]National Library of Wales. Bute MSS. Box 70, vol. 13, letter dated 15 February 1841. Bute, writing when the memory of events at Newport in 1839 was still fresh, hoped particularly that known Chartists would not be employed.

[3]*Merthyr Guardian*, 20 March 1847.

[4]*Ibid.*, 22 September 1860.

[5]*Colliery Guardian*, 4 June 1864.

[6]*Children's Employment Commission. Mines*, Parl. Papers, 1842, XVII, 531.

[7]*Merthyr Guardian*, 18 March, 1 April 1843.

[8]*Ibid.*, 1 April 1843.

[9]Evidence of J. Lewis, *Select Committee on Payment of Wages Bill*, Parl. Papers, 1854, XVI.

[10]*Merthyr Guardian*, 6 March 1858.

[11]*Colliery Guardian*, 26 January 1861.

[12]*Merthyr Guardian*, 1 February 1868.

[13]A. Dalziel, *Colliers' Strike in South Wales* (Cardiff, 1872), p. 81.

[14]W.G. Dalziel, *The Monmouthshire and south Wales Coal Owners' Association* (1895), pp. 9-11. The records of the Association are deposited at the National Library of Wales. This account is based primarily on the 'General Minutes' and on the 'Minutes of the Joint Sliding Scale Committee'.

[15]General Minutes, 14 August, 1873.

[16]*Ibid.*, 19 21, 23 August 1873.

[17]*Colliery Guardian*, 5, 12, 26 September; 10, 17 October 1873.

[18]General Minutes, 20 October 1873.

[19]The effect of Sir George Elliot's proposal was that workers who served out their notice before going on strike could receive their discharge note and would not be penalised if they wished to work at another associated colliery once the strike was over. during the strike the name of the colliery on the note would prevent their being employed.

[20]General Minutes, 7 November 1873. (Underlining in the original.)

[21]*Colliery Guardian*, 2 January, 2 October 1874.

[22]General Minutes, 18 May, 30 June 1888.

[23]*Ibid.*, 19 January 1889.

[24]Shorthand notes of discussion re. revision of agreement, 1889-90, 30 November 1889.

[25]General Minutes, 30 September 1893.

[26]Association circulars, Vol. 3, 24 December 1895, 10 January 1896.

[27]*Ibid.* 21, 27 January 1896; General Minutes, 16 January 1896.

[28]*Cambrian*, 24 March 1896. See also the issues of the *Iron and Coal Trades Review* for March 1896.

[29]Minutes of the Sliding Scale Committee, 7 March 1896.

[30]*Ibid.*, 7, 14 March 1896; *Cambrian*, 3 April 1896.

[31]General Minutes, 25 October 1898.

[32]*Iron and Coal Trades Review*, 23 June, 7 July 1899. The issue for 7 July gives a list of the employers' questions. The men had to agree to dismissal if they were found giving inaccurate answers.

8. MINERS AND THE LAW OF CONTRACT, 1875-1914[1]

One of the distinguishing characteristics of the conduct of industrial relations in the South Wales coalfield in the years immediately preceding the First World War was the widespread use made of the legal system. It is not the purpose of this article to illustrate, explain and comment upon that general issue, but simply to draw attention to one little-noticed aspect: the use made of the law about breach of contract. The contention is that cases of breach of contract played a significant role in conditioning the relationship between miners and coalowners. It will also be suggested that the South Wales experience was in this respect unusual and thus to demonstrate the dangers of assuming that generalisations about social behaviour and attitudes drawn from the United Kingdom (or, as in this case, the England and Wales) experience can be applied to Wales (or some part of Wales).

The received view is that after the law was changed in 1875 breach of contract was little used in British industrial relations. Wedderburn draws attention to the widespread use of breach of contract prosecutions before 1875 and indicates a substantial decline after the passage of the Employers and Workmen Act of that year.[2] The nature and significance of the change in the law which was then introduced makes such a proposition not merely plausible but reasonably probable. It is, however, more difficult to demonstrate with any confidence. The intention, therefore, is to start by recalling briefly the change in the law before examining the use made of its provisions nationally (or rather in England and Wales), and to use that basis as a standard of comparison with South Wales.

The under-lying assumption alike of English law and of mainstream economic theory has always been that the agreement between employer and workman is a voluntary compact freely entered into by two parties (individuals) equally placed in terms of knowledge and (bargaining) strength. It is an assumption which still under-lies the theorising in each of these disciplines. For much of the nineteenth century, however, legal practice not merely imposed the injustice compounded in this fiction, but by way of precaution added a few crucial distinctions to weight the game decisively in favour of the employers. The Master and Servant Act of 1823 laid down that a workman who broke his contract became liable for criminal charges and could be imprisoned for up to three months with hard labour. A group of men acting together in breach of contract could be charged with criminal conspiracy. Under the same Act a Master who broke his contract could be subject at most to a civil action for damages or unpaid wages. The voices of the economists were not to be heard ringing through the land in protest at these substantial interventions in the free working of the market.

In addition, the whole apparatus and mechanism of the law worked to aggravate and deepen these initial distinctions. A single J.P. could issue a warrant for the summary arrest of the workmen. From 1848 (Jervis's Act) the use of a summons, in place of a warrant for arrest, became the normal procedure in England and Wales, though not in Scotland. Even in England and Wales the use of the warrant was still possible and was, moreover, occasionally employed. This was the experience suffered by some Durham miners who in 1863 were engaged in a dispute and proceeded against by the coalowner and 'in the middle of the next night twelve of them were taken out of their beds by the police and lodged in Durham lock-up on the charge of deserting their work without notice'. Cases brought could be heard by a single J.P. and the only punishment that could be given was imprisonment, the alternative of fines or damages not being available.[3] The Master and Servant Act of 1867 operated particularly on this last aspect by substantially modifying the penalties imposed. The number of prosecutions remained high.[4]

It is generally suggested, with much reason, that the blatant discrimination by the law in favour of employers and against the workers was mostly laid to rest in 1875. The labour leaders of the time, whose organised political pressure was one of the important influences on the outcome, had been especially concerned to throw off the liability to criminal charges. They succeeded in having criminal liability for breach of contract of service restricted to public utility workers and to cases where the workers' action had entailed danger. As the Webbs put it: 'The Master and Servant Act of 1867 was replaced by an Employers and Workmen Act . . ., a change of nomenclature which expressed a fundamental revolution in the law. Henceforward master and servant became, as employer and employee, two equal parties to a civil contract.'[5] There was much validity in this judgement. A special section of the 1875 Act made magistrates' courts courts of civil jurisdiction in cases involving less than £10 in disputes between employers and manual workers.[6] The intention and the effect was to provide a cheap process which would be accessible to workers as well as employers. None the less the verdict of the Webbs begged a number of questions. The assumption remained that any bargain represented a voluntary agreement between two equal individuals. But the reality was that the parties were not equal, not in the striking of the bargain and not in the ability, despite the legal reforms, to go to law. Moreover, although the change in the title of the Act was important and symbolic, attitudes were and remained deeply entrenched. Certainly judges well into the twentieth century slipped easily into the nomenclature of 'master and servant', although they would perhaps plead that they were simply using the technicalities of their trade.[7]

The strong impression is given that after 1875 little use was made by employers of breach of contract cases as a weapon in industrial relations. Much of the evidence for this is necessarily negative. The topic virtually disappears from the basic books on the history of trade unions, the labour movement and labour law—books which dealt with the injustices of the pre-1875 situation. There is certainly no repetition of the confident assertion made about the old Master and Servant Act that it has been effectively used by employers to break strikes.[8] Nor does abuse of breach of contract law appear as an item of complaint by labour representatives before such bodies as the Royal Commission on Labour in the 1890s. The statistical evidence will need to be examined more closely later but two points of immediate relevance may be made here: there was, despite the easier access, a substantial decline in the number of breach of contract cases brought after 1875 (from an average of about 10,000 cases a year to a little over 6,000); and the records of individual police courts indicate that a significant (but indeterminate) proportion of these were brought by, mostly individual, workmen claiming wages which they considered to be due to them.

It is against this subdued background that we need to assess developments in the South Wales coalfield which, it will be argued, ran in a counter direction. The evidence is partly statistical but, for the crucial period in the first decade of the twentieth century, more reliance is placed on the records of the local courts, the reports of cases in the

PROCEEDINGS BEFORE JUSTICES UNDER THE EMPLOYERS AND WORKMEN ACT 1875

Table 1. Persons proceeded against, and as a proportion of population, in Glamorgan County (1), Durham County (1), and the remainder of England and Wales

	Glamorgan		Durham		Remainder England and Wales	
	Persons proceeded against	Per 10,000 popul.	Persons proceeded against	Per 10,000 popul.	Persons proceeded against	Per 10,000 popul.
1880	384	10.9	221	3.7	5762	2.3
1881	457	12.6	396	6.6	5912	2.4
1882	321	8.6	1109	18.2	6653	2.6
1883	259	6.7	990	16.0	6072	2.4
1884	380	9.6	1496	23.9	5890	2.3
1885	278	7.0	754	11.9	5040	1.9
1886	291	7.2	286	4.4	4315	1.6
1887	293	7.1	720	11.1	4355	1.6
1888	621	14.6	1307	19.8	4001	1.5
1889	389	8.9	1655	24.8	5732	2.1
1890	364	8.2	363	5.4	6596	2.4
1891	495	10.8	1615	23.6	6385	2.3
1892	374	8.2	260	3.8	4996	1.8
		Ave. 9.3		Ave.13.3		Ave. 2.1

(1) Police Districts (i.e. excluding Boroughs and County Boroughs).

Source: Judicial Statistics.

Table 2. Persons proceeded against, England and Wales, 1880-1913.

Year end. Sept.		Year end. Sept.		Year end. Dec.	
1880	6,367	1890	7,323	1900	7,224
1881	6,765	1891	8,495	1901	7,501
1882	8,083	1892	5,630	1902	7,916
1883	7,321	1893(1)	5,661	1903	8,842
1884	7,766	1894	6,828	1904	
1885	6,072	1895	6,625	1905	4,995
1886	4,892	1896	7,325	1906	4,564
1887	5,368	1897	7,111	1907	
1888	5,929	1898	7,109	1908	6,410
1889	7,776	1899	7,428	1909	6,526
				1910	6,247
				1911	6,500
				1912	5,865
				1913	5,055

(1) From 1893, calendar year.

Source: From 1893, calendar year.

press and the proceedings of the Coalowners' Association. The judicial statistics, normally so fecund and helpful—even if they do have to be handled with extreme caution—can only serve as indicators on the topic of breach of contract. The statistics have three substantial limitations. They do not distinguish between cases brought by workmen and cases brought by employers. Perhaps more seriously, after 1893 they are only available on an England and Wales basis. Up to 1893 the figures for actions under section 4 of the Employers and Workmen Act had appeared under criminal statistics in the tables of 'offences determined summarily' (Police—Table 7) and were given separately for each police district. In 1893, on the occasion of a review of the criminal section of the judicial statistics, the figures for breach of contract cases under the 1875 Act were re-allocated, one consequence of which was that from then on the figures were only available in the form of an aggregate figure for England and Wales.[9] Finally, the series both before and after 1893 suffers, like most official judicial statistics, from some shortcomings. In particular, they are not complete: before 1893 this seems to have been because not all police districts supplied the necessary return, whilst a note to the table for 1909 indicated that 'the figures are obtained from the police who have no direct concern in many of the cases to which they relate, and it has, therefore, always been recognised as probable that their accuracy is only approximate'.

The official statistics can, therefore, only serve as indicators. They do, however, yield a very strong indication of the main point to be established: that the experience of South Wales was at variance with that of England and Wales as a whole. This strongly emerges for the period up to 1893 from the figures in Table 1. The table also serves to draw attention to another important feature: it is no way the intention to suggest that South Wales was necessarily unique. To establish this point the statistics for Durham, as well as Glamorgan, have been included. Their inclusion points to another characteristic: the higher usage of the Act seems to have been particularly related to the coal industry and this aspect will need to be embraced in any attempt to 'explain' the South Wales experience. The evidence before parliamentary committees lends qualitative support to the view that coalowners, almost alone, continued to make persistent use of the law of contract 'as an instrument of industrial discipline'. The figures reveal that the usage of the Act in both Durham and Glamorgan was always substantially greater than over the country as a whole.[10] Thus the strong probability is that the statistics for England and Wales, the only figures available after 1893, conceal a proportionately higher level of cases in so marked a mining district as South Wales (Table 2).

The kind of cases which are of most immediate concern are those brought by employers as a means of imposing industrial discipline or curbing trade union growth. There are good reasons for believing that for cases of this sort the extent of what is concealed behind the national figures is greater than might seem to be indicated by the numbers of Glamorgan cases in the pre-1893 returns. Some adjustment for example, though of a relatively minor sort, would be needed to accommodate the fact that some cases were taken to the County Court. They cannot, however, be unscrambled from the Civil statistics: newspaper reports testify to the use of this method in South Wales but also suggest that it was small scale.[11] Of much greater significance was the fact that the number of cases recorded in the statistics was not necessarily a good guide to the number of persons affected. This was especially true of the cases that we are mostly concerned with, the cases brought by employers where it frequently happened that awards made in court were then applied to other workmen who had not been summoned. An unexceptional example is the case brought by Crawshay Bros., Cyfarthfa Ltd. in 1907. Dis-satisfaction at the failure of the hitchers to secure a wage advance led to a half-day stoppage without notice. The Company summoned 24 workmen and was awarded 4s. 6d. damages against each. The award was then applied to 132 other men who had been involved in the stoppage. At most, therefore, the judicial statistics would have recorded that 24 men had been proceeded against under section 4 of the 1875 Act,[12] and not that the company had received damages for breach of contract from 156 men.[13] Occasionally the numbers so involved could be very large indeed. Thus in a case where 12 men were summoned in 1896 it was said that collieries employing 4,000 men were stopped.[14] These were obviously not included in the number of 'persons proceeded against' in the judicial statistics.

An additional way in which there was a large but indeterminate under-statement in the figures arose from out-of-court settlements. It was a common occurrence for summonses to be issued and then withdrawn either before a first hearing or following a request for adjournment. In such cases the men, knowing that they had stopped without notice and would lose in court, might—if the amounts claimed for damages seemed reasonable—be advised to settle outside and thus avoid the court costs. Such cases were not included in the returns. Their significance can be indicated both from the contemporary press and from the coalowners' records. In 1900, for example, the United National Colliery Co. summoned 17 men who absented themselves for three days without notice from the company's colliery at Risca in Monmouthshire, but it was reported that 'the matter had been arranged between management and representatives of the men for the amount claimed in damages (£1 each).[15] More systematically a table compiled by the coalowners on actions taken against the men for illegal stoppages from December 1904 to November 1912 showed that damages totalling £1950. 5s. were awarded by the courts whilst twice as much (£3932. 11s. 10d.) was recovered 'by agreement'.[16]

It is clear that the number affected by actions taken by employers against their workmen in the South Wales coal industry cannot be even approximately quantified. It is equally clear, however, that such actions were relatively common-place: the numbers actually summoned, even if that were known on anything less aggregated than an England and Wales basis, would only reveal the tip of the iceberg. Verdicts in cases brought were habitually applied to many others who had not been summoned, and many cases were settled out of court. It can, however, be shown that the extent of the use made of the 1875 Act by the coalowners varied over time and some consideration needs to be given to this before an attempt is made to explain the use made of this law (the 1875 Act) in this industry (coal-mining) in this region (South Wales).

The long-run incidence of cases brought by the coalowners against the miners for breach of contract can no longer be recaptured. The figures are only available for individual police districts up to 1893 and even then do not discriminate between cases brought by employers and those brought by workmen, still less do they provide information industry by industry. For a brief period from 1904 to 1912, however, there is a fairly full record available of the use made of this particular aspect of the law by the South Wales coalowners. As we shall see these employers quite frequently summoned their workmen for breach of contract in the early twentieth century. It would be misleading, however, to suggest that this behaviour was typical of the entire period between 1875 and 1914. The more fragmentary evidence for the years before 1900 suggests two strong, but ultimately impressionistic, conclusions: that miners involved in an 'illegal stoppage' always risked being summoned for damages for breach of contract; but the probability of this being activated was generally low. Thus H.W. Martin, speaking for the Dowlais collieries belonging to G.K.N., asserted in 1903 that 'for years past' the Coalowners' Association had paid out indemnities to members affected by illegal stoppages even in cases where the member concerned had not summoned his workmen for damages. Martin claimed, indeed, that of 78 occasions before 1902 in which indemnity was paid by the Association where men struck without notice only one summons had been issued.[17] The inference might seem to be that before about 1900 the South Wales coalowners had rarely made use of the law on breach of contract. Against this, however, it needs to be noticed that Martin was apparently referring to a particular category of colliery disputes—those relating to the maintenance of established colliery customs about work practice. Certainly an earlier categorical statement on behalf of Lockets Merthyr Co. that the company 'intends taking out summonses against every man who stops work without notice'[18] would suggest a higher level of legal activity. More specifically a search through a sample year of a local newspaper in the mid-1890s revealed six cases being reported in which colliery workmen were being summoned by their employers for breach of contract under section 4 of the 1875 Act.[19] Prosecutions clearly took place and seem to have been common enough to make their possibility part of the knowledge and experience of the miners in this coalfield, but it was still far from being probable that any stoppage without notice would lead to a summons for damages: even for members of the Coalowners' Association which paid out indemnities to its members for losses incurred on such occasions, the decision whether to prosecute seems to have rested with the members concerned.

What seems to have decisively changed sometime around 1900 was that the Association removed or reduced this discretionary element from members wishing to claim indemnity. Cases seem to be reported more frequently in the press and, in July 1902, the Association explicitly recommended its members to prosecute miners who stopped work without notice.[20] In November of the same year the legal offensive was intensified by the decision of the Lewis Merthyr Co. (which, in effect, almost certainly meant the decision of the old die-hard war-horse Sir W.T. Lewis), on the advice of the solicitor of the Coalowners' Association, to deduct fines from wages. Kenshole, the solicitor, said that it was 'the first time fines have been deducted but it will have a very good effect if the principle is established.'[21] Which it was, both locally and nationally through a later case also brought by the Lewis Merthyr company and which the men unsuccessfully fought as it progressed from the local stipendiary, D. Lleufer Thomas, to the Kings Bench and then the Appeal Court.[22] A year later, in 1903, these two aspects were brought together in a decisive tightening of the Association's procedures. In June a committee of the Association recommended, and in November a special meeting of the Association accepted that it should henceforward 'be obligatory on Members to prosecute and this course should be a condition precedent to the payment of Indemnity by the Association for such illegal stoppage'. The number of men to be prosecuted and the amount of damages were left to the individual member (but under the general advice of the Association's solicitor); fines were to be deducted from wages due or by distress; the proceedings would be conducted at Association expense by the Association solicitor; when any judgement was obtained against those who had been prosecuted the rest of the men would be given a choice of paying the same amount (less the court costs) or they were proceeded against; from the damages recovered the company would deduct its own costs and pay over the balance to the Association's indemnity fund.[23] There were just three dissentients to this policy: the owners had decisively decided to make the fullest possible use of the legal weapon provided by the 1875 Act.

The deterrent effect was undoubtedly substantial. There was a substantial fall between 1902 and 1904 in the number of stoppages without notice, but the number of cases which had to be brought was still quite high (Table 3).

The number of stoppages in 1904 and 1905 was exceptionally low. It is, however, very doubtful if it can be concluded that these were years of peaceful industrial relations on the South Wales coalfield. The number of stoppages without notice was small, but the extent of legal confrontation was large. The Association's solicitor appears to have approved the issue of summonses in almost all cases: the amount of damages obtained was substantial (£782 for December alone in 1904, and £1,824 for 1905); and many men were involved (at least 5,000 miners had to pay damages from actions brought under section 4 in 1905). Many, including some coalowners, felt that so tight a legal rein was provocative and led, if anything, to sullen quiet rather than harmony. Whether so tight a hold could have been maintained is uncertain but the undoubted relaxation that took place in 1906 was triggered by pragmatism rather than policy. In an appeal case in 1906 the miners, whilst

Table 3. Stoppages and Damages at Associated Collieries 1900-1912

	Number of Stoppages				Damages Recovered from Stoppage Without Notice		
	Total (i)	With Notice (ii)	Without Notice (iii)	Number of Stoppages (iv)	Total Damages (v) £	Awarded by Court (vi) £	Settled out of Court (vii) £
1900	55	28	27				
1901	56	13	43				
1902	94	23	71				
1903	65	19	46				
1904	18	7	11	(Dec. 4 only)	782	782	-
1905	31	15	16	10	1,824	393	1,431
1906	53	28	25	3	55	7	47
1907	44	23	21	8	689	145	544
1908	30	14	16	11	389	69	320
1909	131	109	22	9	297	40	257
1910	85	51	34	15	883	130	753
1911	14	6	8	13	523	308	215
1912	n.a.	n.a.	n.a.	7	443	158	285

Source: Coalowners' MSS.

unable to secure a decision preventing the deduction of damages from wages due, won a ruling from the House of Lords that such deductions could not be made by the employers without an explicit order of the court for a distress warrant. At much the same time a Departmental Committee was sitting to consider the operation of the Truck Act which involved the general question of deductions from wages. The Association's solicitor thought it prudent to advise members not to enforce their rights too strictly.[24]

In the circumstances it became difficult for the Association to withhold indemnity payments from members who had not issued summonses or had not insisted on recovering the full damages awarded in court. The change may have been due to 'temporary legal difficulties' but it was not so easy to revert to the tight regime which had been imposed by the resolutions of July, 1902 and November, 1903 which had first recommended and then insisted that members should 'prosecute' their workmen before indemnity claims arising out of 'illegal stoppages' would be met. The Truck Act, was, it is true, unchanged[25] but the Association's rule was harder to enforce because, as Kenshole pointed out, it had been passed before the House of Lords ruling at a time when damages could be set against wages.[26] To accommodate the change the Association left its rule intact, but, instead of insisting that members enforce in full the payment of damages before paying indemnity, decided simply to reduce indemnity claims by the amounts that should have been obtained from the men.[27] It meant that there was still a very positive policy of taking legal action for breach of contract against miners who left work without notice.

As usual, the limitations of the evidence and the complexities of social situations make explanations hazardous. It would, however, be unreasonable to refrain from making some suggestions as to why employers in the South Wales coal industry continued to use the law on breach of contract as an explicit weapon in the conduct of industrial relations, and to offer some general observations on this experience.

On the face of it there is a plausible case for the argument that the 1875 Act should not have made much difference to employers wanting to use the law to prevent illegal stoppages. In one sense, of course, the Employers and Workmen Act 1875 represented a radical change: it effectively ended criminal liability by workmen for breach of contract so workers could not be fined or imprisoned as a matter of course for stopping work without notice. None the less the employer was still left with what might seem to be an effective deterrent in the form of a civil action for damages. Given the assumptions that an individual 'master' and each of his individual 'servants' were equals in making contracts and enforcing them before the law, the 1875 Act had removed an 'anomaly' under which one party had been liable for a civil action and one for criminal action. But it had not removed the unreality behind the basic assumptions. A worker's only bargaining power rested on his ability to withdraw his labour, and this was most effective if it could be done immediately and in conjunction with other workers. The 1875 Act left employers with the ability to sue workers for damages if such actions involved a breach of contract.[28] Moreover, actions in a magistrate's court were cheap, quick and convenient, and it seems reasonable to think that it would be more attractive to an employer to be able to collect damages after a successful summons than it was to have some of his labour force locked up in prison.

So far as this argument has strength, however, it would apply generally to all employers. But what seems to need explanation is why the continuance of legal action over stoppages without notice seems to have been confined, in any widespread or systematic sense, to employers in relatively few trades, amongst which the coal industry seems to have been prominent. More specifically, for the more restricted purposes of this article, what needs explanation is the use made of the 1875 Act by the coalowners of South Wales. To approach these issues it would be necessary to know what, negatively, induced most employers to forego the use of the law; and what, positively, induced some other employers to see the law as an effective instrument of business.

The most substantial recent historical survey of the ending of the old Master and Servant legislation suggests that employers' use of the criminal law against breach of contract by their workmen was already declining before 1875,[29] and the strong implication is that the decline continued after 1875. The disuse is attributed to three factors:[30] the desire of the new craft unions for better relations with their employers; the trend towards shorter contracts; and the distaste of larger firms for such methods. None of these is entirely convincing since the representativeness of the craft unions is dubious and the implied employer-acceptance of unionisation had no relevance over most of industry, whilst many contracts had always been short and most firms were always small. The real claim being made is that 'the law of master and servant was something appropriate to capitalism in its early stages which the big capitalist had, as it were, outgrown in 1875.'[31] Large issues are raised here but for the present purposes it is enough to mention such small doubts as the fact that the South Wales actions at the turn of the century were mostly taken by very large firms indeed, and point to attempts made in the 1870s and 1880s to use the law to impose discipline, break strikes and weaken trade union organisations. At all events, any weight placed upon the factors mentioned would need to be reinforced by other considerations. One of these would be the simple fact of the custom of the trade. Coalowners had made use of the legal provision for breach of contract: cotton made virtually no use of them.[32] Moreover, many masters felt that a civil action for damages gave them no remedy since the workmen would seldom have the resources to pay the damages: without some punitive element they believed there was no adequate deterrent to instil obedience and discipline.

There were strong reasons inherent in the coal industry which made labour relations particularly important and perhaps also enhanced the attraction of the degree of control offered by the Employers and Workmen Act. Labour costs formed a higher proportion of total costs, but the basis of the wage bargain could shift easily with changing geological conditions making for a fruitful source of disputes at individual pits. Often these were disputes where the miners felt that they needed, and were most likely to succeed by, immediate action but the normal contract was relatively long so the owners had strong reasons for its enforcement. An indication of the sources of dispute can be gained from a table compiled from the records of the coalowners for the first decade or so of the twentieth century (Table 4). The industry, moreover, did not lend itself to easy and detailed supervision by foremen whilst its dangers made the need for a disciplined labour force greater than in most other industries. All these factors were particularly applicable to South Wales where, for example, geological conditions were exceptionally difficult and variable, and where the standard agreement was for a month's notice. Disputes could spring up quickly and lead to instant, but typically short-lived stoppages. These, despite the long notice formally required, were mostly tolerated although individual employers would occasionally invoke the law which was always there as a background threat. But around 1900 a number of factors came together

Table 4. Causes of Stoppages at Associated Collieries, 1900-11

	Without Notice		With Notice	
	Stoppages	Pits	Stoppages	Pits
Non-Unionist	40	71	121	203
Demand increased wages/allowances	32	36	15	20
Sympathetic	21	30	4	11
Funerals	23	29	(1)	(1)
Meetings	14	15	(1)	(1)
Hauliers	76	90	(1)	(1)
Fixing of Price List	(1)	(1)	40	49
Enginemen and Stokers	(1)	-	23	42
Refusal to accept awards	(1)	-	4	4
Eight Hours Act	(1)	-	86	191
Miscellaneous	134	183	43	56
TOTAL	340	454	336	576

(1) Not given separately in source: probably included in Miscellaneous.

Source: Coalowners' Mss.

in South Wales leading the coalowners to make a much more systematic and deliberate use of law on breach of contract as a weapon in industrial relations.

The crucial change was the organisation of a strong union amongst the men. The deliberately humiliating terms which the owners imposed upon them after the bitter six-month lock-out of 1898 led to the formation of the South Wales Miners' Federation (S.W.M.F.) To stimulate and retain membership the union organised 'show cards' and one-day stoppages at individual pits. At the same time the owners, often conscious of what they considered to be inexorably rising costs because of declining labour productivity, were increasingly drawn to challenge entrenched customs—rights to house coal, early finishing at holiday times, miners stopping work if there was a fatal accident or to attend the funeral, rights to used timber etc. The owners were also alarmed at the rising costs of the Workmen's Compensation Act of 1897, which constituted a separate source of frequent legal conflict between owners and men, and which was again especially important in South Wales because of the high rate of accidents. But whilst the sources of conflict mounted the machinery for settling them, which had always been inadequate, remained unimproved. Disputes, if the restrictive rules allowed them to be considered at all, went before the Joint Sliding Scale Committee (up to 1902) or the Conciliation Board (from 1902) and would normally be referred to a member from each side to meet and consider. But since the members of the committees were busy owners and union leaders meetings above and below ground at the appropriate collieries were not easy (or could be made to be not easy) to arrange, deputies were inadmissible, disagreements were frequent but could not be resolved by arbitration which the owners saw as an interference with the right to manage. In these circumstances disputes could easily drag over a year or more causing increasing frustration. And finally into the friable atmosphere were dropped the broad legal decisions of the 1890s and 1900s unfavourable to trade unions. The Taff Vale decision roused particular enthusiasm amongst the South Wales coalowners,[33] and the general euphoria encouraged a more active use of the legal system to curb unionism, impose discipline and deter aggressive action by the men. In 1902-3 this approach, it needs to be emphasised, was put on a systematic, formal and concerted basis by one of the most powerful employers' associations in Britain. The use of the law on breach of contract was formally written in to its rules, a step no other employers' association seems to have taken.[34]

Was it successful? It was certainly substantial. In the eight years from December 1904 the coalowners' records indicate that 80 actions were successful in recovering damages from the South Wales miners and these actions involved 102 pits. From these are excluded other cases which, for one reason or another, were withdrawn and also, possibly, those in which damages were awarded but not enforced. There are also clear indications of a strong deterrent effect. In 1902 there had been 71 stoppages without notice at Associated collieries (see Table 3). In 1903 the number fell to 46; in 1904 to 11; in 1905 it was 16. Of course, the use of the courts was far from the only factor determining the number of 'illegal' stoppages, but the sharp shift in proportion between stoppages with and stoppages without notice suggests that its influence might have been significant. From 1901 to 1903 there were three 'illegal' stoppages for every one for which due notice was given (160 to 55); over the next eight years the stoppages with notice exceeded those without (253 to 153). None the less doubts must remain about the deterrent effect. For example, during the years from 1900 to 1911 there were altogether some 340 stoppages without notice, affecting 454 pits, at the collieries belonging to the Coalowners' Association—and a similar number of stoppages with notice (see Table 4). It may be that this represented an effective curb on miners taking industrial action but, if so, the state of industrial relations in the industry has hitherto been painted in roseate colours. Much more certain is that the coalowners' policy failed to crush the S.W.M.F. whose membership of 104,000 in 1899 was 138,000 in 1910 (and had reached 145,000 in 1908). Indeed, the membership figures if anything under-stated the failure to tame the union. The South Wales coal industry had for the last quarter of the nineteenth century been regarded as an area of relatively weak mining unionism: by 1910 it was viewed quite differently.

If the success of the policy was uncertain, its wisdom is still more suspect. It encountered opposition. The S.W.M.F. was the most natural source of this resistance but, in a direct sense, was necessarily ineffective in most cases. The fact of stoppage without notice was easy to establish and difficult to refute. None the less the union was able to ensure that the men involved in these cases were defended and their grievances were publicly aired. The role of 'the Fed' as general protector was being hammered out and it can hardly have been the intention of the coalowners to encourage this process. At the same time the occasion of the court hearings was often made into a public demonstration. Less obviously, but not surprisingly, the policy also encountered opposition from within the coalowners association itself. The most significant disagreement revolved around whether the Association should adopt a mainly conciliatory or a mainly aggressive stance in dealing with the miners, the disagreement between the hawks and the doves. Some internal dissent was therefore more or less unavoidable. In mid-1903, for example, when the policy of summonsing for stoppages without notice was still only a 'recommendation', Christmas Evans of the Dinas Main Colliery Company stated categorically that they 'do not intend prosecuting their workmen as they had never yet summoned their men'. Such action, he considered, simply created more ill will.[35] William Evans of Crawshay Bros. took a different tack, arguing that it was 'injudicious to make prosecution compulsory' because the Association would then be taking over too much of the power of management from individual undertakings.[36] Too much should not be made of the internal dissent on this issue: at the special Association meeting in November 1903 only three voted against making it compulsory to take legal action against their workmen for stoppages without notice.[37]

More significant were actual legal constraints. It has already been seen that the Lords' decision against the direct automatic deduction of damages from wages due made some coalowners less keen to try and collect the damages awarded; and that the sitting of a Departmental committee on the Truck Act led the Association solicitor to urge prudence and caution—at least temporarily. There were also occasional expressions of disquiet by local magistrates. In one such case at Pontypridd the stipendiary (Ignatius Williams) clearly felt that an arrangement could have been made and expressed his displeasure by awarding the company damages but no costs; in another the Chairman at Bridgend regretted that the management had held on over a 'trifling sum' and pointedly praised the men's solicitor for his conduct of the case; in a case at Blaina the company was awarded nominal damages and no costs, the Chairman adding that he 'was sorry these cases came before them.'[38] In a 1908 case involving Powell Duffryn, where feelings ran very high, the Merthyr Stipendiary, Sir T. Marchant Williams was disinclined to give damages although the breach of contract was undeniable. He urged the parties to settle. The summonses were later withdrawn and the case went to the Conciliation Board.[39]

So far as actions for breach of contract were concerned, however, none of these restraints could be effective. In themselves they represented only occasional mild irritants in the pursuit of the policy. The real issue was always the judgement as to whether the gains (in finance, in curbing unions, in instilling discipline, in reducing stoppages) outweighed any real or imagined losses (where most commentators would stress such intangibles as loss of harmony, co-operation and good-will with their work-force—in short, the possible worsening of industrial relations). The coalowners seem to have placed a quite different stress in assessing the restraints upon them if such can be judged from a remarkable passage in the evidence before the Royal Commission on Trade Disputes in 1906. The Association's solicitor (Kenshole) was questioned by Sir William Lewis, who throughout the last quarter of the nineteenth century dominated the South Wales Coalowners' Association and whose hawkish hand was still frequently to be seen:

> **Q.** 1871 (Sir W.T. Lewis). But are there not great difficulties in obtaining the money especially when the men may cease working at the colliery and there is no money to be added?—If there is no money in the hands of the employer, and as many of the men are single men, the only remedy would be to have them committed to prison, which would never do of course *as it would mean imprisoning a large number of men.*

> **Q.** 1872. (Mr. Sidney Webb). Why would it never do?—I mean to say it would never do to imprison half of your workmen, *because you would be simply depriving yourself of their services . . .*
>
> **Q.** 1874. (Sir Godfrey Lushington). It is rather a troublesome thing to bring 500 actions against 500 workmen?—It is troublesome *and for this reason, that on the day when the case would be heard all your pits would be idle and you could not get any recompense for that.*
>
> **Q.** 1875. (Sir W.T. Lewis). You said in reply to Mr. Webb that they might recover the amount of their loss but in practice there is nothing of the kind because on that day of the hearing of the case the collieries are stopped? That is so.
>
> **Q.** 1876. And as they are not stopped through the action of the workmen, consequently the employer cannot get any redress?—*There is no redress in respect of that stoppage.*[40] (italics added).

The attitudes which such a passage suggests are only a mild reinforcement of a general impression received from examining the record of industrial relations in the South Wales coalfield in the decade or so before the First World War. There is no doubt that the Welsh coalowners genuinely felt themselves to be increasingly threatened. It does not follow, however, that the only response was to heighten their intransigence and intensify the aggressiveness of their stance. That rested on rarely-stated assumptions, such as the belief that a miners' union could only be a mortal enemy. It should not have escaped them that other employers, both within and outside their industry, came to different conclusions: in the 1906 inquiry, for example, the only area in which breach of contract cases were raised as a contentious issue was South Wales. At all events the final outcome would seem to suggest that the coalowners had made the wrong choices. The systematic use of the law over breach of contract as an explicit weapon in the conduct of industrial relations was one, relatively minor, expression of these choices, but it was symbolic. It is difficult to attribute wisdom to policies which by 1910 had produced a more or less total breakdown in labour relations on the coalfield: *Labour Strife in South Wales Coalfield* was the almost unavoidable title of a book, sympathetic to the coalowners, written at the time.[41]

For those who look to echoes from the past a recent authority noted that the 'only significant recent example of the use of the law of contracts of employment as part of a system of industrial relations seems to have been the practice of the coal-mining industry of bringing actions . . . as test cases for the resolution of industrial disputes, and as an instrument of industrial discipline.'[42] The cases cited covered not only the 1930s but stretched into the post-nationalisation period of the 1950s. Those who liked their historical parallels laid on with the trowel might savour rather the bringing of a successful action in 1902 by non-unionist miners against the S.W.M.F. leading to the union making a public apology for placarding men in arrears with subscriptions.[43] A gentler irony might be contained in the evidence given on behalf of the National Coal Board to the Donovan commission in 1966. Rejecting fines and damages as effective ways to stem unofficial strikes, the spokesman stated that 'you would be getting into an impossible situation if you are going to impose legal obligations upon people, interfering with their freedom of action, although they may be misguided about the use of it on occasion.'[44]

(Such enlightened views did not last: in 1984 and 1985 the Board used—was encouraged by the government to use—the courts, along with all the other instruments of the State. The industry, as so often, was the prisoner of its history.)

(Originally published in *Llafur,* 4,2, 1985, pp. 36-51.)

Notes

[1]Much of the basic research for this article was done by Dot Jones whose cheerful and reliable assistance is grateful acknowledged.

[2]K.W. Wedderburn, *The Worker and the Law*, 1971 edition, pp. 76, 85.

[3]S. and B. Webb, *The History of Trade Unionism* (1920 edition), pp. 249-50.

[4]*Ibid*., p. 253; and D. Simon, 'Master and Servant' in J. Saville (ed.), *Democracy in the Labour Movement* (1954), pp. 160-200.

[5]S. and B. Webb, *op.cit*., p. 291.

[6]The Employers and Workmen Act (1875), section 4. Larger claims went to the County Court which dealt with most civil claims.

[7]For examples see F.R. Batt, *The Law of Master and Servant* (1967 edition), pp. 246, 270, 425, 428, 457. The book's title is itself expressive even allowing for the fact that the first edition appeared in 1929.

[8]D. Simon, *op.cit*., p. 168.

[9]Since proceedings under the Act were civil and not criminal, the figures from 1875 to 1893 had—strictly—been misplaced. The more curious feature, however, was that in 1893 they were re-allocated not to the civil statistics but to a separate table (xiv) of 'Quasi-criminal matters' alongside proceedings under orders for maintenance, school attendance and possession.

[10]For anyone mainly concerned with Durham the other, equally interesting, feature is the very wide annual fluctuation ranging from 221 (3.7 per 10,000 population) to 1655 (24.8 per 10,000 population).

[11]See, e.g., *South Wales Daily News* (SWDN), 7 Aug. 1900, 5 Dec. 1900. In a sample of three years only 7 such cases were found in 1900, 14 in 1903, and 8 in 1908. All of these were cases brought by a workman or workmen and, if this could be taken as typical, would mean that the omission of County Court cases was still less serious for our purposes.

[12]'At most' because the normal practice at the court was to hear details of just one or two cases, each side agreeing that the findings should then be applied to however many were summoned.

[13]*S.W. Coalowners Ass. Mss.*, Cardiff District Board Mins., March 1907.

[14]*S.W.D.N.*, 16 and 17 Oct. 1896. In this case the owners, J. Lancaster and Co., were awarded no damages and only nominal costs.

[15]*S.W.D.N.*, 21 and 22 June 1900.

[16]*Coalowners Ass. Mss.* Details of Stoppages without notice when damages were recovered from the workmen, Jan. 1913.

[17]*Coalowners Mss.*, Cardiff District Board, Minutes, 20 Feb. 1903.

[18]*Ibid.*, 17 April 1896.

[19]See *S.W.D.N.*, 5 March, 15 April, 6 June, 10 July, 16 Oct. and 18 November, 1896.

[20]*Coalowners' Mss.*, Association Minutes 5 July 1902.

[21]*Ibid.*, Cardiff District Board Minutes, 4 Dec. 1902. It is interesting, and it may be a significant indication of attitudes, that the Coalowners (and even the Association's solicitor) persistently talk of 'prosecutions' and 'fines'. Each of these terms was appropriate for criminal proceedings but not for the 'summonses' or 'applications' for 'damages' which applied under the civil law of the 1875 Act.

[22]Porth Police Court, 18 May 1909; K.B.D., 14 Dec. 1909; C. of A., 20 April, 10 May 1910.

[23]*Coalowners' MSS.*, Association Minutes 9 June, 28 Nov. 1903.

[24]*Coalowners' Mss.*, Cardiff District Board, 18 May 1906.

[25]The Departmental Committee on the Truck Act had reported in 1908 (Cd. 4442) but its recommendations were totally ignored.

[26]*Coalowners' Mss.*, Association Minutes, 20 Sept. 1907.

[27]*Ibid.*, 11 November 1907.

[28]The Act also, of course, gave workers an inexpensive method of pursuing individual grievances over wages due or wrongful dismissal (i.e. not due notice). And the Act was often so used by individuals. But workmen did not usually use this law until after they had been sacked: the Act offered no possibility for re-instatement, but taking action under it could lead to dismissal.

[29]Daphne Simon, 'Master and Servant' in J. Saville (ed.), *Democracy and the Labour Movement*, pp. 160-200.

[30]*Ibid.*, pp. 190-2.

[31]*Ibid.*, p. 195.

[32]*Ibid.*, pp. 172, 190.

[33]The General Manager of the Taff Vale Railway whose obduracy and persistence led to the decision threatening trade union funds was presented with a silver candelabra and his wife with a brooch.

[34]Coalowners' Association. Appendix A (rules 78A).

[35]*Coalowners Mss.*, Cardiff District Board Minutes, 13 July 1903.

[36]*Ibid.*, Association Minutes, 9 June 1903.

[37]*Ibid.*, 28 November 1903.

[38]*S.W.D.N.*, 19 and 26 Nov. 1896; 8 Jan. 1904; 17 Oct. 1896.

[39]*Ibid.*, 26 Aug. 1908.

[40]*R.C. on Trade Disputes*, 1906.

[41]D. Evans, *Labour Strife in the South Wales Coalfield, 1910-11*, 1911.

[42]M.R. Freedland, *The Contract of Employment*, 1976, pp. 2-3.

[43]*Coalowners Mss.*, Cardiff District Board Minutes, 16 Jan. 1902.

[44]Royal Commission on Trade Unions and Employers' Associations, Minutes of Evidence, 4, N.C.B., p. 822.

See page 206

9. THE STRIKE OF 1898

Even at the time it was clear that the miners' strike[1] of 1898 marked a watershed in the development of industrial relations in South Wales. But it was not clear then, and has not since been made clear, exactly why and in what ways this struggle marked a turning-point. It is part of the purpose of this article to examine this question.

The point that has usually been made[2] is that the substantial defeat of the Welsh miners in this struggle induced them to end their long semi-organised separatism in union affairs and throw in their lot with the youthful Miners' Federation of Great Britain,[3] and that this move thereby sealed the fate of the sliding scale as a means of regulating wages in the coal-field. This is true enough so far as it goes, but it does somewhat distort the sequence of events. After their defeat the miners rushed 'as penitent Welshmen' to enter the fold of the M.F.G.B.: this desire to become associated with the larger body was, however, in part merely symbolic of the more fundamental change which had taken place—the determination to have a strong organised union in South Wales itself. Moreover it was not because the Welsh miners joined the M.F.G.B. that the sliding scale was doomed; it is truer to say that the Welsh miners emerged from their experience of the 1898 strike determined to abandon the sliding scale and to organise themselves to the achievement of this objective. By joining the M.F.G.B., with its basic policy of opposition to sliding-scale arrangements, they gave formal and explicit expression to this determination.

All this may seem to amount to no more than over-nice changes of emphasis. But it is not without wider significance. One of the most recent historians of the Welsh miners has stressed that successful organisation in Wales was largely dependent upon the provision of leadership from England.[4] Hence it is the connection with the M.F.G.B. which is the over-riding feature distinguishing post-1898 developments in South Wales from those which had gone before. But this picture of the divided Welsh tribes inertly awaiting the arrival of an English Messiah is in several respects overdrawn and unsatisfactory. Two brief points must suffice to illustrate this. It seems, for example, much more plausible to look for explanations of the variations in the experience of union development in South Wales, as opposed to England, in terms of the different markets served by the different coalfields. Thus the two major coal-exporting districts of South Wales and Northumberland and Durham had more in common with each other than either of them had with the Midland coalfields which produced for a home market and which formed the original nucleus of the M.F.G.B. It is thus not without significance that Northumberland and Durham did not finally join the M.F.G.B. until 1908, clinging to their separatism for nearly a decade after South Wales.[5] The second point is that, even after South Wales had joined the M.F.G.B., there is little evidence of its dependence upon English leadership. The first two Conciliation Board agreements in South Wales (in 1903 and 1905) were made, in some important respects, in direct opposition to the wishes of the M.F.G.B. Much more important was the clear way in which South Wales, in several of the major issues of the mining industry before 1914, itself provided the initiative: in the struggles over abnormal places and the minimum wage it was the M.F.G.B. which was led, indeed almost dragged, by South Wales. All this is difficult to reconcile with a thesis of an innate inability of Welsh miners to create and maintain an organised union.

There were many reasons making for disunity amongst the Welsh colliers. Here it is only possible to mention, without evaluating, a few of them. The South Wales coalfield contains the full range of coal from anthracite to bituminous. Hence several quite sharply different markets were served. In addition the valley formation of the coalfield tended to isolate the various districts geographically. Moreover, the very rapid rate of growth after 1875, faster than that of the other coal-exporting districts, meant a constantly increasing labour force and a steady influx of population from other (usually rural) areas, which greatly magnified the problems of organisation. Finally, the long existence of the sliding-scale system of wage regulation, with its apparent automatism of operation, provided a strong institutional barrier to union development. 'Why should we contribute to a union' (was the attitude of many colliers) 'when our wages are automatically regulated?' And it was irrelevant that this attitude was founded on a misconception of how the sliding scale operated. Most of these basic causes of disunity were not markedly weaker after 1898, but their effectiveness as barriers to the growth of a powerful organisation became much reduced. The reasons for this must be partly sought in the impact which the 1898 strike had upon the attitudes of the men.

Before dealing with this, however, it is necessary briefly to consider the discussions which took place on three major issues in the years immediately preceding the stoppage. These issues—the Workmen's Compensation Act, restriction of output, and the discharge note—all happened to come to a head around the same time and the acute disagreements which they provoked between the owners and the colliers formed the prelude to the stoppage itself. They thus helped to condition the hostile attitudes which hardened during the strike and formed an essential part of its background.

Thus the passing of the Workmen's Compensation Act for industrial injuries in 1897 was regarded by many owners with dismay. Although they exaggerated its effects[6] it did add to their costs of production and hence increased their determination to resist wage demands. To the men it was a major matter of principle, and there was some resentment at the virulence with which the Bill was opposed and at the pressures brought upon the men, after its passage, to contract out of its operation.

Feelings before the strike had also been embittered by the collapse of a strong effort to secure the operation of a scheme to control output in South Wales. There was widespread belief that coal prices—and hence wage levels—were often pushed to artificially low levels by price-cutting and speculative selling. Restriction of output had long been a recurrent theme amongst the miners but had normally been pursued by them on a unilateral basis. In 1896, however, stimulated by the publication of a scheme for this purpose by a leading coalowner,[7] an attempt was made to secure joint action with the owners on this issue. Under pressure from the men the Coalowners' Association, although rejecting the possibility of joint action, eventually agreed to devise a scheme to be considered by all coalowners. This was drawn up by Sir William Lewis, but coalowners representing more than half the total output of South Wales made their participation conditional upon its acceptance by owners controlling 95 per cent of total output. There was never the slightest likelihood of such a target being reached, especially as the owners naturally roundly rejected the miners' offer to bring the dissentients into line. Indeed, owners controlling over 10 per cent of the total output, including a large number of very small operators, did not even reply to the circulars which were sent out.[8] Thus the men were eventually informed, in mid-1897, that the owners had decided not to continue with the scheme.

There was wide-spread dissatisfaction at this result. Many felt, and with some justification, that the Owners' Association had never been sincere in their attempts to get the scheme adopted. The stillborn nature of this desultory attempt at output control also led many colliers to question the nature of the substantial identity of interest between owners and men which had long been stressed to them. In this instance, where the aim had been to prevent unduly low prices, the joint interest had seemed to them to be particularly prominent, but it had been insufficient to induce the owners to participate. At the same time the gingerly approach of the owners to the whole exercise roused strong suspicions that the owners had only embarked upon it to delay consideration of the demands which the miners had been making for revision of the sliding-scale agreement. At all events, it is suggestive that within a month of the formal burial of the scheme the men voted to give notice to end the sliding scale agreement and thus started the chain of events leading to the strike of 1898. Nor was it surprising that the insistence upon a minimum wage-rate being incorporated into any new agreement formed a prominent feature in the men's programme. Once the owners had declined to operate any control over output in order to maintain prices (and hence wage-rates), the request for a minimum to be written into the scale was the natural alternative.

Yet another issue which raised heightened feelings in the years immediately preceding the 1898 strike was that of the discharge note. This was a certificate given to each worker who satisfactorily completed his contract of service at one colliery and which had to be produced before he could be engaged at another. It had a long history in South Wales.[9] Its use, which could be justified on perfectly reasonable and valid grounds, had, however, always led to intense conflict because of the wide possibilities of its misuse as an instrument of victimisation. For present purposes it is only necessary to note that in 1896, after twenty years of intermittent operation of a partial discharge-note system, the employers decided to adopt the full use of the discharge note on a permanent basis. This meant that nobody could be employed without producing a discharge note, that all engagements were to be made by the manager himself, and that no worker who had been working at a colliery where a strike was in progress was to be employed. The operation of this system proved highly effective and produced a correspondingly sharp reaction. Indeed, one local newspaper commented that no matter has 'met with such universal condemnation at the hands of the workmen' since the great strike of 1875.[10] At a meeting called to consider this situation a strong minority favoured an immediate strike without even waiting to discuss the matter with the employers, and, when it was discussed, the certainty that its retention would lead to a general stoppage induced its withdrawal by the owners.[11] But for the next two years many of the owners still hoped for its re-introduction and, almost to the end, this formed one of their terms for the settlement of the 1898 stoppage. Even when this direct demand was dropped—itself a measure of the intensity of the men's feelings on this issue when they were defeated on all else—an unsuccessful attempt was made to incorporate the substance of the discharge-note system into the administration of the Compensation Act. Again it is not the details which are important but the contribution which the resurrection of this issue made to the general attitude of bitterness.

This gathering climate of conflict helps to explain why the impact of the 1898 stoppage was so powerful. But a fuller explanation of this impact is to be found in the course taken by the strike itself. To understand this, some of the salient features of the struggle must be briefly recounted.

Although the men gave the necessary six months' notice to end the existing sliding-scale agreement on 30 September 1897, it was not until 12 February 1898 that the first meeting was held to discuss a new agreement. At the beginning of March the owners gave a month's notice to end their contracts with their individual workmen.[12] When this expired, without any agreement having been reached, an arrangement was made to postpone the notices for nine days, but no actual negotiations took place during this period and many of the men ignored the extension. Thus on various dates between 1 and 9 April the Associated collieries came to a halt: all were idle on Monday, 11 April. After a brief meeting on 12 April the two sides did not meet again until the end of May when there was a further failure to agree. This prompted two major attempts at conciliation first by Lord Dunraven and then, in July, by the Board of Trade. Both were rejected by the owners. After a few more abortive meetings, and with the position of the men becoming more and more desperate, the employers, on Saturday 27 August, made a final offer which gave very little concession to any of the demands of the men and they abruptly stated that this offer would only remain open for five days. A miners' general conference on 31 August bowed to the inevitable. Work resumed in the first week of September. But there was no illusion that the settlement represented an agreement in any meaningful sense of the term: it was a solution enforced by the owners on the defeated colliers.

The men had initially asked for various alterations in the existing sliding-scale agreement and not for an abandonment of the sliding-scale principle. In particular they asked that the scale should incorporate either a minimum percentage below which wage-rates should not fall whatever the price of coal, or a scheme for restriction of output to prevent prices from falling excessively. The owners countered with their own proposals for modifying the scale agreement, mainly a reduction in the percentage change in wage-rates for each shilling increase (or decrease) in price; the abolition of the miners' monthly holiday (Mabon's Day); and the introduction of the discharge note. As the conflict continued, the men's demands hardened into a complete abandonment of the sliding scale and the substitution instead of a conciliation board with an independent chairman and a minimum and maximum wage-rate on the model of the Federated Areas of England. The owners dropped their demand for a revision of the scale in their favour and insisted on the existing scale and the abandonment of Mabon's Day. The final solution was on the owners' terms, with the slight concession to the men that if, during the course of the agreement,[13] wage-rates fell below 12.1/2 per cent above the standard rate, then the men's side would be free to give six months' notice to end the agreement even if the allotted four years had not expired. This was in no sense a minimum: it simply allowed the miners to end the scale agreement early if this situation arose—and it also ensured that any subsequent negotiations would take place against a background of trade depression which would be unfavourable to the miners.

The obduracy which characterised the struggle reflected a basic divergence of attitude. On the men's side was the consciousness that wage-rates had declined steadily since 1894.[14] This strengthened their determination to secure improved terms when conditions became more favourable. Moreover they considered that better terms were feasible since at the time of the last upsurge in prices and activity they had, in 1890, secured a scale which gave them advances in wage-rates of 10 per cent with each increase of a shilling in the selling price, which the owners drove down to 8.3/4 per cent in 1892 when the level of activity had once again fallen away. In 1897, therefore, at the first signs of a revival in trade, there was a strong demand to end the current sliding scale and this was decided upon despite the advice of the more moderate leaders (such as Mabon) that it would be wiser to wait until the revival was more marked. The men, apart from a significant minority, were by no means firmly opposed to the continuance of the principle of the sliding scale; they were fully determined that its conditions would have to be modified in their favour.

On the owners' side, too, these years had been trying and disappointing. Although the range of experience was inevitably very wide, a substantial number of companies reported much reduced profits or actual losses. This was not simply the normal result of falling prices; it was also reinforced by rising costs. It must be borne in mind, however, what is meant by this. Costs were rising, not in the sense that absolute costs were higher than, say, during the boom years of 1889-91, but in the sense that costs formed a higher proportion to price in, say, 1897 than in 1885 when prices were at about the same level. Profit margins were thus being squeezed. In these circumstances (and given the fact that in coal-mining, wages formed a high proportion of total costs) the owners, whilst they almost universally wanted the sliding scale to continue, were convinced that (at the worst) its terms could not be modified against them. Indeed, many of them felt that revisions in their favour were essential; and it is clear that the revisions which they proposed represented more than the normal bargaining counter to the demands of the men, since the owners' side clung to some part of their demands throughout the struggle and despite the background of a steadily improving situation.

These convictions help to explain the shape and length of the conflict which extended from April to September. The diametrically opposing positions of the two sides left no range over which bargaining was possible. But the flavour of the struggle arose much more directly from the tactical positions adopted by the two sides. The attitude of the owners was symbolised by an incident right at the outset. In the autumn of 1897, the workmen had been balloted on the issue of giving the necessary six months' notice to end the current agreement. The result (41,245 for and 12,014 against) had led to what then seemed a routine and formal handing in of notice. But despite the substantial majority the owners took counsel's opinion on the validity of this notice on the basis that the number of favourable votes (41,245) was less than half of the total number of men working under the scale agreement. The matter was still not allowed to rest when counsel gave as his opinion that this was no valid ground for objecting to the notice.[15] The miners' leaders were, blandly informed that although 'the Association are advised that the notice given . . . is invalid the Employers decide not to insist upon their rights.'[16] If the men's leaders felt any gratitude for this gracious treatment, they managed to control it remarkably well.

A much more serious source of discord arose over the somewhat related question of plenary powers. At almost every joint meeting the owners' chairman, Sir William Thomas Lewis (later Lord Merthyr), challenged the extent to which the men's representatives were free to negotiate. There were strong reasons for Sir William's insistence. If the men's representatives did not possess full powers they might not be able to make any concessions: negotiation would be impossible. The other danger was that any agreement reached might be repudiated by the general body of the miners. Despite the cogency of these considerations, the wisdom of the owners' insistence on this issue is open to question. The owners' attitude in itself played a significant part in inducing the men to withhold plenary powers from their representatives: the men resented what they considered to be an attempt to dictate to them how they should run their affairs. The anxiety of the owners that the men's representatives should be given full powers tended to make the men look suspiciously on their own leaders. Many thought that the attitude of the owners could only be rooted in the belief that the men's leaders—several of whom were well known to be cautious, moderate and pacific—would be prepared to abandon at the negotiating table the principles laid down at the delegate meetings. Thus as the owners grew more insistent on this point, the men became more and more obstinate. At the opening negotiations the men's representatives had had full powers: these were withdrawn at the delegate meeting of 12 March.

The reaction upon public opinion was also a significant feature: both sides spent much effort (by press interviews, manifestos etc.) to win over public opinion. In this respect the owners' rigid insistence on the men's leaders securing plenary powers was almost certainly unwise. It was this difficulty more than anything else which prevented any joint meeting being held for nearly two months after the strike had actually started. The most general public reaction seemed to be that the owners were adopting an excessively dictatorial attitude over the ways in which the miners conducted their own affairs: the public, which was much affected by the strike, mostly felt that efforts at settlement were being postponed over a mere technicality.

Nor did the inconsistency with which the owners applied their principle escape notice. Thus when notices ran out at the end of March and the owners thought some settlement was possible if the stoppage could be delayed, they did not hesitate to negotiate with the 'unauthorised' men's representatives an agreement to continue working for a further nine days. This negotiation was even more extraordinary in that the men's leaders had to accept the continuation at the same wage-rates as had ruled in March even though everyone knew that the regular sliding-scale audit, which the owners had earlier refused to take, would have revealed that an increase was due to men even under the existing terms. Thus the owners, who had rejected the men's leaders as being unauthorised to negotiate, accepted them 'as competent to bind the men to work after 31 March on terms lower than were fairly their due'.[17] In face of these circumstances, which the owners had created for themselves by their refusal to allow the regular audit to be taken, the public was much less shocked by the action of some sections of the men in deciding not to work the extra nine days than they were annoyed at the inconsistency with which the employers pursued their insistence upon plenary powers for the men.

It is true that the rigidity of the employers was justified in the sense that the miners were eventually forced to give their representatives full powers. But the cost of extracting this had been high. Public opinion had been partly alienated; the men's representatives consistently and publicly humiliated (both by being imperiously rejected by the owners as 'unauthorised', and by having to plead repeatedly with their constituents for an explicit statement of their trust); and the general resentment of both leaders and rank and file against this 'interference' by employers hardened resistance. By the time this issue had been settled at the end of May[18] even the most moderate leaders had abandoned the sliding-scale principle as a basis of settlement and insisted upon a Conciliation Board (or an umpire for disputes) and a minimum wage-rate. This hardening of attitudes made any real negotiated settlement unlikely: the owners' tactics, probably based on the hope of securing large concessions from the moderate leaders, had largely defeated their own ends.

The attitude of the employers towards the conciliation attempts which were made alienated public sympathy even more clearly and aroused a lasting antagonism amongst the men. On 20 June, Lord Dunraven offered to put Dunraven Castle at the disposal of representatives of both sides and, if desired, he was ready to preside over any conference. The employers' Emergency Committee replied that they had determined 'not to entertain any suggestion placing the settlement . . . into the hand of third parties'.[19] The miners then appealed to the Board of Trade to appoint a conciliator under the 1896 Conciliation Act. Sir Edward Fry was appointed for this purpose. It was expected that the owners, however, half-heartedly, would give this official attempt at peace-making a trial; few were prepared for the abrupt and high-handed manner in which Sir Edward's mission was rejected. On 9 July, Fry requested the Owners' Chairman to call upon him. Sir William went and authorised Fry to make a note of their meeting. This recorded that Sir William had called 'merely out of courtesy' and declined 'to admit any intervention of the Conciliator or any other person appointed by the Government or otherwise . . .'[20] Press comment was almost universally unfavourable,[21] the men were confirmed in their growing belief that the owners were determined to enforce a complete surrender. This view was further fortified at the end of July when the owners announced that the terms which they had placed at the pit-heads on 16 July were an ultimatum which it would be 'impossible' to vary.[22]

There was also widespread felling that the arrest of David Morgan (Dai o'r Nant) was a direct attempt to bring pressure on the miners to end the stoppage. Morgan was sentenced to two months' hard labour at the Glamorgan Assizes at Swansea, on 8 August, on a charge of intimidation arising out of an incident at Aberaman No. 9 pit two years earlier, in 1896.[23] The timing of this certainly raised strong suspicions that the owners were pressing charges because of Morgan's intransigence during these latter stages of the 1898 strike. David Morgan's temperament was certainly a formidable barrier to the capitulation of the miners which was daily becoming more inevitable. Always excessively prickly at the conference table, too obstinate, too inflexible to adjust his views, his anticipated refusal to bow to the inevitable was likely to prolong resistance.

There is, it must be firmly stated, no evidence at all to support the charge that the coalowners were motivated by any desire to get Morgan out of the way at a crucial stage in the conflict. But from the present point of view—suggesting that this was one of the sources of the exceptional bitterness engendered by the 1898 strike—this hardly matters. It is only necessary to show that the miners (and many others) *thought* that David Morgan's imprisonment was motivated by a vindictive desire to put him safely behind bars. And of this assumption there is plenty of evidence. At numerous protest meetings throughout the coalfield this point was repeatedly made.[24] Several other factors added to the vehemence of the miners' indignation: David Morgan was by this time an old man and a sick man; it was also widely thought that the sentence was in any case particularly harsh since Morgan, both at the actual incident in 1896 and during the strike which followed, had generally exercised a restraining influence on the men. But the core of the protest was always the belief that he was being punished not for what had happened in 1896 but for his beliefs in 1898. This viewpoint seemed to gain some confirmation from the strange manner of his release on 9 September. Two weeks earlier the Home Secretary, despite influential appeals for mercy,[25] had refused to intervene. Yet suddenly 'down came an order, peremptory as it was laconic, to discharge the prisoner forthwith', three weeks before he was due to be released. In a leading article, the *South Wales Daily News* forcefully committed itself to the view that this sudden change was only explicable in terms of the ending of the coal strike. The men returned to work on Monday, 5 September; David Morgan was released the following Friday.[26]

A comparable indignation was roused by the action of the owners in preventing the Boards of Guardians from granting relief to the men. The closure of the stoneyards was enforced on the argument that work was available for the men at the pits (on the owners' terms). But whatever the legal subtleties, many felt (and remembered) that this was a particularly harsh turn of the screw.

At no stage was the tactical maladroitness of the owners more evident than at the ending of the struggle. On Thursday, 25 August, Lewis Miles, secretary of the men's provisional committee, 'phoned to ask for a meeting with the owners. This was arranged for Saturday, 27 August. At the meeting the men's side pressed hard, but unsuccessfully, for concessions. At 8.40 p.m. the meeting was broken off and several of the owners, as they left the building just before nine, told reporters that there was 'no settlement'.

A few moments later, however, a messenger dashed out and brought them back, and soon after a provisional agreement was announced. After the initial break-up, the men's representatives had met and decided that further resistance was useless. They accepted the owners' formula of allowing the miners to give notice to end the agreement before its four-year term expired if the wage-rate fell to less than 12.½ per cent above the standard rate. This was in no sense the minimum wage-rate which, during this last day, was the only point the men had tried to hold out for, but it was clearly all that could be extracted without a further fight. The owners gave the men until Thursday, 1 September, to hold a delegate meeting to ratify the agreement.[27]

This delegate meeting was held on Wednesday, 31 August. Despite the evident plight of the men, there was still much resistance to the terms of settlement which were virtually dictated by the owners. Finally, however, they were ratified by 61,912 to 37,077 with 8,800 neutral votes.[28] One incident during the discussion epitomised both the resentment of the men and the tactical clumsiness of their employers. In the middle of the debate, a telegram was received from the owners' chairman, Sir William Thomas Lewis, to the effect that no better terms than those arranged on the previous Saturday could be expected. When this was read, one delegate shouted, '"Oddi wrth bwy mae hwnna, Mabon? Oddi wrth yr Hollalluog?" (Who is that from, Mabon? From the Almighty?) "Yn agos iawn" (Very near it), was the prompt reply of the chairman, which elicited a shout of laughter.'[29]

The delegate meeting left one issue over. Their representatives were instructed to make one last effort to secure some modification over the monthly holiday (generally known as 'Mabon's Day'). The owners had insisted that this should be abolished. The men felt strongly about this: it gave them a holiday on the first Monday of every month (to which much of their social activity was geared), it gave them a chance to meet and discuss their affairs (the monthly meetings of all the district unions were held on Mabon's Day), and it was at least a gesture towards the idea of restriction of output to which, since their wage-rates were geared to the price of coal, they attached much significance. The owners' well-founded objections were expressed largely in terms of the loss of output (and hence increased costs of working) on the days following the holiday: after Mabon's Day there was frequently much absenteeism on the Tuesday, and even the Wednesday, following. The men's leaders were, however, prepared to substitute Saturday for Monday as the day of the holiday, arguing that this would meet most of the owners' objections since Saturday was already a shorter working day, and it would leave the weekend to allow for the recovery of those who celebrated the holiday with more enthusiasm than discretion. But when they met the employers' representatives on 1 September to plead for this concession they received a blank refusal: the owners wanted unconditional surrender. Mabon, the most consistently moderate of the men's leaders, made a dramatic appeal: '"If you force us . . . to sign this agreement today, which provides for the abolition of the holiday, you will compel us to adopt an agreement which we know, and which you in your inner hearts also know, cannot be carried out. I appeal to you for our sakes as leaders to grant some tangible concession to go back to the men. Surely our services to the community and to the coal trade deserve some better treatment at your hands than that which you now offer us. I entreat you . . . to give us something to go back to the men which we can recommend and which we can advocate. Without it enduring peace will be impossible.

You are now asking us practically to put the halter round our necks."'[30] But it was of no avail. The following day, Mabon derided the settlement as 'not based on justice and goodwill,' the owners having 'insisted on their pound of flesh' and made the men 'tread the path of humiliation'.[31] For Mabon forthrightly to denounce an agreement which he had himself only just signed was an eloquent testimony of the way in which even the most cautious, peaceful and conciliatory amongst the men were driven into bitterness by the tactics adopted by the owners.

This is, perhaps, the real importance of the conflict. It started with a considerable majority of the colliers still well-disposed towards the sliding scale: it ended without a single voice being raised in its defence. The sliding scale had passed from being an agreement negotiated between two sides into a settlement enforced by the owners: it was irretrievably associated with a humiliation which the colliers were determined to eradicate. It was this determination which gave impetus to the surge towards a stronger organisation which followed the closing of the strike. Perhaps this was largely inevitable, but it is instructive to compare the situation with that of 1875 when the sliding scale was first established as the general method of wage-regulation in the south Wales coalfield. In 1875, too, the men had been roundly defeated after a long contest. But on the earlier occasion the owners, once they had secured their substantial wage reduction, had been prepared to listen to the pleas of the men's leaders to 'take something back to the men,' and had accepted the principle of the sliding scale.[32] The defeat was thus softened since the men's leaders could argue that, although they had lost the fight on the immediate issue, the sliding scale would in future mean that wage-rates would not be arbitrarily decided by the owners. It was partly because the humiliation of defeat was blunted in this way that the end of the 1875 strike was followed, not by a drive towards greater organisation, but by a continuation of the decline of unionism which had started in 1874.[33] In 1898, however, it was not possible—and nobody attempted—to disguise the total nature of the defeat. Indeed, this was emphasised by all the leaders and all drew the same lesson: organise, organise, organise.

It did not escape notice that the miners had suffered their most crushing defeat at a time of a rising market, conditions which should have been strongly in their favour. This was attributed to their entry upon the conflict with virtually no funds and only very loosely-organised unions.[34] The decision to affiliate to the M.F.G.B. followed upon this. The view that association with a larger body would be a source of greater strength was, of course, a strong argument in favour of joining the English federation. But this argument had applied, and been appealed to, ever since the formation of the M.F.G.B. a decade earlier. Previous moves to join the M.F.G.B. had, however, always foundered on the attachment of the Welsh colliers to the sliding scale: the experience of 1898 weaned them, almost unanimously, from this. It was not that joining the M.F.G.B. killed the sliding scale; it was rather that once the sliding scale was discredited by being associated with an enforced settlement, there was no longer any obstacle to prevent the South Wales miners from joining the M.F.G.B.

What has mainly been attempted here is some explanation of why attitudes—on both sides—hardened in 1898. In so far as attitudes are important in industrial relations, this is some contribution to an understanding of the later turbulence of labour relations in the South Wales coalfield. Too much should not be made of this, however. The fundamental causes of conflict lay much more in the economics of the Welsh coal industry than in the personalities or the group psychologies which were involved. But this is a question which extends beyond the modest purpose of the present essay.

Notes

[1]For much of its course the 1898 stoppage had elements of a lock-out rather than a strike: but this distinction is not important for the present purpose.

[2]R. Page Arnot, *The Miners*, Vol. I, (1949), pp. 280-8; Clegg, Fox and Thompson, *A History of British Trade Unions Since 1889*, Vol. I, pp. 124-5; Ness Edwards, *History of the south Wales Miners*, Chap. 1.

[3]Hereinafter referred to as M.F.G.B.

[4]E.W. Evans, *The Miners of South Wales* (Cardiff, 1961), p. 216.

[5]Arnot, *op.cit.*, p. 369. There were, of course, special reasons for the aloofness of Northumberland and Durham—particularly their peculiar position on the eight-hour question. But their general reluctance to accept the "English" leadership of the M.F.G.B. because of their divergent interest as a coal-exporting area stands out clearly. See, e.g., their attitude in the great stoppage of 1893. Clegg, *op.cit.*, pp. 104-7.

[6]The official estimates of the Welsh coalowners, expressed by Sir W.T. Lewis, put the extra cost at *3d.* a ton, but companies were able to insure against their liabilities under the Act at a cost of around *1d.* per ton. For some contemporary comments on this see, e.g., *South Wales Daily News* (hereinafter referred to as *S.W.D.N.*), 1 March, 6 Aug., 26 Sept. 1898.

[7]D.A. Thomas, *Some Notes on the present state of the Coal Trade in the United Kingdom*, (1896).

[8]Minutes of Coalowners' Association, Vol. 17, 12 June 1897.

[9]See, Chapter 7 above.

[10]*Cambrian*, 24 March 1896. See also the issues of the *Iron and Coal Trades Review* for March 1896.

[11]*Cambrian*, 3 April 1896. Minutes of Joint Sliding Scale Committee, 7 and 14 March 1896.

[12]At the same time the owners refused to allow the normal audit of selling prices to take place: there was therefore no means of knowing what, under the existing agreement, the wage-rate should be from April onwards.

[13]The owners had also stiffened their terms in that they insisted on any settlement running for 4 years instead of the 3 years which they had earlier stipulated.

[14]In April 1897 there was a slight rise from 10 to 11.1/4 per cent above the standard rate (which was based on the levels which had existed in 1879); in April 1894 the rate had been 30 per cent above the 1879 standard.

[15]Counsel (A. Lawrence Q.C.) stated that the sliding-scale agreements were silent on this issue. He did point out that the agreements only bound the actual signatories, so that objection could technically be taken because not all the men's signatories to the agreement had signed the notice, but he thought it would be most unwise to press this point.

[16]*Coalowners MSS.*, Scrap-book on 1898 strike, compiled by W.G. Dalziel.

[17]*S.W.D.N.*, 2 July 1898.

[18]*Ibid.*, 25 May 1898.

[19]*Coalowners MSS.*, Scrap-book, 20 and 23 June 1898.

[20]*S.W.D.N.*, 14 July 1898.

[21]The *S.W.D.N.* published a wide selection of comment from British papers on 15 July 1898.

[22]Scrap-book, Dalziel to Lewis Miles, 30 July 1898; *S.W.D.N.*, 1 Aug., 1898.

[23]*S.W.D.N.*, 9 Aug. 1898.

[24]See, e.g. *S.W.D.N.*, 10, 11, 12 Aug. 1898.

[25]One petition being prepared a few days after David Morgan's imprisonment already contained over 30,000 signatures including 7 Justices of the Peace, 8 County Councillors, 22 doctors, 13 solicitors, 60 clergymen and ministers and 196 colliery managers, officials and owners. *S.W.D.N.* 15 Aug. 1898.

[26]*Ibid.*, 10 Sept. 1898.

[27]*Ibid.*, 29 Aug. 1898, and Scrap-book.

[28]*Ibid.*, 1 Sept. 1898.

[29]*Ibid.*

[30]*Ibid.*, 2 Sept. 1898.

[31]*Ibid.*, 3 Sept. 1898.

[32]It is interesting to note that Sir William Lewis (then Mr.) had been one of the chief advocates of granting this concession to the men in 1875.

[33]This was, of course, only part of the explanation: the decline of unionism after 1875 was also attributable to the continued depression in trade. In the same way, the drive towards unionism after 1898 was stimulated by the improved conditions of trade.

[34]This 'explanation' is deficient in at least two important respects. It ignores the extent to which the men's defeat stemmed from the determination of the owners not to make concessions. That the owners held so resolutely to their demands—despite the heavy costs and the sharply rising market in which several non-associated owners were making very large profits—suggests that the owners had a very real feeling of grievance about which they felt very

strongly indeed. It also suggests that Sir William Lewis performed a remarkable feat of leadership. In the second place it greatly exaggerates the importance of reserve funds in industrial conflicts. The highly-organised South Wales Miners' Federation of the following decade rarely had any substantial reserve funds but was able to sustain several important conflicts.

10. THE ROAD TO TONYPANDY

In the spring of 1911 it was said: 'Anything is better than the state of anarchy and red riot such as prevails at Tonypandy to-day.' This was not the voice of Winston Churchill who, as Home Secretary and contrary to Rhondda mythology, exercised a strong restraining influence over the use of the military. Nor was it the voice of D.A. Thomas, seeking to make up in the Hills the power he had been denied in the House. It was not even the voice of that stern and unbending old war-horse Sir William Thomas Lewis, who probably derived some secret guilty relish from the discomfiture of the up-start 'D.A.' Instead the words were those of a veteran trade unionist, W.E. Harvey of the Derbyshire Miners Association.

Harvey's outlook was doubtless somewhat jaundiced. He—and Thomas Ashton—had come to South Wales in March 1911. They were sent by the M.F.G.B. as peace-makers but were greeted at Tonypandy by a crowd which made its hostility uncomfortably explicit and which bluntly advised them to 'Go back to England'. But there was much justification for the view-point which Harvey expressed. In the course of the year-long stoppage at the Cambrian Combine there were several outbursts of violence.[1] On November 2, 1910 a workmen's train was attacked at Aberaman. On November 21 there was a four-hour conflict between police and strikers at Tonypandy and Penygraig, followed by rioting at Aberaman on the following evening. On March 22, 1911 the appearance of the M.F.G.B. emissaries, Harvey and Thomas Ashton, provoked further outbreaks spread over two days, and there was a final substantial clash on 25 July at the Ely Pit. The most celebrated occurrences, however, took place on November 7 and 8, 1910, involving sustained attempts by the strikers to close down the pumping engines at the Glamorgan Colliery, Llwynypia, and culminating in the so-called 'Sack of Tonypandy'. This latter incident involved the indiscriminate smashing of shop-windows and some looting of their contents. (Perhaps the process was not as uncontrolled as it seemed: at all events, the crowd with a nice regard for priorities, left intact the windows of the chemist's shop owned by Willie Llewellyn, one of the Welsh heroes of the already legendary 1905 rugby match against the All Blacks!)

During this period police were—from time to time—drafted into the Rhondda and Aberdare valleys from 21 county or borough police forces spread as far afield as Devon and the North Riding. In addition, nearly 1,000 men were sent from the Metropolitan Force,and troops drawn from the Royal Munster Fusiliers, the West Riding Regiment, the Somerset Light Infantry, the Lancashire Fusiliers, the Hussars and others were sent into the area. There were 224 formally reported police injuries and an indeterminate (but large) number of strikers received injuries of varying severity. There was one fatality—Samuel Rays who died from blows received when the police repulsed the crowd outside the Glamorgan Colliery on November 8. At the moments of conflict the method most widely used by the disaffected colliers was to gather on the hillsides and bombard the police with stones. Something of the zest of the police response—when they could get to grips with their tormentors—may be gauged from the fact that on the morning of November 9, 1910 some 300 police batons were sent up to Llwynypia to replace those broken—some on mandrils, some on skulls—during the previous night.

How are we to explain the substantial turmoil which has been so briefly indicated? What *was* the road to Tonypandy? Perhaps I should begin by being more explicit about what it is that I am trying to explain—especially as there are (at least) two quite different questions which could be raised. The first would be to ask why there was a violent outburst at that particular spot at that particular time. The answer would—I imagine—centre around the detailed origins of the strike at the Cambrian Combine. That, however, is not the question which will be addressed in this paper. It is, however, also possible to use Tonypandy simply as a symbol and to raise the broader issue of why the South Wales miners became increasingly militant in the first decade or so of the present century.

It is this second question which is to be the immediate concern. An obvious objection to such an approach would be that many would consider such concern to be superfluous. Miners are militant, and none more so than those in South Wales. This is the general impression and it is certainly the entrenched mythology. Moreover it has recently been given more tangible confirmation by Knowles's statistical study of strikes. Knowles established that between the years 1911 and 1945 the most strike-prone industry in Britain was coal-mining, and the most strike-prone region was South Wales. Thus there might seem to be no particular need to account for the militancy of Welsh miners in the early twentieth century.

It is, however, central to the current argument that the pre-eminence of South Wales in British industrial conflict was, in 1911, a relatively new phenomenon. It has to be conceded that a possible weakness of the current argument is that it is not easy to demonstrate that before 1900 the Welsh miners were seen in a quite different light. The statistics used for Knowles' study, do not go back into the nineteenth century. None the less there is much strong—though circumstantial—evidence to support the view that the Welsh labour movement was relatively passive until the

1890s. There had, of course, been previous outbursts of violence and significant industrial unrest. The 1820s and 1830s, for example, had witnessed the Scotch Cattle episodes in Monmouthshire, the Merthyr riots of 1831 and the Chartist march on Newport in 1839. And in the 1870s the South Wales coalfield was affected by three major stoppages in the space of five years. In addition throughout the period there were intermittent strikes at individual collieries, the kind of stoppage which seems to be inseparably connected with coal-mining, especially in an area like South Wales where the physical condition of the seams—and hence the basis of the wage-agreements—was constantly shifting.

None the less for virtually the whole of the last quarter of the nineteenth century, one of the outstanding characteristics of the South Wales coalfield was the relative peace of its industrial relations. In 1875, as part of the general agreement to end the long stoppage of that year, a sliding scale was introduced to regulate changes in the general level of wages. Thereafter, for a generation, sliding scale agreements were—albeit with difficulty—re-negotiated without provoking any general stoppage. The dominant philosophy of this period in trade union circles—partly reflecting the fragility of the movement after the eventual defeats of the 1870s—was one which stressed the mutuality of interests between employers and workmen. Contemporary comment certainly did not look upon the Welsh miners as leaders, much less militant leaders, on the labour front: quite the contrary. And the Webbs in depicting the trade union scene at this time saw the Welsh miners as backward, dismissing their unions as disjointed and company-dominated: a view which was basically endorsed—though couched in blander language—by the more recent historians of British trade unionism.[2]

By 1914 the impression was quite different. The first decade of the century saw a large number of—usually short—stoppages at individual pits over the Non-union issue. In 1910 there was the year-long Cambrian stoppage over abnormal places. And it was on the initiative of South Wales that this issue was broadened out into a demand for a minimum wage, which led to the first really national coal strike of 1912. South Wales was, moreover, also well to the van in the substantial re-adjustment in attitudes that was taking place at this time in the British labour movement as a whole. Everywhere old leaders were being challenged and old aims questioned. But nowhere was this process more evident than amongst the South Wales miners, and a—perhaps the—most symbolic publication, *The Miners' Next Step* with its explicit syndicalist programme, also originated in this region.

The contention, then, is that—at least for a couple of decades after 1875—the miners of South Wales were not a significant force in trade union development in Britain and were regarded by contemporary observers as being pliant, ineffective and generally lagging behind their English counterparts. But by 1914 they had become a prominent and influential segment of the labour movement with a reputation for initiating aggressive actions and policies. The change took place somewhere around the 1890s with the strike of 1898 acting as the water-shed—if it is legitimate to look for anything as decisive as a water-shed in social events. The contention is, then, that there was a perceptible change in industrial relations in the Welsh coal industry around the turn of the century—that about this time the road took a decisive turn in the direction of Tonypandy, and that these developments call for an explanation.

This background has perhaps been over-long: the preamble has, as it were, degenerated into a meander. The excuse—and hopefully the justification—has been the need to establish that the pertinent question to be asked is not: why has there always been a fair degree of industrial strife in South Wales? It is rather: why should South Wales have become so prominent in industrial relations at this time?

It is because they fail to answer this particular question that some of the traditional explanations are, it seems to me, significantly deficient.

We shall return to this in a moment. First, however, it might be helpful to make a few very brief, but more specific, comments on some of these traditional explanations. Thus—to take perhaps the most frivolous of them—it has sometimes been asserted that the strike-proneness of South Wales reflects the racial characteristics of the Welsh—that volatile and fiery Celtic temperament that we're so used to reading about whenever there's a great sporting occasion like a rugby international or a coal strike. But it is difficult to reconcile this with one of the best established facts of the development of the coalfield in the half-century before the First World War: namely, the very marked extent of labour migration. As Professor Brinley Thomas has recently demonstrated, 'at the beginning of this century Wales was absorbing population at a rate not much less than the United States.' This absorption was, moreover, overwhelmingly concentrated in the Welsh colliery districts. Between 1861 and 1911 Glamorgan alone received 427,000 migrants.[3] This is not in itself an indication of the extent to which the 'Welshness' of the population had been diluted. Many of the migrants were drawn from other Welsh counties; and the exceptionally high rate of natural increase on the coalfield would have been predominantly of Welsh origin. None the less the fact that over one-third of the inhabitants of Glamorgan in 1911 had been born outside Wales should act as a sharp warning against making too facile a correlation between the industrial unrest of the region and the presumed racial characteristics of its inhabitants.

Another cautionary note should arise from the observation that Irish workers in Wales were generally viewed by their fellow-workers as the most docile section of the labour force. There were, in fact, very few Irishmen amongst the colliers but in the ironworks, where they were more common, they were widely regarded as the section most likely to accept wage cuts and most easily persuaded to serve as black legs. Yet the Irish are often attributed with the same Celtic traits of character as the Welsh—and those who make such attributions would probably not regard the Irish as being less pugnacious than other groups. It is not intended to suggest that the comparative industrial pliancy of Irish workers was in any sense a consequence of their nationality. They were quiet, not because they were Irish, but because they usually constituted the poorer section of the community, and commonly worked as unskilled labourers—the most easily substitutable, and hence the most vulnerable, section of the labour force. Their attitudes are more plausibly explicable in terms of their economic situation than as a reflection of racial characteristics. It is the central argument of this paper that the same is true of the South Wales miners.

It was the view of the commissioners investigating the causes of industrial unrest in Wales during the First World War[4] and it is a view which has echoed down the years—that a major cause of the unrest in the region was the unsatisfactory social conditions. The basis of this argument has, indeed, become so familiar that it scarcely needs re-statement here. The way in which the narrow valleys forced residential building to straggle along the steep valley sides, which discouraged corporate life and made for overcrowding and lack of recreational areas. In addition the pace of the migration had produced an ill-balanced population with an excess of unmarried males. Altogether the Commissioners depicted an environment of sombre gloom, which contributed to industrial unrest by producing a discontented population. They concluded: 'there can be no doubt that . . . the workers feel deeply discontented with their housing accommodation and with their unwholesome and unattractive environment generally,' and that this discontent greatly contributed to industrial unrest.[5]

None the less it is not clear that social conditions in South Wales were significantly worse than elsewhere. They may have been, but an acceptable assessment on this would need to take into account some offsetting factors. Thus, for example, the steep valleys which constricted the area of industrial activity and habitation also meant that the hills above and between the valleys were both accessible and empty. Escape from the squalors of industrialism was in many areas only a walk away. Again, the stress upon the ways in which the straggling lateral development along the valley sides mitigated against the emergence of a sense of community should not pass unchallenged. Many of the facilities of community life were lacking or inadequately provided but it would be absurd to presume that therefore corporate spirit was stunted. Absurd, that is, in fact of the vast amount of evidence to the contrary.

Thus E.D. Lewis's study of the Rhondda[6] has presented a picture of a lively, active and highly social community, and this picture is amply confirmed by a reading of the contemporary press. No doubt the particular character of the popular culture of the region was largely determined by the dominance of non-conformity. The chapels were the centres of a constant social activity and provided much of the stimulus for the numerous *eisteddfodau* and *cymanfaoedd canu*. These cultural festivals formed the basis of a literary and musical activity which was vigorous and, in a few very limited fields, such as choral-singing, undoubtedly reached high standards. The chapels, of course, also exercised a powerful dampening effect upon those social activities of which they disapproved. Their influence, however, can be over-stated: such entertainments as whippet racing, boxing and wrestling matches, foot-races, handball, cycling, pigeons and rugby all claimed their adherents and all made their contribution to a richly-embroidered social climate.

It is also frequently implied that changes in company structure re-acted considerably on industrial relations. It is argued that the replacement of firms which were largely family-owned by the impersonal company changed for the worse the relationship between owner and worker, especially with the tendency for these companies to be grouped together in large combines. The owners ceased to live in the area and hence lost individual contact with the men. This trend was certainly marked and must have had some of the repercussions which are suggested, but it seems unlikely that it can be made to bear the weight of a general explanation of the difficulties in South Wales. The tendency for the limited liability company to become the typical unit of industrial organisation was a trend which affected most industries, but its coming was not inevitably associated with growing industrial unrest. Industries other than mining, regions other than south Wales, experienced these changes to at least a similar degree: there was nothing particularly distinctive in the corporate structure of the Welsh coal industry.

One aspect of this development of company organisation which is sometimes emphasised is the gradual spread from about the end of the nineteenth century of methods of cost accounting. Again there seem to be no strong reasons for thinking that the South Wales experience in this respect was markedly different from that of other industries and areas. And even if it was this would simply raise the issue of why cost accounting should have become more developed at this time: it is a symptom, rather than a substantial cause. None the less the effects upon industrial relations of a more widespread use of cost accounting would tend to be more marked in coal mining than in most other industries simply because labour cost formed a high proportion of total cost in mining. Thus managers naturally turned first to the detailed break-downs of labour cost when seeking ways of economising. There were, as will be seen later, particularly strong pressures inducing cost reductions in the South Wales coal industry but the real causes of friction lay in the sources of these pressures rather than in the system of cost accounting which was merely an instrument for effecting them.

In addition to the various incidental comments already made most of the explanations so far discussed suffer from a more general defect. They do throw light upon the issue of why there should have been industrial unrest in South Wales: but this—as was suggested earlier—is only a partial formulation of the problem. It is also necessary to explain why industrial relations in the South Wales coal industry were more difficult than elsewhere and also why this heightened conflict emerged somewhere around the 1890s. The explanations thus far offered are all defective on one or both of these counts. Thus, for example, the most simplistic account—that which emphasises the volatile nature of the Celtic temperament—could (even if the criticisms which substantially undermine its validity are ignored or discounted) at best serve as an explanation of why labour relations in South Wales were more difficult than elsewhere: but it is difficult to believe that the Celtic temperament suddenly

House Plans Approved per 10,000 Population
Based on 15 Local Authorities in South Wales 1881—1913

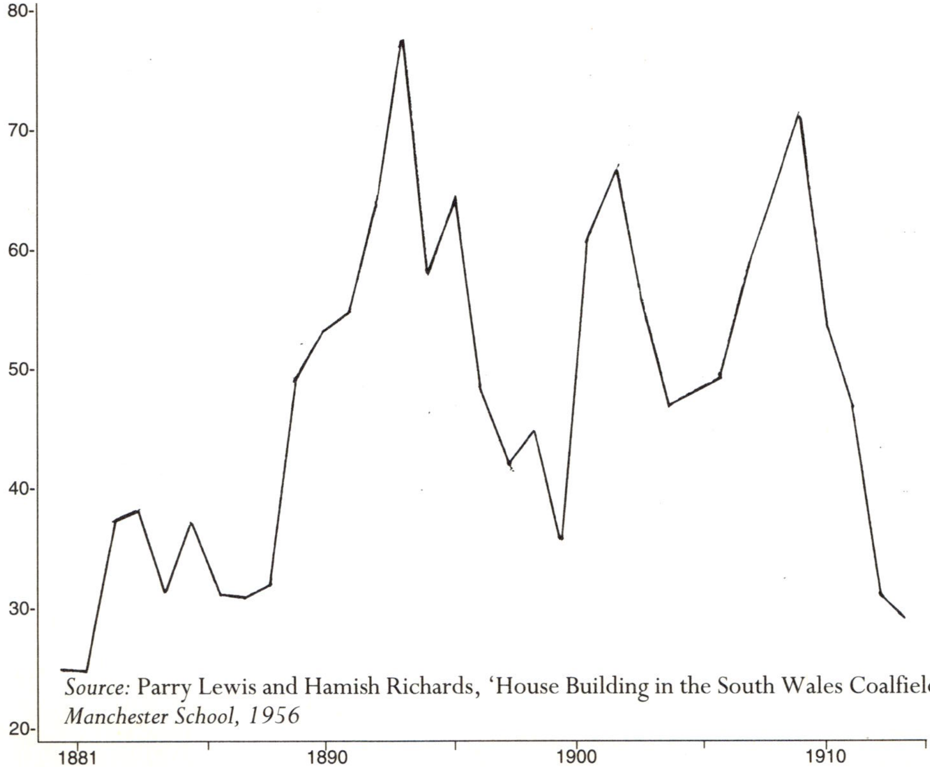

Source: Parry Lewis and Hamish Richards, 'House Building in the South Wales Coalfield 1851-1913', *Manchester School*, 1956

became more volatile somewhere about the turn of the century. The same general point could be made, though much less sharply, about the arguments relating to the general social conditions of the region particularly where these are related to the valley formation of the area. It is not at all clear, for example, that the housing situation in South Wales was worsening (see graph). Parry Lewis and Hamish Richards were especially concerned to show how building activity exhibited a long (20 year) cycle, but their figures also suggest that there was a slight secular tendency for the number of houses built per 10,000 population to rise in the first decade of the twentieth century. At all events they certainly don't suggest that the housing position was becoming worse. On the other hand it might well be possible to demonstrate that the move towards the emergence of the limited company as the typical form of industrial organisation was quickened in the 1890s, but there is no evidence that this development was sharper in South Wales than elsewhere.

It could also be plausibly argued that a powerful reason for industrial relations being characteristically more difficult in coal mining than in other industries arises from the fundamental conditions under which the industry is conducted. Thus, for example, although a basic price list may be negotiated the conditions to which it is supposed to apply may be constantly altering. The seam may alter in thickness or in character, the roof may vary, the presence or the amount of water may fluctuate, bands of clod (stone) may appear in or over the coal. In an industry where detailed supervision by management was impossible (or, at least, was not practised) such vicissitudes could—and did—easily lead to friction. The South Wales coalfield was generally acknowledged to be more geologically faulted than most and hence perhaps more prone to disagreements arising from these sources. But, until they were brought together in the general issue over payment for working in abnormal places in 1909-10, the geological variations usually resulted in restricted disputes confined to individual working places or to work in a particular seam or district of a mine. They provided a continuous source of petty disputes but were not decisive factors in producing a general picture of unrest. Certainly, there is nothing to suggest that the geological conditions in South Wales dramatically worsened at the end of the nineteenth century.

Let us now see if it is possible to open up an alternative—and, possibly, more fruitful—approach to the problem. The first thing to notice is that one of the outstanding characteristics of the South Wales coal industry was that, compared with the other major British coalfields, it was a relatively high-cost area. So far as one can judge this was true at least well back into the nineteenth century. At the time of the initial Admiralty trials of steam coals in the 1840s it was noticeable that the prices quoted for Welsh coals were generally higher than those from other districts.[7] Since at that time Welsh coals were not yet established for steam-raising purposes and Welsh owners were acutely anxious to secure the seal of naval approval, it is reasonable to conclude that this higher price reflected higher costs rather than a heavier demand. The somewhat more reliable indicators of labour productivity which are available later in the century confirm this impression. In terms of output per man-year labour productivity in South Wales was consistently lower than in the other major coalfields. Thus between the early 1870s and 1914 output per man-year in South Wales fluctuated between about 90 and 95 per cent of the average for Great Britain as a whole.

This lower productivity (and hence higher cost) characteristic of the South Wales coalfield has been a permanent feature, and was as evident in (say) the 1960s as in the 1860s. Thus in, for example, the year ending March 1964 the output per man-shift for the south Western Division of the N.C.B. was 23.9 tons, the lowest of all the divisions, and compared with an average for Great Britain of 33.4 tons. The cost per ton of saleable output was higher in South Wales than in any other division.[8] All the evidence suggest that this has been a more or less constant feature of the industry.

The relatively high cost nature of the Welsh coal industry has been in several respects of crucial importance to the development of the industry. In the present context it need only be considered from one aspect. Its higher cost basis means that to secure normal profits Welsh coal would have to sell at a somewhat higher price. This it was able to do in the nineteenth century because of the emergence of a special demand for its steam-raising qualities. This ability to command a price premium was essential to the development of the South Wales coal trade because of the need to cover higher costs. Hence it was not until the comparatively late emergence of a market—the steam coal market—where the special advantages of South Wales coal were able to command a premium that its exploitation became really rapid around the middle of the nineteenth century.

Thus the price premium commanded by Welsh coal during the last century was as much a sign of the weakness (higher costs) of the trade of the region as of its strength (superior quality for steam-raising). And in any event there were severe restraints upon the size of the price premium. If Welsh coal prices became too high in relation to other coals the advantage of its steam-raising qualities were neutralised.

The high cost basis of the Welsh coal trade thus made it especially vulnerable to competition: it controlled only a relatively specialised trade arising from its peculiar steam-raising qualities.[9] It is true that in 1914 most of the threat was still in the future.[10] None the less there was a consciousness that the fundamental reason why Welsh coal sold at a higher price than that of other regions was because it cost more to produce and that this could only be covered by the existence of a special demand.

These factors alone, however, would not—given the strong secular increase in the demand for steam coal—have created acute difficulties before 1914. They were made much more significant because of their inter-relationship with the productivity trends in the industry. As the graph and table indicate the thirty years before 1914 saw a sharp fall in output per head which dropped by some 25 per cent.

Number of tons produced per head per annum (South Wales and Mon.)

	Average of		
	1880-4	1903-7	1910-14
Output per head of			
(a) total employed	306	264	230
(b) underground workers only	360	312	270

This decline in productivity was a general phenomenon in the British coal industry at this time[11] but for reasons that have already been indicated it had especially potent implications for the industry in South Wales. From the owners' point of view the limited price premium which Welsh coal commanded and the vulnerability of the specialised South Wales trade meant that the higher costs arising from lower productivity could only be very cautiously passed on. In some of the other coal districts, especially those which were mainly dependent on the home market, the problems brought by declining productivity

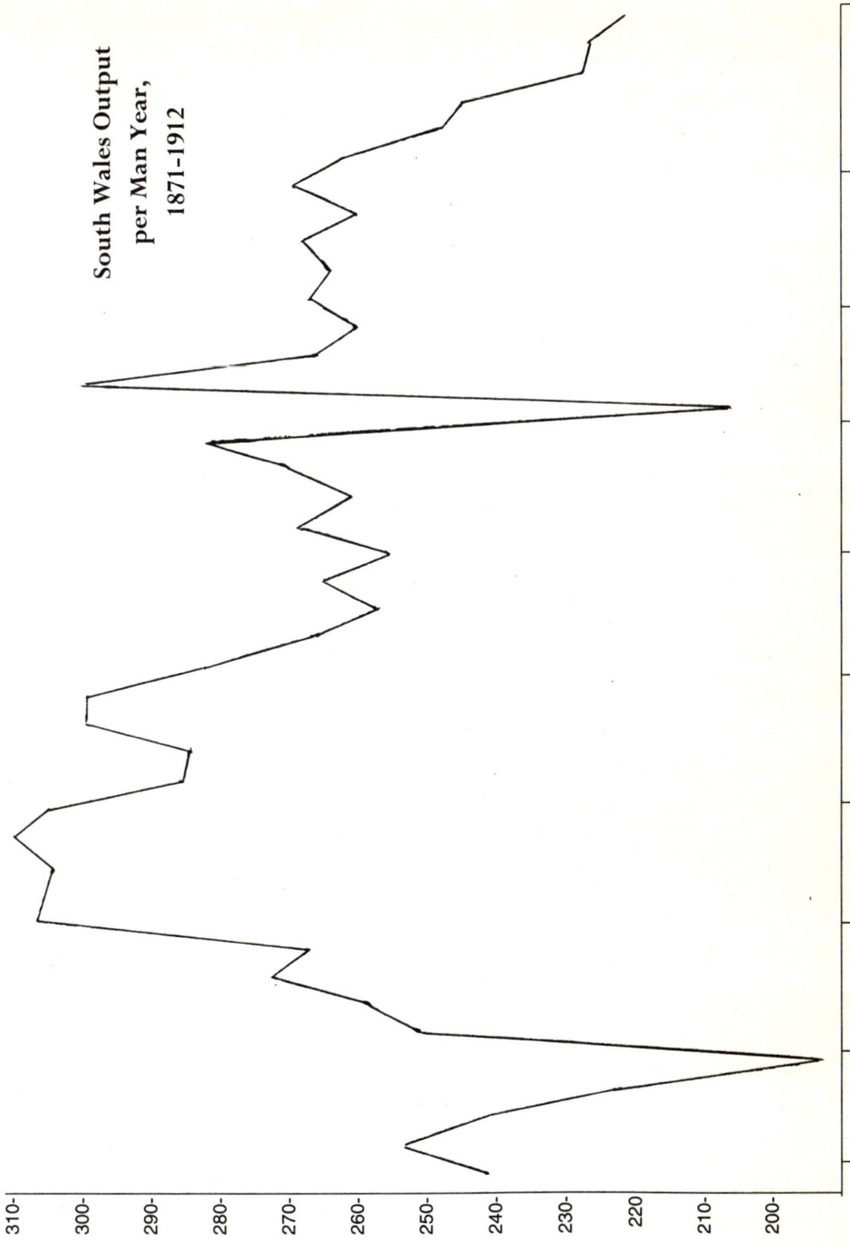
South Wales Output
per Man Year,
1871-1912
310-
300-
290-
280-
270-
260-
250-
240-
230-
220
210-
200-
1871
1880
1890
1900
1910

were much less acute. Prices could be increased in response to changes affecting all those competing in the market. In the exporting districts the position was more difficult: the existence of competitors who would be unaffected by the British productivity trends imposed an extra degree of restraint in price adjustments. And no district was more dependent upon foreign trade than South Wales where, even if coal shipped as bunkers is excluded, over one-half of the total output was shipped overseas in the years just before the First World War. Welsh owners thus had strong incentives to keep down costs.

The repercussions of this upon industrial relations can be more clearly seen when the significance of these trends for the wage-earners is also considered. For the hewers, who were the most important section of the miners, the vital consideration was that their earnings were directly related to output. This piece-rate basis hence meant that the declining trend in productivity reacted adversely upon their earnings—their annual output was tending to fall and, other things being equal, this would reduce their annual earnings. They thus had a strong incentive, even apart from any efforts at improvement, to press for the wage-bargain to be revised in their favour.

Both sides then were under pressure from the impact of declining productivity—the owners because it was increasing their costs; the colliers because it was eroding their earnings. This was already evident in the 1890s. Indeed, it was this situation which was ultimately behind many of the difficulties which led to the long conflict of 1898. But there were two influences in the decade before 1914 which brought these pressures to bear much more sharply.

The first derived from the trend in the cost of living. This rose fairly continuously after the mid-nineties. It was, of course, a general influence tending to reduce the real wages of all wage-earners. Its impact was not confined simply to miners, still less only to South Wales miners: but it did serve to reinforce the other unfavourable influences which were operating at this time on the level of earnings of the South Wales miners.

The second influence was more direct as it derived from the Eight Hours Act. The evidence collected by the Departmental Committee on the Miners' Eight Hour Day established that the hours worked in South Wales were longer than those of any other major coalfield, except Lancashire.[12] It followed directly from this that the cut in hours would have a greater proportional effect in South Wales than in most other coal fields.

From the owners' point of view the effect of the Eight Hours Act was—then—to produce a rise in costs. Unless substantial readjustments were made the same total wages would have to be paid to those who worked on day-rates—though not to those who were paid piece-rates—and these would be spread over a smaller output, which would also have to bear the same overhead costs as before. From the point of view of all those who were paid on tonnage rates it meant that their earnings would be lower than before. Thus the effect of the Act was very similar to the declining trend in productivity: it raised costs and lowered earnings. But there was this important difference: the productivity trend, though seemingly inexorable, was very gradual; the Eight Hours Act was necessarily abrupt. Thus the Act gave a highly dramatic expression to trends that had long been evident.

It was largely for this reason that it was primarily in South Wales that the implementation of the Eight Hours Act led to bitter and prolonged dispute. Only in South Wales did the coal-owners insist that the introduction of the Act meant a cancellation of the existing Conciliation Board agreement. They pressed for revisions in the existing agreements in order to offset the increased costs involved in the Act and they also sought to use the 60-hours clause of the Act (which allowed a man to work a total of 60 hours a year in excess of the statutory hours) to impose a system of regular overtime working. The owners secured no very solid concessions from this stratagem; a few clauses relating to the implementation of the Act were incorporated into the existing (1905) agreement, which was otherwise allowed to run its course. But this agreement itself expired only nine months later so the coalfield was almost immediately plunged into a further period of uncertainty and disruption. And even the brief time between these two negotiations was dominated by a bitter legal struggle over the 60 hours issue, a struggle which in December 1909 was finally decided in favour of the owners, who then refused to withdraw their claims for damages against all those men who had declined to work the extra hour since the Act came into force.

It was in this highly-charged atmosphere that the new agreement was negotiated. Each side produced an extensive list of revisions which would tilt the balance towards its own advantage. This was natural: but in 1910 these were far from being simply ritualistic proposals. Each side was acutely aware that the working of the Eight Hours Act had in some important aspects made it worse off; productivity had perceptibly fallen reducing earnings and raising costs. Neither side was yet prepared to push the issue to a fight, but each, conscious of its very real grievances, was bound to be dissatisfied with the compromise agreement which eventually emerged.

This uneasy peace did not last long. It was broken by the looming problem of abnormal places,[13] which largely dominated industrial relations in the industry for the next two years. Amongst the revisions which the workmen had tried to secure in the negotiations of 1910 was a clause giving a minimum wage to men working in abnormal places. The final settlement was silent on this issue, but it was one which could not be ignored because it arose directly out of the basic difficulties which we have been examining. With costs persistently rising—because of falling productivity accentuated by the Eight Hours Act—the owners were naturally anxious both to cut down on costs and, as far as possible, to keep them under their control. Hence they tended to reduce the allowances which it had long been customary to pay to men working in abnormal places, and also to insist that these allowances were not a customary right due to the men but a gratuity entirely at the discretion of the owners. This latter position they had established in the courts in 1908, even before the Eight Hours Act was passed. The colliers, whose earnings capacity was threatened by the declining productivity trends, were determined not simply to re-assert their customary right to some allowances for work in abnormal places, but to secure a specific minimum payment for such work.

This was not an issue where any easy compromise was possible. If the owners met the men's demands, even partially, then costs would again rise and the owners' control over them would be weakened. On the other hand, for the men to accept the owners' arguments would mean an acceptance of a further erosion in their earning-power. It was this battle that was initially joined in the nearly year-long Cambrian strike from which it blossomed out into the national campaign for a minimum wage in 1912. South Wales, which a generation before had been considered the laggard in industrial action in the coal industry, had become the spear-head of this entire movement.

This transformation then—leading as it did directly to Tonypandy—had been brought about by the pressure of the general economic trends facing the industry. In particular the persistent decline in productivity from the 1880s had led to increased costs of production for the owners and threatened the earnings of the colliers. For an area whose market was dominated by the export trade, it could not be assumed that the problem could be automatically resolved by passing on the higher costs to the consumers. Both sides were therefore driven towards a greater intransigency. The effects of this were partly seen in the strike of 1898, but became even more apparent in the first decade of the twentieth century, when they were reinforced by a rise in the general level of prices (tending to depress real wages) and by the effects of the Eight Hours Act.

The obvious way out of the productivity impasse might seem to be by the adoption of new technical methods which would raise productivity and reverse the adverse trends of costs and earnings. It is often said that the South Wales owners were reluctant innovators and that the workmen strongly opposed new methods. This view seems, moreover, to be confirmed by the very limited progress made in mechanical mining in South Wales before 1914. Although this is not the place to argue the case there is, however, much to suggest that the greatest obstacle to the introduction of mechanical mining was neither entrepreneurial torpor nor colliers' conservatism. It was rather the very difficult geological conditions of floor and roof in South Wales which defeated persistent efforts to use the machines then available.

Be that as it may, the fact still remains that productivity continued to decline during these years. And the pressures of this on industrial relations were pervasive. In the absence of any dramatic technological developments the rising costs resulting from declining productivity could only be held in check by the coal-owners—in one way or another—attacking wages, since wages still represented much the greatest part of the cost of production. The logic of that was ominously intensified by the fact that the same trend in productivity was eroding the earnings of the colliers. And anything that the men did, or attempted, to reverse or halt this trend was bound to lead to further increases in costs.

The object of this paper is to suggest that the emergence of these trends goes far to explain the timing of the worsening of industrial relations in the South Wales coalfield from about 1890 onwards since the effects of declining productivity were to push each side towards a course of action that was bound to bring it into conflict with the other. It also helps to explain why the difficulties were particularly acute in South Wales which was especially vulnerable to these trends for at least three reasons. Firstly, South Wales had always been a high-cost area; secondly, it was also subject to greater restraint on its prices (and hence costs) because it was primarily a coal-exporting region in direct competition with coal from other countries; and lastly the Eight Hours Act, which tended to accentuate the adverse productivity trends, acted with particular force in South Wales where the hours of working had customarily been longer than in most other British coalfields.

It could thus be plausibly argued that economic trends constituted the most important source of industrial unrest in the South Wales coalfield in the years before 1914. It is also pertinent to note that one other basic economic trend acted as a major factor which, despite all the difficulties, still worked to ease matters during these years. For as long as the secular trend in demand and output was strongly upwards this acted to cushion the impact of industrial difficulties: when this cushion was removed after 1914 the problems of the coalfield became vastly more intractable.

No doubt in this over-rapid dash along the road to Tonypandy, a number of ideological toes have been trampled upon and a few academic shins hacked. It should therefore be made explicit and clear that it is not intended to suggest that the factors mentioned were the only ones of any importance. There were—in a sense—many roads leading to Tonypandy—the sociological, the political, the personal. But it is suggested that the path which uses the economic trends as signposts is much the most direct road to Tonypandy.

(This essay was originally given as an address to the A.G.M. of the Society for the Study of Labour History at its meeting in Swansea in September 1972. It was printed in *Llafur*, 1,2, 1973, pp. 41-53.

The general policy of printing these essays more or less unchanged from their original form has been maintained here. But as Chapter 2 above indicates, I would not now place the same stress on the *persistent* decline in productivity. The essential argument would still survive this change of mind: but much more weight would be placed on the effect of the Eight Hours Act on productivity. More pertinent, it is necessary to refer to important later work on this subject by David Smith: i.e. 'Tonypandy 1910; definitions of community', *Past and Present*, 87, 1980; and 'From Riots to Revolt' in Herbert, T. and Jones, G. (eds.), *Wales 1880-1914*, Univ. of Wales, 1988.)

[1]The brief account of the riots is based on D. Evans, *Labour Strife in the South Wales Coalfield, 1910-11*, Cardiff, 1911, and on reports in the *Western Mail* and *South Wales Daily News*.

[2]S. and B. Webb, *Industrial Democracy*, 1920 edition, pp. 208-11, 237; Clegg, Fox and Thompson, *A History of British Trade Unions Since 1889*, 1964, pp.15-23.

[3]Brinley Thomas (ed.), *The Welsh Economy: Studies in Expansion*, Cardiff, 1962. pp. 8, 15, 16.

[4]*Commission of Enquiry into Industrial Unrest*, Wales, 1917.

[5]*Ibid*., p. 23.

[6]E.D. Lewis, *The Rhondda Valleys*, London, 1959, Ch. XI.

[7]*Reports on the Coals Suited for the Steam Navy*, P.P. 1847-8 (915), xxviii; 1849 (1086), xxxii; 1851 (1345), xxxiii.

[8]National Coal Board, *Report and Accounts*, 1963-4, vol. II.

[9]This argument would apply even more forcibly to the anthracite trade where costs were generally higher still and which catered for a still more specialised demand. The price of anthracite was high because its cost of production provided a high floor below which price could not fall in the long run.

[10]J.H. Clapham, *Economic History of Modern Britain*, vol. III, pp. 63-4, 125, 161, 166.

[11]A.J. Taylor, 'Labour Productivity and Technical Innovation in the British Coal Industry, 1850-1914', *Economic History Review*, 14.1, 1961.

[12]Despite this, the implementation of the act in Lancashire raised no real difficulties.

[13]An abnormal working place could very crudely be defined as one in which a normally skilful and diligent collier was unable—because of such conditions as the crushed or faulted nature of the coal or the amount of water—to earn an adequate wage.

11. THE NEW UNIONISM IN SOUTH WALES, 1889-92

Despite the existence of a few books dealing with particular industries, the detailed story of the development of trade unionism in South Wales has, as yet, hardly begun to be told. Naturally enough, attention has been generally concentrated upon the miners and tin-plate workers.[1] These formed compact, coherent groups whilst, in addition, they —particularly the miners—played a predominant role in the development of industrial society in South Wales. Trade union growth amongst other workers has been neglected, amongst other reasons, because they formed less compact groups, were numerically less important, and were often relatively late in developing any union tradition. Part of the purpose of this article is to draw attention to the beginnings of organisation amongst some of these groups and to suggest that their unions were in some ways different in character from the older unions of the region and that these differences have had some significance for Welsh life and culture. Its main purpose is the simpler and more limited one of providing a brief sketch of a few eventful years in the trade union history of the region. For the most part developments in the mining, iron and steel, and tin-plate industries have been overlooked in order to concentrate attention upon less familiar fields. It needs to be explicitly noted that this approach necessarily involves some distortion of perspective.

The more general writings on labour development around 1890 give scant attention to events in South Wales.[2] This is not surprising. South Wales was following trends which had their origins elsewhere: the struggles of the London gas workers, match-girls, and dockers are rightly highlighted as the initiating actions in the new impulse towards trade union growth. In addition the strikes in South Wales in 1890 and 1891 were part of a general unrest and form only incidents in a widespread outburst of activity. They do not, therefore, command the attention which attaches to the Taff Vale strike of 1900 (insignificant in itself but leading to the famous judgement by the law Lords) or to the Cambrian strike of 1910 (which was the first major step towards a legal minimum wage for miners)—strikes which raised issues of fundamental importance to the whole trade union world. They merit some resurrection, however, both for their local significance and because such impression as is left by the general textbooks suggests that South Wales was relatively backward and quiescent in labour affairs at this time.[3] This latter impression is hardly consistent with the evidence provided by a reading of the local press.

In fact, South Wales seems to have shared to the full in the great leap forward in trade union growth between 1889 and 1891. This rapid advance was encouraged by the revival in economic activity in the late 1880s and was given its particular force and direction by the rise of the new unionism symbolised by the success of the London dockers in 1889. The participation of South Wales in this movement can be seen, first, in the considerable degree of union-building which took place in the region. In some cases this was achieved through an extension of the activities of societies which were already established in the district. Thus, for example, the Amalgamated Society of Railway Servants (A.S.R.S.) besides increasing its recruitment at existing branches, opened new branches at Pontypridd and Ton-du in the first quarter of 1890,[4] and the numerous unions in the building industry grew rapidly through the same means.[5] This could not, however, form the typical method of any marked expansion in South Wales where the already-established organisations were comparatively few and largely confined to the relatively small groups of skilled craftsmen. Thus at the opening ceremony of the Roath Dock in Cardiff in 1887—before the new movement got under way—there was a great parade of friendly societies and trade unions which marched through the town on its way to celebrate the event. The unions which were represented, however, were all organisations of craftsmen, the processions being made up of carpenters and joiners, plumbers, boiler-makers, shipwrights, masons, tailors, engineers, steam-engine makers, plasterers, iron moulders, and printers. Nearly all of these were the members of the local branches and lodges of well-organised national societies. In addition, the numbers of the individual craft contingents were usually comparatively small, although the carpenters mustered over six hundred.[6] In the same year the annual Trade Union Congress was held at Swansea where, as contemporary comment made clear, active trade unionism was confined to a still more restricted group. 'Now if trade unionism is weak anywhere, it is weak at Swansea. There are few such centres of industry as Swansea, and there are fewer still where so many of the toiling thousands neglect to combine for their general well-being . . . The steel smelters . . . the copper smelters, spelter makers and others have no semblance of (a union) . . . There is at Swansea a Trades Council on which twelve different trades are represented, but last year the membership represented on the council was only 550 . . .'[7] The composite impression is one of a region in which trade unionism, in the major towns, was limited to a small range of skilled trades which gave employment to only a tiny proportion of the total working force of the district. Any considerable leap forward would necessarily have to break out of so constricted a field.

This process took place on quite a formidable scale. A few organisations like the south Wales and Monmouthshire Clerks' Association were formed as early as 1887,[8] but most of the activity was concentrated into the last part of 1889 and the first half of 1890. This reflected both the peak of the boom (with general prosperity and a low level of unemployment) and the effect of the spectacular success of the London dockers in the autumn of 1889. The men at Spillers' flour mills in Cardiff, the saddlers in the towns and in the valleys, the tramway workers, riggers and boatmen, blacksmiths, bakers, and confectioners form a sample of the groups which, hitherto unorganised, began to launch and join their own unions.[9] Even such normally passive sections as the shop assistants displayed considerable enthusiasm as the South Wales and Monmouthshire Shop Assistants' Union spread throughout the region and eventually amalgamated with the National Union of Shop Assistants.[10]

However, the most important and characteristic feature of the movement, in South Wales as elsewhere, was the growth of unions catering for the unskilled workers and usually based upon low contributions. In the railway industry, for example, the Railway Workers' Union was founded as a rival to the older A.S.R.S. Unlike the latter body the R.W.U. eschewed friendly benefits and hence kept its subscriptions at a level low enough to attract all shades of labour in the industry. Branches of the R.W.U. were formed in South Wales[11] but their recruitment was an addition to, rather than a substitute for, the considerable numbers who were already flocking into the A.S.R.S. The extension of the Dock, Wharf and Riverside and General Labourers' Union of Great Britain and Ireland (Ben Tillett's dockers organisation, affectionately known in South Wales as 'the union with the long name') was much more successful, effective, and significant. Following rapidly on the London success a branch of the union was set up in Cardiff in November 1889, and soon spread to Newport and Swansea.[12]

The dockers' organisation in South Wales fulfilled the three distinct functions attributed to general labour unions.[13] It operated, though only in a most muted fashion in South Wales at this time, as a class union; it organised the labourers who were ineligible for the old-type craft unions; and it served as a residual union, drawing in those—of varying degrees of skill—who, for one reason or another, had not been covered by other unions. Thus besides their recruitment at the docks the Dockers' Union soon spread into other fields. The Hauliers' and Porters' National Union, which was started in Cardiff at the end of 1889 and had branches at Barry and Newport, decided in March 1890 to amalgamate with Tillett's organisation, whilst the copper workers at Morfa and Tai-bach were also recruited.[14]

Unlike the Dockers' Union, Will Thorne's Gas Stokers' Union—the other major general labourers' union—was not very prominent in South Wales at this time, although it was claimed that it had enrolled most of the gas workers of South Wales by the end of 1890.[15] The chief rival to the Dockers in this region was the National Amalgamated Labourers' Union. This was, despite its impressive title, a purely local body. It was a particularly interesting organisation because, although it was of the 'new' unionism in that its appeal was to the general labourers, it was of the 'old' unionism in its maintenance of friendly benefits and generally conciliatory attitude. Although its higher subscriptions, as compared with the Dockers' Union,[16] meant that in less prosperous times labourers would be unable or unlikely to continue membership, the N.A.L.U. enjoyed considerable success between 1889 and 1891. Its significance as an indicator of local trade union development was further enhanced in that it was launched before the London dock dispute had developed. Its founder was Albert Kenny who, before settling in Cardiff, had been one of the earliest organisers of the Sailors' Union, having opened branches at Newport and Cork and served at Dublin and Whitehaven. By the beginning of 1890 Kenny claimed that the N.A.L.U. had three branches of about 500 each at Cardiff, 200 members at Blackweir, 200 at Penarth, 50 at Cadoxton, 245 at Chepstow, 572 at Swansea, and was planning to extend to Lydney and Gloucester. The union had enrolled dock labourers, iron-ore men, ballast men, deal springers, hydraulic-crane drivers, pitwood men, engineers, stevedores, and hauliers. The solid core of membership was thus at the docks, but the workers at Isca foundry at Newport, the Cardiff copper-workers, the patent-fuel works, as well as seamen, firemen, and some railway-yard labourers of the Taff Vale Railway had also joined. 'We mean to organise even the agricultural districts', was Kenny's comment. Despite their obvious competition for membership there does not appear to have been any animosity between the Dockers and the N.A.L.U. Kenny did not, however, anticipate any amalgamation between the two bodies, as the absence of friendly benefits in the Dockers' Union made its purpose quite different: Kenny hoped rather for an eventual alliance with the Sailors' Union and the A.S.R.C., upon the rules of which his own organisation had been based.[17]

It is important that the flavour of intense activity and enthusiasm which the labour movement of the region enjoyed at this time should be conveyed and also that the extent to which these events dominated the local news should be appreciated. These considerations did much to condition the attitudes of both men and employers in the struggles which ensued. Perhaps the atmosphere may best be suggested by citing a few of the more bizarre and untypical incidents. Thus the contagion of unrest spread from their elders to the schoolboys of Swansea who conducted their own strike in October 1889, and were fined 10s. (with the option of a week's imprisonment) for the accompanying assaults on teachers. A plaintive letter in the local press encouraged housewives to join in the general ferment of organisation by suggesting the formation of an Amalgamated Society for Distressed Wives to protect them from drunken and neglectful husbands.[18] But this campaign for a living wage made no further progress. There were, however, more earnest indications that the example of Annie Besant, no less than that of John Burns, had been noted. The girls engaged in unloading potato ships and the laundry-women at Messrs. Vaughan of Cardiff won some concessions after brief strikes.[19] Examples such as these suggest the extent to which the ferment of the time had permeated to even the most helpless elements in industrial society. Such indications encouraged extravagant hopes amongst the workers and prompted employers to believe that the alternative to standing firm was the opening of the floodgates of revolution.

These attitudes were hardened by the extent to which the new movement led to industrial disputes. Various sectors of the building industry were involved in frequent stoppages. These were usually highly local in character, concessions gained by the men in one town leading to similar stoppages in neighbouring districts.[20] The tramway men were particularly aggressive, those at Cardiff striking three times in six months in 1889.[21] There were numerous other strikes and stoppages—at Spillers' flour mills in Cardiff, at the Landore Alkali Works, at the Star patent-fuel works, the iron-moulders at Morriston, and so on—but most of these were skirmishes. The decisive struggles, as was clearly recognised at the time, were those involving the railwaymen and the dockers.

Railway unionism in South Wales was not the product of the new unionism of 1889. Following upon a number of meetings of railwaymen in South Wales in 1871, there were representatives from Merthyr, Cardiff, Pontypool, Aberdare, and Newport at the famous general delegate meeting in London in June 1872 at which the A.S.R.S. was founded.[22] Moreover, South Wales provided—in the person of Canon Jenkins of Aberdare—the president of the Society between 1873 and 1875, whilst Cardiff, with 270 members in 1875, was the third largest branch.[23] Thereafter the society, in Wales as elsewhere, was largely dormant, concentrating during the 1880s on its friendly society activities to the substantial neglect of trade matters. Nonetheless, there had been some tradition of unity providing a useful preparation for the outburst of activity amongst the railwaymen of South Wales in 1890.

A more immediate benefit to the Welsh railwaymen's movement arose from the fact that Fred Evans, one-time general secretary of the A.S.R.S., was living in Cardiff at this time. This exceptionally able and clear-sighted organiser did much to control and fashion the tactics which made the Welsh movement outstanding in its success. In a series of pungent, cogent, highly literate articles in the major local Liberal newspaper (he wrote for the *South Wales Daily News* under the pseudonym of 'An Old Trade Unionist'), Evans carefully prepared the ground by mobilising public sympathy and encouraging the men to take a firm, bold course. Nothing was rushed. The campaign was opened in the autumn of 1889. Letters were sent to the local newspapers setting out the excessive hours which were commonly worked, a series of local meetings was held and a strong recruiting campaign launched. On Sunday, 8

December 1889, a large demonstration meeting of all local railwaymen was held in Cardiff—it being carefully explained and emphasised that, although the men were reluctant to stage activities on the Sabbath, their duties left them no other time. At the meeting the national programme launched at Birmingham was wholeheartedly adopted with its demand for a ten-hour day, a six-day week, overtime at time and a quarter, and Sunday work at time and a half. About the same time Edward Harford, the general secretary of the A.S.R.S., wrote to all companies asking them to receive deputations to discuss the terms of the national programme.

The men proceeded with studied restraint. By mid-February 1890, apart from a formal acknowledgement from the Taff Vale Railway, all the companies of the district had ignored Harford's letter.[24] To avoid the charge that the Union was coming between the companies and their servants, deputations of workmen were appointed by the men from each company to wait upon their directors. Fresh petitions were presented and the resolution of the men was hardened when, at the beginning of March, the directors of the Great Northern Railway of Ireland gave way to their men under the threat of strike action. But at yet another mass meeting on 27 April it was reported that the Barry Dock and Railway Company had given no reply, written or verbal; the Rhymney Railway Company had seen a deputation and offered an eleven-hour day, which the men had rejected; and the Taff Vale Company had also received a deputation, but not yet given a reply. It was decided that the Barry and Rhymney men would now ask the executive committee of the A.S.R.S. to take up their case and offer the companies arbitration, and the same course would be followed with the Taff Vale if no satisfactory response were received in the next fourteen days.[25] At the end of June a further joint meeting of the men of all the companies at Cardiff was attended by Edward Harford, the general secretary of the A.S.R.S. He reported that the Barry Company had not responded to the offer of arbitration and the Rhymney Company had declared they had nothing further to offer, and that the men of these two companies had placed their notices in his hands. The Taff Vale, exercising more discretion and subtlety, had made a more reasonable offer to some sections of their men.[26] Much now hinged on the attitude of the Taff Vale men, who might be split by this offer. In the event a strike ballot showed a large majority in favour of rejecting the company's offer and of acting with the men of the other companies.[27] On 24 July 1890 notices were handed in.

While the notices were running out there was a substantial display of unity on the men's side. The dockers expressed their full support as did a number of other unions (including the aristocratic Amalgamated Society of Engineers) and the Cardiff Trades Council. The rival railway unions—the R.W.U. and the A.S.L.E.F.—promised their full backing.[28] At the same time the men continued to maintain their conciliatory attitude. They modified their terms by indicating a readiness to accept a sixty-hour week rather than a ten-hour day (although Evans thought this unwise as a major part of their case had turned on the evils of excessive hours). Harford wrote a moderately-phrased letter to the directors expressing a readiness to negotiate and followed this up with a letter to the press pledging the men to accept arbitration by Lord Brassey, Lord Aberdare, or some other suitable person. The companies, for their part, further alienated public sympathy by their failure to display any interest in these gestures: they allowed several days to elapse before deigning to reply to Harford's letter and then turned down his suggestion of negotiation. Not till the eve of the strike did they make any move and then, through the mediation of Alderman David Jones, an ex-mayor of Cardiff, they agreed to receive a deputation from the men. This, however, was abortive since, after keeping the deputation waiting in a corridor for over an hour, the directors then refused to receive them as Harford was accompanying them.[29]

One source of the intransigence of the companies had derived from the agitation amongst the dockers. This was important from two standpoints. It served to underline the extent to which there was general labour unrest in the district and in this atmosphere it was easy to foster the belief that all employers must stand firm. It was also widely understood that the dockers were demanding the exclusion of all non-union labour. In fact, this formed no part of the dockers' demands.[30] The dock employers, nevertheless, encouraged this misrepresentation of the men's position since they found the 'threat to free labour' a convenient bogey to raise and since they wished to suggest that the exclusion of non-unionists was a general aim amongst all trade unions. The railway workers had never raised this issue but there was a serious danger of the railway dispute—where public sympathy was strongly behind the men—becoming confused with more general issues. William Riley, the president of the Cardiff Chamber of Commerce, was strongly endeavouring to have the dockers' dispute fought out by the railway companies; and his statements and threats were, as the press pointed out, far more inflammatory than those of such so-called 'firebrands' as Ben Tillett.[31] More specifically the two issues threatened to merge because of the peculiar position of the Bute Dock Company. Although the interests of this private company, still mainly owned by the Bute family, were overwhelmingly in the docks they also operated railway facilities around the docks and were thus drawn into the railway dispute. Their representative was Sir William Thomas Lewis (later Lord Merthyr) whose opposition to the idea of unions was inflexible. His attitude and influence as one of the outstandingly able men of the district undoubtedly did much to set the faces of the railway directors against concessions, negotiations, or any other signs of 'weakness'. But on the day that the railway strike started the dockers, with considerable magnanimity, cut much of the ground from under this approach by announcing that they would waive all their claims until those of the railwaymen had been settled.

The intransigence of the directors had also partly derived from the belief that they would be able to import a considerable supply of labour. When the strike finally started on 6 August 1890, however, this illusion was soon shattered. Traffic was stopped entirely and pickets succeeded in meeting and sending home all potential blacklegs without any suggestion of force or violence. At once the attitude of the railway companies became more pliable: these events enabled the initiative at the joint meetings of railway directors to pass to those who had advocated a more conciliatory policy. Fortunately, the chief amongst these was William Inskip, the chairman of the Taff Vale Railway, the largest of the companies involved in the dispute. At the close of the first day of the strike, when it was obvious that the men had succeeded in securing a complete stoppage and after the dockers had made their gesture of solidarity, Inskip met Harford at the Park Hotel, Cardiff. Harford was ready, indeed anxious, to meet Inskip more than half-way, but the men turned down the proposals for settlement which he produced. However, a line of communication had been opened and eventually on 14 August, after eight days of complete stoppage of the railways (and hence, to a considerable extent, of the docks and collieries as well), a settlement was reached between Inskip and Harford and confirmed at a mass meeting of the men.

In some ways the railwaymen had won only a very limited victory. Harford's achievement as general secretary of the A.S.R.s. had been that of quietly nursing the society from the low ebb which it had reached by 1883, carefully building up numbers and finance. Confronted with an actual strike his first reaction was to end at once this drain upon the union's wealth. Thus the South Wales settlement did not, in fact, concede in full any of the demands of the men, although even after a week there was still no traffic moving, public support was still firmly with the men, and they were fully backed by all sections of labour in the district—especially by the dockers and the miners who were themselves seriously affected by the railway standstill. None the less there was no doubt that it had been a victory for the men. The companies had made substantial concessions and, no less important, the settlement had in the event been negotiated directly with the general secretary of the A.S.R.S. without even the presence of deputations of workmen. In face of the attitude of the companies right up to the outbreak of the strike, the railway stoppage of 1890 forms a substantial landmark in the history of industrial relations in the district.

These development had been made possible by several favourable circumstances. The men's claim had not merely been a good one but had been demonstrated to be well-founded. The ground had been carefully prepared and every reasonable possibility of conciliatory action exhausted before resorting to the strike weapon. Moreover, the men themselves—and those in other trades likely to be affected—had been organised and educated into attitudes of full support. The importance of these considerations only became clear in the following year when the dockers finally struck and demonstrated how few of these lessons had been assimilated.

For their detailed demands for better wages and conditions the Cardiff dockers could have made a strong case. The protracted delays of the employers could also have been used to their advantage; the public, no less than the dockers themselves, seemed exasperated by the way in which the opening of negotiations was continually delayed because Sir William Lewis was in Germany or Scotland or the U.S.A.[32] Even in the most favourable circumstances, however, the dockers were faced with a more formidable task than that which the railwaymen had tackled in mid-1890. Much of the dock labour was casual and unskilled and hence easy to replace; it was organised by a number of different unions amongst which it would be difficult to secure smooth co-operation. Moreover, the dockers were opposed by Sir William Lewis, the chief agent of the marquis of Bute and an ardent believer in the rights of 'free labour' which he saw threatened by trade union ideas. A stern, strong, severe man, but also sincere, just, and courageous, he combined a rigid inflexibility on what he considered to be essentials with a supple tactical sense.

In the event the dockers precipitately chose to make the occasion of their fight one which sacrificed most of their advantages and magnified their considerable disabilities. Their prospects of victory, which had never been outstanding, soon became hopeless. The stoppage began on Tuesday, 3 February 1891, when six coal tippers refused to load the *Glen Gelder*, a vessel whose master declined to engage any members of the Seamen's Union.[33] The sailors' fight with the Bristol Channel shipowners (who were members of the Shipping Federation founded the previous autumn) had long been coming to boil alongside that of dockers with the Bute Dock Company. At a mass meeting at Cardiff on 2 February the dockers and sailors had agreed to take joint action against the Shipping Federation which was vigorously attempting to suppress the trade union movement. But by doing so, and by making this the basis for a stoppage without notice the next day, the dockers placed themselves in a completely false position. They were now fighting the sailors' case for them. Moreover, the issue had specifically become that of trade union versus free labour. An important trade union principle was, no doubt, involved but it was bad ground on which to wage a direct conflict. Indeed, a few months earlier Ben Tillett, in submitting the dockers' claims, had taken some care to state quite explicitly that they were not aiming at excluding non-unionists.[34] Public opinion in the area, whilst not as hostile to the unions as it seems to have been elsewhere,[35] was much more hesitant in its support on this sort of issue than where the more easily-judged matters of wages and conditions were concerned; the employers were generally and naturally bitterly opposed; and there was little possibility of compromise on such basic principles.

The decisive consideration was the attitude of the Dock Company which—superficially at least—was not directly involved. Thus at Newport in the previous year 2,000 dockers had struck without notice because of the refusal of a captain to engage a union crew. Despite a telegram from Tom Mann advising against their spontaneous strike and threatening to withhold strike pay, the men were completely successful because the Dock Company agreed to the men's request to turn the vessel out to the buoys. This sympathy of the Alexandra Dock Company with the men's views—or its reluctance to oppose them—was enough to persuade the captain concerned to recruit a union crew.[36] It was unlikely, however, that the Bute Dock Company would adopt a similar attitude. The exclusion of non-unionists was against Sir William's deepest principles whilst he was not likely to have overlooked that the dockers' precipitate action gave him a strong tactical advantage in his own dealing with them.

The situation, indeed, was one which Sir William found no difficulty in handling. The squabbles between the Shipping Federation and the Sailors' Union, he could, and did, protest, were no concern of his. The occasion of the stoppage—the blocking of individual ships—meant, moreover, that the men came out piecemeal and without notice. At first only half-a-dozen coal tippers were involved and even when their 300 fellow-tippers joined them (ostensibly, because Sir William had taken out summonses for breach of contract against the tippers directly involved) Sir William, who had long prepared for this contingency, had no difficulty in replacing them with imported labour. After a week the docks were almost back to normal working, a crucial consideration being that the coal trimmers, who were not members of the Dockers' Union but organised into a protection society run and managed by their petty-master gang leaders, gave full support to their employers and agreed to work with the 'blackleg' tippers.[37]

Tom Mann came down to Cardiff to join Tillett in endeavouring to save something from the wreckage —the men had initially acted without the authority of the executive committee—by attempting to open negotiations. The shipowners gave him some encouragement but Sir William calmly informed him that, since the men had left and their places had now been filled, there was nothing to negotiate.[38] Sir William's cool, curt attitude tended to transform the issue into that of securing simple recognition for the existence of the union. This, together with his bland assumption that the dockers had no grievances of their own, worked to command much more public sympathy for the men. This could be of influence, however, only if the strike could be made effective. The only hope for this was to extend the area of conflict. But the attempts to do this merely demonstrated that Sir William's contemptuous treatment was based on a correct reading of the situation. The attitude of the railwaymen was here decisive; although they owed the dockers a substantial debt of gratitude from the previous autumn, the railwaymen delayed making any decision. The miners, with more justification and greater candour, told Mann it would be impractical for them to refuse to cut coal intended for the Bute Docks: they could not know for which docks any particular tub of coal was destined.

In an attempt to disguise and repair this lack of unity a great conference of all the unions of the South Wales district was arranged to discuss the strike and to consider the formation of a general labour federation.[39] This meeting appointed a deputation, including Harford and Mabon, to wait on Sir William to ask him to reconsider his decision not to reinstate the tippers who had struck. Sir William conceded nothing saying simply that the old workmen could, as vacancies arose, apply along with others and no questions would be asked as to whether they were union members or not. The conference, despite the pleas of Harford and Mabon, at first refused to accept this. At an adjourned meeting, however, it was decided that a deputation of the old workmen should wait on Sir William. After a friendly discussion the strike was called off, although Sir William still made no concessions, the dockers' leaders taking what comfort they could from the fact that Harry Orbell, the local organiser for the Dockers' Union, was allowed to be present at this meeting. At the same time (15

March 1891) the Seamen's Union also capitulated, the Shipping Federation insisting that J.H. Wilson, the general secretary, should withdraw the blockage on ships at Cardiff before they agreed to enter into discussion with the union. The defeat could not be camouflaged, although the unrealistic hope was fostered that the general delegate meeting of all the trades in the district which it occasioned would lead to the formation of an effective federation of all South Wales unions.[40]

The railway and dock strikes of 1890 and 1891 have been recorded in some detail. This has not been done solely because of the inherent local interest of these incidents nor to point the obvious lessons that spring from their sharply contrasting fortunes. It is rather that they illustrate several of the salient trends in Welsh trade unionism at this time. They demonstrate, for example, the force of the impact which the new unionism had in South Wales. A few years earlier it would have been inconceivable for the railway workers of the district to have acted with such unanimity or for the dockers to have been tempted to behave with the tactical rashness which they displayed in February 1891. Under the influence of the new movement the base of trade unionism in South Wales, as elsewhere, was substantially broadened. The colliers, tin-plate workers, and, to a lesser degree, iron-workers already had some tradition of organisation, but this was now extended to a number of other groups. The effect of this was most clearly seen in the ports where trade unionism had hitherto been largely confined to a minority of skilled artisans. Thus even at the beginning of 1890, when the movement was still gaining impetus, it was said that the thirty or so delegates at a meeting of the Cardiff Trades Council represented 13,000 members of trades societies[41] and there is ample evidence of a similar vigour at Newport and Swansea.

All this helped to make the district a leading centre of the British labour movement. The numerous visits paid to the region by the oustanding national personalities are perhaps some indication of the importance they attached to South Wales. All the acknowledged leaders of the new unionism movement—Mann, Burns, and Tillett[42]—spent some time in South Wales. Tillett, indeed, was a frequent and familiar visitor doing much to build up the district as one of the most important centres of the Dockers' Union, a position it retained until at least 1910.[43] In addition, Harford of the railwaymen,[44] John Hodge of the steel smelters, and J.H. Wilson of the seamen were prominent in the region.[45]

The events in South Wales are also interesting because, to some extent, they foreshadow the later triple alliance between railwaymen, miners, and dockers which, for a decade after 1912, loomed so large in British industrial relations. The Cardiff railway and dock strikes, in so far as they represented the triple alliance in microcosm, illustrated both the strength and the weaknesses of such an arrangement. The success of the railway strike in 1890 owed much to the support of the dockers and miners. It is true that neither of these groups struck in sympathy; this was not necessary. But the dockers gave invaluable assistance by postponing their own demands, and both miners and dockers played an important part by quietly and cheerfully accepting the widespread unemployment which a railway strike inevitably entailed for them. In 1890, as in the more formal alliance of later years, its effectiveness—since it involved neither amalgamation or federation—depended on common action and mutual support. This was secured in 1890 because all knew and accepted exactly what the railwaymen were trying to achieve. In 1891 common action and mutual support were lacking because the dockers chose to strike without notice and on the issue of non-unionism and 'free' labour. Neither the miners nor the railwaymen had been consulted on this and neither was prepared to lend unqualified support.

The most important and permanent trend, however, was that towards national unions. The days of the local independent unions were numbered. Most of the new unions formed in Wales at this time were offshoots of general British organisations to which they were either from the outset attached or quickly became linked.[46] Labour organisations in Wales, as elsewhere, were being drawn into wider associations embracing Britain as a whole. The trend was inevitable but the impact of the new unionism of the early 1890s was important in this respect because it marked a substantial leap forward. The great amalgamated societies of the skilled workers had long been organised on this basis; in the early 1890s it became the general pattern for unskilled and semi-skilled workers; in the next decade the miners and tin-plate workers of South Wales were drawn into closer association with unions embracing Britain as a whole.

In some respects this general trend had peculiar and far-reaching implications for South Wales. The often vigorous forces of regional loyalties were reinforced in Wales by a growing awareness of national consciousness. Nowhere were Irish events watched with greater interest, nowhere were Irish aspirations more warmly endorsed. This interest largely derived from the parallels which were drawn between Irish and Welsh nationalism and was demonstrated by the enthusiasm which the Young Wales (*Cymru Fydd*) movement evoked for a few years after its formation in 1886. So long as trade union development in South Wales was contained within locally-based organisations there was some hope that they could serve as vehicles for these nationalist aspirations; but when they were drawn within the framework of a general British movement the unions became, on the contrary, a potent source of Anglicisation.

National sentiment undoubtedly played some part in the debates on labour organisation which figured so prominently in the mining and tin-plate industries in the 1890s. Rarely explicit and never dominant, this consideration none the less affected such matters as, for example, whether the South Wales miners should join the Miners Federation of Great Britain[47] and the slow crumbling of the independent Welsh-centred union for tin-plate workers. Its impact is still more clearly seen in the recurrent discussion of such topics as self-government for Wales, disestablishment, and land reform at the trade union meetings of miners and tin-plate workers as well as in the frequency with which such leaders of the Young Wales movement as Lloyd George and D.A. Thomas were invited to address their meetings. A negative indication of the possibilities is perhaps even more revealing: these issues do not appear amongst the topics discussed at the gatherings of, for example, the railwaymen and the dockers. The character of their meetings was determined more by their English links and leaders, whilst their unionism was in any event centred upon the already more anglicised towns.

(Originally appeared in *Welsh History Review*, 4, 1963, pp. 413-29. There is some later relevant documentary material in Hopkin, D. and Williams, J., 'New Light on the New Unionism in Wales, 1889-1912, *Llafur*, 4,3, 1986, pp. 67-80.)

[1]See, e.g. D. Evans, *Labour Strife in the South Wales Coalfield, 1910-1911* (Cardiff 1911); N. Edwards, *The South Wales Miners' Federation* (1938); E.W. Evans, *The Miners of South Wales* (Cardiff, 1961); and the relevant chapters in J.H. Jones, *The Tin-plate Industry* (1914); W.E. Minchinton, *The British Tin-plate Industry* (Oxford, 1957); and J.H. Morris and L.J. Williams, *The South Wales Coal Industry, 1841-75* (Cardiff, 1958). The iron and steel workers, apart from those connected with the tin-plate industry, have been more neglected although much may be gleaned from *Men of Steel* by One of Them (Sir Arthur Pugh, 1951). Since this essay was written a major work on the miners has appeared: Smith, D. and Francis H., *The Fed*.

[2]See, e.g. S. and B. Webb, *The History of Trade Unionism*

[3]This impression has largely arisen from the Webbs' views of the miners' unions in South Wales (S. and B. Webb, *op. cit.*, p. 434), but in the absence of other evidence this judgement-disputable even for the miners-tends to be attached to all labour movements in South Wales at this time.

[4]*South Wales Daily News* (hereinafter referred to as *S.W.D.N.*), 13 January, 25 February 1890.

[5]See, e.g., S.W.D.N., 28 April 1890, for formation of branch of the Amalgamated Society of House Decorators and Painters at Pontypridd, and ibid., 5 May 1890, for formation of a branch of the Carpenters' and Joiners' Union at Aberavon.

[6]*S.W.D.N.*, 25 August 1887.

[7]*Ibid.*, 2 September 1887.

[8]*Ibid.*, 30 November 1887.

[9]See, e.g. *ibid.*, 23 and 28 November, 9 and 10 December 1889; 6 January and 3 March 1890.

[10]*Ibid.*, 22, 25, and 27 January, 12 and 28 February 1890; 16 September 1981.

[11]*Ibid.*, 4 December 1889.

[12]*Ibid.*, 30 November and 21 December 1889; 20 February 1890.

[13]E.J. Hobsawm, 'general Labour Unions in Britain, 1889-1914' *Econ.Hist. Review*, ii, 1 (1948-49), 123.

[14]*S.W.D.N.*, 3 March, 31 July, 8 and 11 September, 24 November 1890. Later the dockers most important diversification in South Wales was their substantial recruitment amongst tin-plate workers. Minchinton, *op. cit.*, pp. 125-7.

[15]*S.W.D.N.*, 31 December 1890.

[16]There was an entrance fee of 2s. 6d.(12.5p) and weekly subscription of 5d.(2p.) The Dockers' Union, which offered only trade benefits, levied 1.5d or 2d a week. (Less than 1p.)

[17] *S.W.D.N.*, 1 and 15 March 1890.

[18]*Ibid.*, 10, 18 and 21 October 1889.

[19]*Ibid.*, 5 and 24 March 1890.

[20]For examples see *ibid.*, 17, 26,28, and 30 April, 3 and 5 May 1890.

[21]*Ibid.*, 6 February, 28 June, 1 and 2 July, 15 October 1889. They had much cause for discontent. In mid-1889 the hours of conductors, who were mostly boys, were said to be from 8 a.m. to 11.30 p.m. (except for about one week in six when they finished at 6.30p.m.) with a short dinner break which might fall anywhere between 8.45 a.m. and 6 p.m. For this they received from 12s to 16s a week (60 to 80p). The employers- the London and Provincial Tramways Company—tried, unsuccessfully, to demand a £2 deposit from their conductors as surety for good behaviour.

[22]G.W. Alcock, *Fifty Years of Railway Trade Unionism* (1922), pp. 39-40. 74, 82. A further branch was opened at Swansea shortly afterwards on 27 October 1872, whilst Wyatt, the delegate from Aberdare, achieved the dubious distinction of being one of the three delegates to the general meeting who were discharged by their companies as soon as the meeting was over. (*Ibid.*, pp. 90, 97-8)

[23]Ibid., pp. 140, 183-5

[24]*S.W.D.N.*, 14 February 1890. Fred Evans later summed up the attitude of the companies: 'I paraphrase Timon of Athens' invocation to the gods as a chorus for directors to sing to their men— "For these our present friends, as they are to us nothing, so in nothing bless them, and to nothing are they welcome".' (*Ibid.*, 1 April 1890.)

[25]*Ibid.*, 28 April 1890.

[26]*Ibid.*, 30 June 1890.

[27]*Ibid.*, 21 July 1890.

[28]See, e.g., *ibid.*, 28 July 1890.

[29]*Ibid.*, 28 July, 1, 2, 4, 5, and 6 August 1890.

[30]This does not mean that it was not an integral part of the dockers' intentions. They were not asking the employers to use only union labour because, Tillett said, they could deal with non-unionists in their own way. (*Ibid.*, 7 August 1890.)

[31]*Ibid.*, 7 August 1890.

[32]*Ibid.*, 6 December 1890.

[33]*Ibid.*, 4 February 1891.

[34]*Ibid.*, 8 September 1890.

[35]J. Saville, 'Unions and Free Labour', in A. Briggs and J. Saville (eds), *Essays in Labour History* (1960).

[36]*S.W.D.N.*, 16, 17, and 22 July 1890.

[37]*Ibid.*, 9 February 1891.

[38]*Ibid.*, 17 February 1891

[39]*Ibid.*, 4 March 1891.

[40]*Ibid.*, 5, 13, 14, and 16 March 1891.

[41] *Ibid.*, 14 February 1890.

[42] J.H. Clapham, *An Economic History of Modern Britain*, 111, 320.

[43] Alan Bullock, *The Life and Times of Ernest Bevin*, 1 (1960), 29.

[44] Indeed, three general secretaries of the A.S.R.S.—past, present and future—were active in South Wales at this time in the persons of Fred Evans, Edward Harford, and Richard Bell, who first rose to notice during these years when he was transferred by the G.W.R. from Landore to Carn Brea in Cornwall because of his trade union activities. *S.W.D.N.*, 20 April, 6 July 1891.

[45] Wilson, indeed, perhaps spent more time than he wished in South Wales, being imprisoned for six weeks on a charge of riotous assembly. *S.W.D.N.*, 8 April 1891.

[46] Not all the unions launched at this time followed this pattern. There were some indigenous independent creations, such as the Welsh Artisans Union formed in 1890. But it is clear that these were not typical.

[47] This is perhaps reflected in the common reference to the M.F.G.B. as the 'English Union' as meetings of Welsh colliers.

12. THE CLIMACTERIC OF THE 1890s

A generation ago Phelps Brown and Handfield-Jones launched the idea that the 1890s were a turning-point for the British economy. It was an inspired touch to entitle their essay 'The Climacteric of the 1890s'.[1] Attention was arrested by the resonances of this term as commonly applied to the human condition to indicate a time of 'fundamental bodily change'. Applied to the economy, however, the intention of the authors was to draw attention to what they saw as a critical period. The assertion is that after a long period of confident and persistent, though not necessarily steady, economic growth the British economy was perceptibly checked in the period around the turn of the century, and that this marked a definite break in trend and not just a cyclical downturn. There was a deceleration in the progress of productivity improvement and this arose from tardiness in applying technical changes. The argument thus reinforced vague criticisms about falling enterprise, and intensified concern on this issue soon led to the assertion that by the late nineteenth century 'the British entrepreneur had lost much of the drive and dynamism possessed by his predecessors of the classical industrial revolution'.[2]

Claims as dramatic and sweeping as an 1890s climacteric and entrepreneurial failure have naturally not stood unchallenged. There have been disputes about dates. From the outset Coppock[3] accepted the concept of the climacteric but wanted it pushed back to the 1870s. The debate became enmeshed, as was probably unavoidable, with the longer-standing issue of whether the years from c.1873-1896 constituted a 'Great Depression'.

A much stronger response was provoked when the hypothesis of entrepreneurial failure was directly challenged. Perhaps this was partly because one source of the challenge was by the proponents of the new economic history. Making a more explicit use of economic theory they—and especially McCloskey and Sandberg[4]—seemed to demonstrate that British entrepreneurs at the time behaved in an economically rational manner. The extent to which these entrepreneurs applied new methods and shifted to different products was, given the relative factor prices, consistent with an hypothesis of maximising returns. The elegant demonstrations of the cliometricians have not, however, resolved the issue of entrepreneurial capability. Partly this is because doubts remain about the quality of the data being used and, more fundamentally, about the appropriateness of the neo-classical theory for the problem to which it has been addressed. More recently, it has been strongly questioned from within the neo-classical tradition whether a satisfactory short-run rate of return does indicate a 'correct' allocation of resources[5]—though this point has not yet been explicitly applied to the argument about late Victorian and Edwardian entrepreneurs.

Beyond these more or less technical considerations, however, the debate has not been resolved because the participants are nursing quite different concepts of 'the entrepreneur'. There are at least two radically different views of the function of the entrepreneur which are embodied in the literature. The one, which may be described as Marshallian, sees the entrepreneur as the provider of a fourth factor of production, organisation, to ensure the most efficient use of the other three—land, labour and capital. The main function of this entrepreneur is to make marginal adjustments to the factor combinations in a way that ensures the maximisation of the short-run rate of return. His time-horizons are short. The other view, which may be described as Schumpeterian, sees the entrepreneur as innovator. The main functions of this entrepreneur are to introduce new methods, supply new products and create new demand. His time-horizons are long. With such divergent and confusing views being held about the basic nature of the problem a consensus on its resolution was never likely. The entrepreneur of the new economic historians, whose marginal adjustments were by definition successful because they earned a satisfactory rate of return, bore little relationship to the entrepreneur who had failed to produce the new chemical dyes and electrical equipment. The entrepreneur which McCloskey thought he had redeemed was quite simply not the same person who had been earlier damned.

A rather different defence of British entrepreneurs was provided by writers like Charles Wilson.[6] This was to accept many of the strictures but to argue that they only applied to parts of the economy and especially to the older heavy industries like iron and steel. The border between entrepreneurial failure and success ran along a structural divide. 'The division can be made—though very roughly and with exceptions—into old industries and new industries, basic industries and light industries, industries largely based on home markets and others on export markets.'[7]

It is hoped that even so abrupt a summary will have suggested something of the complexity of the issues involved. They form an essential background. Fortunately, however, most of the complications in the extensive literature are concerned with the attempts at explanation, and especially the attempt to attribute a break in the rate of growth of the British economy to a decline in business enterprise. There is a much greater level of agreement that there *was* a fall in the rate of growth. Aldcroft and Richardson, drawing on calculations made by Matthews, Feinstein, Maddison, Lomax and others demonstrated that for a whole range of economic indicators the performance of the British economy from c.1900 to 1913 fell below previous levels.[8] This was epitomised by the bare figures for the rate of growth of gross domestic product: in the forty-odd years from 1856 to 1899 this had averaged 2 per cent; from 1899-1913 it fell to 1.1 per cent (a difference between doubling the output of the economy in 35 years and taking nearly 70 years to do so).

It thus seems to be reasonably established that there was a decline in the rate of growth somewhere in the 1890s. In accepting this, however, it is not necessary to give the phenomenon the full significance bestowed upon it by Phelps Brown and Handfield-Jones. Their climacteric implied a fundamental long-run change. But the average growth rate for much of the inter-war period (1924-37) was back up to 2.3 per cent and that level—or more—was sustained for another quarter century beyond 1945. In this perspective the decline of 1899-1913 looks less decisive, not so much a permanent downwards shift as a hiccup.

Fortunately, again, the complications over significance need not for the moment detain us. What is reasonably clear and certain is that the British economy under-went a deceleration in growth in the decade or so before the First World War. Our question is: did Wales share this experience?

Paring the issue down in this way thus relieves us of some of the complications of the more general debate. At the same time, however, its very starkness forces some confrontation with the blunt questions: was there a Welsh economy and, if so, do we know whether it grew faster or slower at this particular period? The questions have been linked because they are, necessarily, linked.

The issue of what constitutes 'an economy' is fraught with definitional niceties. But the essence of the problem can be indicated at a high level of generality. 'An economy' needs some physical geographical basis and it needs to be given some reasonable economic coherence. This can be achieved through political action (the area concerned being the basis for economic and social decision-making by political units or agencies); or through the fact that the area is bound by natural economic links; or because the people (or influential sectors of them) think of the area as a single economic unit.

At the beginning of the twentieth century the concept of a Welsh economy fails most of these tests. It was true that Wales constituted a reasonably well-defined geographical area. But the area was not lent much economic coherence through political action. Despite the recent (1881) passage of an Act of economic significance which related exclusively to Wales (prohibiting the general Sunday sale of alcohol)—and despite the busy huffing and puffing that surrounded the Cymru Fydd movement in the 1890s,[9] Wales was almost never a unit for decision-making in economic policy. Nor did economic activity within the geographical area impose its own natural coherence. There were strong geographical barriers to limit the links between North and South Wales. These, reinforced by traditional ties, meant that North Wales commerce looked naturally to Liverpool and South Wales to Bristol (and, as transport improved, London). People's economic thoughts ran along much the same lines. This was not surprising for managers and capitalists: but even for many who subscribed to the unity of Wales in cultural and social matters, it was natural to turn to England and (perhaps even more decisive in its long-run effects) to English for economic affairs.

These doubts about the reality of a Welsh economy are reinforced by the paucity of statistical data relating to Wales. Figures *do* exist. But they do so mostly as a by-product of information being collected on Great Britain, the United Kingdom or—that most irritating of fictions—'England and Wales'. Wales, then, occasionally appears as a convenient regional unit but more often has to be reconstructed by adding together the figures for individual counties (and remembering to retrieve Monmouthshire from touch) or for North Wales and South Wales (since even in county tables the Welsh counties are often not separately listed—and Monmouthshire still has to be retrieved). All this simply under-lines the obvious fact that Wales was not seen as a meaningful economic unit.

In other respects such considerations are, for the issue presently under discussion, largely academic. This is because the claim that a British climacteric had been discovered rested largely on figures relating to economic growth and to international trade. And on these issues, even if the concept of a Welsh economy had had substantial content for other purposes, there would still have been no separate statistics for Wales. Indeed, for economic growth there were, at the time, no figures for the British economy either. Changes in economic growth require the annual measurement of the national income, which has only been systematically provided since the Second World War. But for the U.K. as a whole national income accounts have been reconstructed retrospectively to carry the series back at least to the mid-nineteenth century.[10] The same has not been done, and probably cannot be done, for Wales precisely because the necessary statistical bricks for such an edifice are still only available for very recent times—and even then their quality is suspect.

The second main statistical foundation for the climacteric thesis was information on international trade and commerce. But this too does not and, in any realistic sense, cannot exist for Wales. Foreign trade statistics necessarily coincide with sovereign political units. It is possible to extract information on the value of goods exported from, and imported through, each Welsh port. But aggregating these would not provide answers sufficient for our purpose: it is at least probable that for Wales viewed as a separate entity the largest volume of foreign trade (and finance) was conducted with England. And for that activity no reasonably reliable indicators exist.

It is clear, therefore, that any discussion of the possibility of a Welsh climacteric will have to reply on more indirect approaches. In the main these involve placing reliance on three main aspects. First, in the absence of any single measure—like an index of industrial output or of national income—which purports to capture the behaviour of the whole of industry or the entire economy, attention is concentrated on the particular experience of a small range of industries. In the case of Wales, and especially industrial South Wales, the exceptional dominance of a single industry in terms of male employment makes such an approach less hazardous and haphazard than would otherwise be the case. Second, it is also possible, in the case of the coal industry, to take up one of the main issues of the general debate: the extent to which the climacteric was associated with a decline in efficiency indicated by falling productivity trends. And finally some attempt will be made to indicate how contemporaries viewed the performance and prospects of the economy. It is realised that such a survey will be even more selective and even more subjective than the other indicators, but it is none the less relevant to enquire whether a change substantial enough to be labelled 'climactic' strongly impinged itself upon the public consciousness of the time.

The figures that are available on the rate of growth of output for some of the major Welsh industries (Table 1) seems to be broadly consistent with identifying a decline in the rate of growth from somewhere about 1890. The rate of growth of coal output falls quite sharply and this is reflected (and magnified) in the figures for coal exports. Tinplate shows a similar downward trend although the exceptionally sharp fall in the 1890s, when there was a drop in the absolute level of output as well as its rate of growth, was caused by the specific collapse of the industry's major market in the United States as a result of the McKinley tariff of 1890. Slate, too, conforms to the pattern although this cannot be satisfactorily indicated on a decadal basis since the output series for slate only begins at 1881. The annual figures, however, show a pronounced peak in the late 1890s which is then followed by an absolute and accelerating decline.

The evidence of the coal industry is in many respects crucial. It is crucial because of the extent to which it came to dominate the Welsh economy from the mid-nineteenth century. In the absence of national income figures this dominance is best illustrated from the occupational distribution of the Welsh population. In 1911 almost one-third (32 per cent) of all men in Wales were engaged in Mining and Quarrying and nearly 90 per cent of these were in coal mining. Since most Welsh counties had no coal this was an extraordinary proportion for a single industry out of the twenty-three occupational groupings used by the census. It implies, of course, an even greater preponderance within the mining counties: Glamorgan and Monmouth, easily the two most populous Welsh counties, each had 40 per cent of the occupied male population in coal mining: in Denbigh over one-quarter (25.6 per cent) of the corresponding population was similarly occupied.

It is significant therefore that the coal industry does, indeed, seem to provide supporting evidence of a break in trend towards the end of the nineteenth century. Two

Table 1

Decadal Percentage[1] Changes. Economic Indicators. Wales 1855-1914

	OUTPUT							EXPORTS			
	Coal										
	N. Wales	S. Wales	N.& S. Wales	Pig Iron	Tinplate	Slate	Lead	Coal	Tinplate	Value of Coal Output[2]	Value of Tinplate Exports
1855-64 to 1865-74	56.3	45.9	47.3	-1.8	N.A.	N.A.	9.0	N.A.	N.A.	103.8	103.1
1865-74 to 1875-94	5.5	42.7	37.4	-11.0	N.A.	N.A.	-20.1	104.4	110.5	10.5	45.1
1875-84 to 1885-94	12.6	42.1	38.9	-3.4	84.2	N.A.	-50.5	79.6	84.8	53.8	39.3
1885-94 to 1895-1904	10.6	32.0	30.1	1.3	-1.6	+5.6	9.5	45.9	-23.3	54.3	-31.5
1895-1904 to 1905-14	5.0	33.5	31.3	8.6	28.9	-23.6[3]	-8.9	43.6	49.2	63.1	

1. i.e. shows increase in the total output for the indicated decade as a percentage of the preceding decade.
2. Output x f.o.b. price of large coal.
3. Includes estimate for 1914.

major items can be cited. The most thorough recent statistical investigation of the coal industry[11] has established a definite break in the annual growth rate for coal output in South Wales. For the period from 1874 to 1914 the rate of growth is 4.21 per cent p.a. until 1890, and 2.88 per cent p.a. after that date. Moreover the significance of this is reinforced because it can be demonstrated that, contrary to the previously received opinion,[12] for the United Kingdom coal industry the average annual growth rate remained steady throughout this period (at just under 2 per cent p.a.). The second aspect relates to productivity trends. For the United Kingdom, Taylor[13] argues that productivity (in the sense of output per man year) was declining from the 1880s. For South Wales, Rhodri Walters[14] paints a more complicated pattern. There is still a substantial fall from about 300 tons per man year in the late eighties (1888) to less than 250 tons in the years just before the First World War. The fall is, however, neither steady nor persistent. Indeed, nearly all the decline takes place at the beginning and the end: either from 1888 to 1890 or after 1906.

Fig 1. Annual Labourer Productivity of Coalmining, 1874-1914

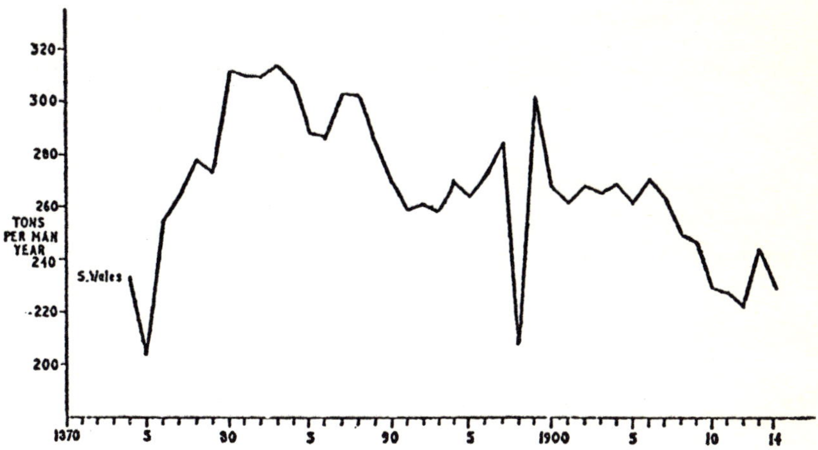

There is thus a respectable body of statistical evidence supportive of a contention that Wales experienced a break in its economic development around 1890. Moreover, the evidence from the major industry of coal-mining indicates not merely that there was a sharp deceleration in the rate of growth but that this was accompanied by declining productivity. This seems to be consistent with another aspect of the general hypothesis of the climacteric: namely, that it was associated with a decline in enterprise and innovation. This, too, is apparently given extra weight by the fact that the degree of modernisation in South Wales before 1914 was lower than in most other coalfields. In 1913 only just over one per cent of output in south Wales was mechanically cut. Nevertheless, the evidence is suggestive rather than conclusive. Closer examination of its statistical basis raises doubts about drawing firm conclusions, and these doubts are reinforced when more qualitative material is brought into consideration.

To start with the productivity propositions.[15] Here the shape of the path taken by the decline in productivity is important. As already noted, the decline in output per man year effectively took place either between 1888 and 1890, or after 1906. In between there were fluctuations (very sharp in 1898 and 1899 because of the long strike and the recovery in output which followed and which was intensified by the Boer War boom), but they were not fluctuations around a discernible downward trend: the level of output per man year in 1906 was the same as that for 1890. The significance of this pattern is that it makes it (on *a priori* grounds) less plausible to seek the explanations of declining productivity in such factors as diminishing returns, less intensity of effort by workers and falling enterprise by owners and managers, factors which would produce their effects persistently over long periods. The two quick burst of declining productivity suggest that rather more weight might be given to *ad hoc* factors.

The exhaustive investigations of Dr. Boyns largely confirm these deduced expectations. His concern was with the United Kingdom as a whole but, fortunately, his most detailed work was on South Wales. The findings here draw upon three layers of evidence: for the coalfield as a whole; for some 64 individual collieries; and, in still more detail, for the operations of two of the major companies, Powell Duffryn and Ocean. These various approaches allowed cognisance to be taken and tests to be made of such variables as days worked, the ages of collieries and colliery size. From all this what emerged was that the most important influences on output per man year were the number of days worked and wage rates. Disregarding the many complications and qualifications the most pertinent conclusions for the immediate purpose were the two negative findings: for the period between 1890 and 1913 the industry did not suffer from decreasing returns to labour nor from generally diminishing returns (i.e., the influence of diminishing returns was being offset by other factors such as technical change). The actual falls in productivity can, however, be substantially explained by *ad hoc* factors. At the end of the period the effect of the Eight Hours Act was followed by the Cambrian strike of 1910-11 and the national strike (the first of a very small number) of 1912. There are also specific explanations, though of a less decisive nature, at the beginning of the period. The Coal Mines Regulation Act of 1887, which reduced the number of hours worked by boys, was followed by Mabon's Day, which was introduced in 1888 and reduced the number of days worked by declaring the first Monday in each month a miner's holiday.

There is, in any event, a simpler interpretation of the overall experience from about 1870, one which would indicate that the stress placed on the fall of productivity in the 1890s is misplaced. This could be summed up by saying that the reason for the 1890s was the 1880s. That is to say, the experience which stands out as exceptional is the very high level of labour productivity from 1880 to 1888. It was an experience which perhaps reflected the opening of a large number of new and well-equipped pits under the stimulus of the extraordinarily high level of prices and profits of the early seventies. On this reading the experience of the 1890s simply meant that after the effects of this big lump of capital investment had been digested there was a reversion to a more 'normal' productivity level. It would be pressing too hard entirely to spirit the problem away in this fashion, but the contemplation of such possibilities does contribute to keeping the productivity issue in perspective.

A further by-product is to lower the presumption that there was a substantial failure of innovation and enterprise. The most usual indicator of this is the slow progress made in mechanical cutting and conveying in South Wales before 1914. This was never a very reliable guide, even when it was assumed that there was a long and continuous decline in productivity to be explained. The conditions in South Wales were never particularly suitable to such machinery, given—and it is an important qualification—that the labour cost of cutting remained relatively low and was fairly directly related to the selling price of coal. The geological conditions in South Wales militated against the use of machinery in two broad ways. The unsettled nature of the seams, with 'working' (movement) of both roof and floor made difficult the smooth, continuous working of the machines. But these conditions also reduced the contribution which could be made by machines since the pressure from the roof often eased the actual problem of cutting the coal: many Welsh miners ended their shift by under-cutting the seam in the sure knowledge that when they returned next morning much of the over-hanging coal would have been brought down. The most general criticisms of technical backwardness were thus always misdirected. The demonstration that there were, in any event, no significant signs of diminishing returns suggest that they were also superfluous.

The conclusion would seem to be that the failure of diminishing returns to show up as a significant factor, must mean that its inherent influence in an extractive industry was being successfully offset. And such a result must have involved a fair degree of innovation and enterprise. Diminishing returns can be held back by more efficient production methods and by the opening up of new coal areas. There is evidence of each in pre-1914 South Wales. In particular underground haulage was improved and, in this and other respects, there was a significant shift towards the use of electrical power. The continued drive towards new sinkings and the tendency to shift towards previously under-worked sectors of the coalfield can be economically illustrated by the following figures:

Number of collieries sunk in Rhondda Valleys		**Dates of sinking of S.W. collieries still in existence in October 1922**	
		All	**Anthracite**
1855-84	60	96	12
1885-1914	7	175	38

It can also be illustrated by a brief extract (already cited in Chapter 2 above) from the *South Wales Daily News* of 1 July 1891—just at the time when the decline in activity was supposed to be taking place. At a meeting of Cardiff Chamber of Commerce it was reported that *at the present time*: 'the new Clydach pit was being developed (and it is rumoured that another was to be sunk); Naval Colliery Co. is going to sink a new pit; Lewis Merthyr Co. to do the same; Tylor & Co. now well on with new Cefn-nant-ddu colliery; Mardy Co. had started new shaft; Dowlais Co. is sinking 2 new shafts; Universal Colliery Co. to sink new pits north of Pontypridd. In Rhymney valley, Llanbradach Co. had found fresh coal; Rhymney Co. is sinking 2 new shafts at Pengam; P.D. Co. contemplated sinking in same area. Universal Co. had started 2 pits at top of Aber valley, a new pit is being sunk at Llanhilleth; E.V. Co. is sinking at Cwm and at Abertillery.' And all this was just around Cardiff area—leaving developments in the Ogmore and Garw valleys.

There remains the problem of the overall growth rate. To the extent that the above arguments undermine, or substantially modify, the notion of a decline in productivity, they dispose of an explanation, rather than of the fact, of a break in economic development. The notion of a downward shift in the pace of development seems to be much more firmly embedded in a lower growth rate. This, moreover, seems well-established for South Wales. The long-accepted view that there was a break in the 1880s in the growth of coal output of the United Kingdom has collapsed under closer statistical scrutiny[16] (pounded from close range by the dreaded Boyns gun); but for South Wales this break has emerged from such treatment even more starkly. Whether the break is tested for 1883 or 1890 it still seems quite decisive: growth rates of 5.5 and 2.6 before and after 1883, and 4.2 and 2.9 before and after 1890. Does this not demonstrate a significant deceleration in economic activity?

What it mostly demonstrates is the danger of using trends in the output of a single industry, albeit one of substantial dominance, as a growth indicator for the economy as a whole. It is almost unavoidable, unless the starting-point is at a very low level of absolute output, that a high growth rate for an individual industry cannot be sustained over time. An annual increase of 5 per cent p.a. means that output is multiplied 130 times in the course of a century (10 per cent would multiply output 16,384 times!). All this is achieved through what Rostow called 'the magic of compound interest'. For the present purposes its significance is that, if the process is surveyed from a point where the absolute levels of output are already high, then the actual subsequent growth rate may not be the most appropriate criterion by which to assess the later development. Changes in the absolute levels of output, manpower, exports and so on may be better guides. If, for example, the pre-1883 growth rate had been maintained until 1913 the output of the South Wales coalfield would then have reached 125m. tons instead of the actual 57m. tons, i.e., five times the 1883 output of 25m. tons instead of just over twice that level. And even on the lower pre-1890 growth rate and the shorter time period for it to operate, output would have reached 75m. tons. Are we to consider that anything which falls short of these levels represents a 'failure'?

The contention is that if attention is focused upon the size of the absolute changes attained in the decade or so before 1914, it is difficult to reconcile these with the implication of relative stagnation contained in the climacteric thesis. Thus in the decade and a half before 1913 the annual output of the coalfield increased by over 20m. tons; an *extra* 13m. tons a year were being exported from South Wales and an *additional* 100,000 men were employed.

The sheer scale of these increases necessarily spilled over into other sectors. One of the most dramatic and pervasive of these was—as Brinley Thomas taught us years ago—population change. The main outlines of the inter-censal findings for Wales in the first decade of the twentieth century are those most usually associated with thriving economies. The buoyancy was undoubtedly directly connected to the activity of the coal industry. In this decade alone the South Wales coalfield absorbed an additional seventy thousand miners. The impression of a *teeming* population can be caught in the accidental phrase of a newspaper reporter at the time of a royal visit in 1912: '. . . all through Treorky', he said, '. . . all through Treorky the coal tips were black with people . . .' The overall population effect of the increase in the number of miners was substantially multiplied: the population of Glamorgan grew in this decade by 261,000 (an increase of 30 per cent), of Monmouthshire by 98,000 (33 per cent) and of Carmarthenshire by 25,000 (18 per cent). Although the birth rate in the coalfield (in common with that of the United Kingdom colliery districts generally) remained higher for longer than in other social and regional sectors, these represented growth rates that exceeded the rate of natural increase.

An additional feature of this decade was thus a substantial net gain by migration.[17] The Glamorgan-Monmouth colliery area gained 130,000 by migration in this decade and for Wales as a whole the gain was 98,000. In the context of the British experience since the middle of the nineteenth century such gains were exceptional. Indeed, they were unique. In each of the individual countries—England,

Wales, Scotland, Ireland—in every decade from 1851 to 1911 there was a net loss through migration with this single exception for Wales from 1901 to 1911. The exception was, moreover, substantial. Proportional to its population, as Brinley Thomas has tellingly emphasised, Wales was for this brief period 'absorbing population at a rate not much less than the United States'. Moreover, this overall result was reached despite quite contrary trends in large tracts of Wales. Five of the (then) thirteen Welsh counties—the four in mid-Wales plus Caernarvon in the north—actually suffered a decline in the absolute level of their population during this decade), the two coal counties of Flint and Denbigh were the only ones to show a population increase of over ten per cent for the decade—though the more important influence may have been the developing North Wales holiday coast.

House-building was another related sector which was influenced by the scale of the economic expansion. The broad pattern which emerges is that house-building in South Wales experienced a substantial boom in the 1890s and again in the 1900s.[18] In each case the level of activity was, proportional to population, comparable with the boom of the early 1870s. A few comments are required both to qualify and to emphasise the significance of this experience. Building is, of course, an industry in which fluctuations in activity are particularly marked. Thus it is not surprising to find that between the two post-1890 peaks there was a down-turn around 1900 associated with the Boer war. The dip in activity at that time was common to the U.K. industry generally and was associated with the usual rising costs (especially interest rates) caused by the war, but the downturn was much much sharper in South Wales than elsewhere. On the other hand, whilst building was generally active in the 1890s the resurgence in South Wales up to

1910 was contrary to the overall U.K. experience. Since the level of building activity is considered to be a major factor determining the general level of economic activity, the buoyancy of house-building in South Wales for much of the first decade of the century acts as an important indicator.

One further sector has been selected for comment, namely the degree to which continuing efforts were being made to extend and improve the capital infrastructure. Most of this consisted of either railway building or, more important, of dock construction. Already by 1890 South Wales had one of the world's most densely-developed rail networks, so the later activity was necessarily most of the nature of minor extensions and improvements. Thus in the period after 1890 the Barry Railway opened an additional 32 miles, the Cardiff Railway 23 miles, the Rhondda and Swansea Bay 17 miles, and the Port Talbot 21 miles. Elsewhere construction mostly took the form of light railways, like the Vale of Rheidol and the Lampeter to Aberaeron lines, although an additional 35 miles were also built for Cambrian Railways.[19] The provision of additional dock accommodation was on an altogether different scale. Indeed, capital expenditure on docks in Wales from the early 1890s to 1910 was higher than it had ever been.[20] The Barry No. 2 Dock, covering 34 acres, was opened in 1898. At Cardiff the Queen Alexandra dock was opened in 1907 at a cost of £1.3m. Its 52 acres increased the Bute Dock system by almost one-third.[21] At Newport a dock extension of 20 acres was opened in 1893 whilst the South Dock extension of 48 acres was finally completed in 1914. At Port Talbot a new dock was opened in 1898 the same year as a 28 acre extension to the Prince of Wales dock in Swansea. A decade later, in 1909, the King's Dock of 70 acres was also opened at Swansea and the Act which had authorised its construction had also provided for still further expansion, which eventually materialised when the Queen's dock was opened in 1920. For the present purpose these substantial undertakings hold a double significance: they represented in themselves major works which would have large multiplier effects; and the readiness to build them is itself a telling indicator of a thriving economy with a confident future.

Most contemporary comment reflects this confidence. There are always instances of foreboding to be found and, with hindsight, they tend more readily to leap out of the page. Nevertheless, the more characteristic impression was the turn of the century assessment that 'in this year of grace 1901 it (Wales) is one of the brightest and most truly civilised spots in the Queen's dominions . . . with the black mineral pouring into the lap of Cardiff, Newport, Swansea and Llanelli, where the argosies of the nations await its arrival to convey it to the remotest parts of the earth . . . (with) the transformation of the Rhondda Valley from a sleepy hollow, into the most active and thriving community in Great Britain or the world . . .'[22] A less lyrical confirmation of the same buoyant judgement was delivered in the sober prose of Professor H. Stanley Jevons. Living in Cardiff and writing in 1914, just before the First World War, he observed that 'A new and urgent demand for more dock accommodation at Cardiff is now being pressed . . . The South Wales coalfield is now producing at the rate of nearly 60 million tons per annum, and the rate of production is pretty sure to increase within 30 or 40 years to about 100 million tons per annum.'[23]

Whatever may be its validity for the U.K. as a whole, the 1890s climacteric hypothesis does not—in the end—correspond to the Welsh experience. The most convincing explanation of this contradiction is still contained within Brinley Thomas's perception of the working of an Atlantic economy. As a descriptive device for the Welsh economy, however, the notion of a climacteric need not be totally discarded. Instead, some would argue, it simply needs to be shifted. It is, perhaps, appropriately used, not for the 1890s, but for the 1920s. In 1907, reflecting the Edwardian confidence and high expectations, Lloyd George had rhetorically asked: 'Why should not South Wales and Cardiff' (this was Ministerial tact—he was in Cardiff at the time) 'develop into one of the greatest manufacturing centres in the whole Empire?'[24] It was not the kind of question that could have been posed with any sense of tact—or credibility—in, say, Merthyr Tydfil or Blaenau Ffestiniog in the 1930s.

(Written for a special conference held at Gregynog, near Newtown, to celebrate ten years of bringing together students from all the Welsh Colleges for discussions on economic history. Later appeared in Williams, J. and Baber, C. (eds), *Modern South Wales*, Univ. of Wales, 1986.)

Notes

[1]E.H. Phelps Brown and S.H. Handfield-Jones, 'The Climacteric of the 1890s', *Oxford Economic Papers*, IV, 1952.

[2]D.H. Aldcroft, 'The Entrepreneur and the British Economy, 1870-1914', *E.H.R.*, XVII, 1964.

[3]D.J. Coppock. 'The Climacteric of the 1870s', *Manchester School*, XXIV, 1956.

[4]D.N. McCloskey and L.G. Sandberg, 'From Damnation to Redemption: Judgements on the Late Victorian Entrepreneur', *Explorations in Economic History*, IX. 1971. Some recent manifestations of a large and growing literature can be seen in the section on Victorian Britain in *Journal of Economic History*, XLII, March 1982. pp., 57-118.

[5]R.H. Hayes and D.A. Garvin,'Managing As If Tomorrow Mattered', *Harvard Bus. Rev.*, 60, 3, 1982.

[6]C. Wilson, 'Economy and Society in Late Victorian Britain', *E.H.R.*, XVII, 1965.

[7]*Ibid.*, p. 198.

[8]D.H. Aldcroft and H.W. Richardson, *The British Economy, 1870-1939*. London, 1969. Table on pp. 4, 11 and the sources given for them.

[9] K.O. Morgan, *Rebirth of a Nation, Wales, 1880-1980*. Cardiff, 1981. Ch. 4.

[10]The most recent comprehensive attempt has been the C.H. Feinstein, *Statistical Tables of National Income, Expenditure and Output of the U.K., 1855-1965*. Cambridge, 1976.

[11]Trevor Boyns, 'Labour Productivity and the British Coal Industry'. Ph.D. Thesis, Univ. of Wales, 1982.

[12]A.J. Taylor, 'Labour Productivity and Technological Innovation in the British Coal Industry, 1850-1914', *Econ. Hist. Rev.*, XIV, 1, Aug. 1961.

[13]*Ibid.*, pp. 48-51.

[14]Rhodri Walters, 'Labour Productivity in the South Wales Steam-coal Industry, 1870-1914'. *Econ. Hist. Rev.*, XXVIII, 2, May 1975, pp.281-2.

[15]The following draws heavily on Trevor Boyns, *op.cit.*

[16]Trevor Boyns, *op.cit.*, Ch. 1.

[17]This paragraph is based on B. Thomas, 'Wales and the Atlantic Economy' as reprinted in Brinley Thomas, *The Welsh Economy*. Cardiff, 1962. Some aspects of the Thomas thesis have been questioned by D. Baines, *Migration in a Mature Economy* 1985) and re-stated in a later essay by Brinley Thomas in his *The Industrial Revolution and the Atlantic Economy* 91993). It is an important controversy, especially for issues relating to the Welsh language, but fortunately it does not impinge on the more specific issues raised in the present essay.

[18]J. Hamish Richards and J. Parry Lewis, 'House Building in the South Wales Coalfield, 1851-1913', *Manchester School*, XXIV, 1956. pp., 289-300, and J. Parry Lewis, *Building Cycles and British Growth*, 1965, esp. Appendix 4 and Ch. 8.

[19]Ernest Carter, *An Historical Geography of the Railways of the British Isles*, 1959. Chs. 14 and 15.

[20]Tom Taylor, 'Capital Formation by Railways in South Wales, 1836-1914'. Appendix I. In Ca. Baber and L.J. Williams (eds.).

[21]M.J. Daunton, *Coal Metropolis: Cardiff, 1870-1914*. Leicester, 1977. p. 28.

[22]*Western Mail*, 1 Jan. 1901.

[23]H.S. Jevons. *The British Coal Trade*, 1915. pp. 109, 111.

[24]Quoted in M.J. Daunton, *op.cit.*, p. 37.

13. OCCUPATIONS IN WALES, 1851-1971

Introduction

The major purpose of this article is to present a reasonably continuous occupational series for Wales over the last century or so, and to draw attention to the more important changes which are revealed. The series has been constructed from the census returns and is therefore subject to the limitations of this source. These limitations have been widely discussed especially in the *Guides to Official Sources*, the introductions to the appropriate volumes at the successive censuses and in a recent chapter by W.A. Armstrong.[1]

For the present purposes, the most obvious and significant effect of these limitations is that, although the returns exist over a long period, comparisons over time have to be made with some care and it is certainly not possible to make a straightforward contrast between the figures given for 1851 and those given for 1971. In particular, as indicated in the tables in the appendix, the total period has been split into two parts, 1851-1911 and 1921-71.[2] The reason for this split is that the form of the occupational census in 1921 was substantially different from that of 1911. Up until 1911 the categorisation which had been used had been a semi-industrial, semi-occupational type, but from the 1921 census onwards two separate studies, one of the industrial distribution of the working population and one of the occupational distribution, have been published. Although direct comparisons between pre-1911 and post-1911 figures are clearly hazardous, the extent of the dislocation varies substantially as between the different occupational orders. Thus some of the orders—like Agriculture, and Mining and Quarrying, where the industrial and occupational groupings largely coincide—are virtually unaffected by the change.

On the other hand, it is not possible to get at all a 1911 figure to correspond to the 1921 order of Administrators and Managers because until 1911 such persons were inextricably mixed up with others under a variety of industries and occupations.

There are several more specific problems which will be mentioned in the course of the discussion of each of our two separate time-periods, but perhaps two further general points should be made in this brief introduction. Firstly, in the course of the hundred and twenty years under consideration there have naturally been changes in the names of many of the occupations as well as the emergence of new occupations and the disappearance of some of the old ones. Some exercise of judgement is therefore involved from time to time in allocating these detailed occupational headings to the broad orders contained in the table. We can only give an assurance that we have tried to be as consistent as possible, and that the problem is in any event a relatively minor one, the number of difficult decisions being quite small and normally involving only small numbers of people. The second general difficulty is of more significance. For our first period, 1851-1911, we have used the 1911 occupational classification and aimed to rearrange the material in the earlier censuses on that basis. It is a process that has involved, especially for the earliest years, the moving around of groups, sometimes quite large, between occupational orders. Again, every care has been taken to make the figures as consistent as possible. The same process was undertaken for the second period, 1921-71, where the material was based on the 1951-61 classification. The problem was, however, much less marked in the later period.

Finally, it needs to be emphasised that the unavoidable restrictions and constraints imposed by the data over so long a time period are substantially modified by at least two important considerations. In the first place we are dealing with quite broad occupational groups—excluding the retired and unoccupied, there are only 22 occupational orders in our table for 1851-1911 and still only 26 orders for the period from 1921 to 1971. Thus many of the problems, like the changes in the names of detailed occupations, dwindle or disappear when such broad groups are being considered. In the second place, the particular occupational structure of nineteenth-century Wales has served to minimise the effect of several of the problems which have been mentioned. In particular the Welsh occupational structure was—as we shall see—for long dominated by a small number of the occupational orders contained in the census, and those orders were moreover the ones—especially Agriculture and Mining—which were least prone to changes in definition and treatment from census to census. It is especially fortuitous that the dominance by occupations that were defined with reasonable consistency was strongest in the years before 1911, the period when shifts in census practices and definitions were most marked.

1851-1911

There is, in general, a tendency for the accuracy and reliability of the census information on occupations to improve over time with the accumulation of experience. The pace of such improvement was naturally especially rapid in the early years. Indeed, following the generally accepted view, we judged that the inadequacies of the first attempt to collect comprehensive occupation figures in 1841 were too large for them to be used. Changes in the census procedures were also quite marked in 1851, 1861 and 1871 but the information for these years was fuller and was mostly capable of being re-allocated on the same basis as 1911.

Two cases warrant special mention because of their overall importance in determining the number and distribution of occupied women. First, one major problem for the census enumerators, especially in the early years between 1851 and 1871, was how to record members of the farmer's household, the indoor or living-in servants. The distinction between those who were mainly helping with the farm and therefore classed as being in Agriculture, and those who were mainly helping inside the farmhouse and therefore classed under Domestic Service, was obviously difficult to make. Experience led to considerable improvement in the census instructions and performance, but there is no way to adjust the figures to allow for this. It can only be noted that between 1851 and 1881 some part of the increase in the numbers in the Domestic Service order, and of the decrease in the Agriculture order, arose because farm servants, especially female farm servants, were being more accurately described. The second case also concerns agriculture and involves the crucial issue of female family workers. The early returns (1851-71) included as occupied in Agriculture all the farmers' wives, sisters etc., over 15 years old. But from the census of 1881 these were excluded from automatic inclusion amongst occupied workers. We have, therefore, removed the female relatives of farmers from our figures for Agriculture from 1851 to 1871 to make them more directly comparable with those for the later census years. This solution has naturally led to some understatement of the number of females occupied in Agriculture in the early years.

A few other groups were more intractable but fortunately their overall significance was quite tiny. The first three of our censuses identified House Proprietors and

Land Proprietors as separate occupational sub-groups. These categories disappeared after the census of 1871, but the problem arises of how to treat the small numbers involved from 1851 to 1871. There was a case for re-allocating them to the Unoccupied group, but it was eventually decided to leave them in the occupational order to which they had been allocated by the census authorities, namely Building and Agriculture respectively. Land Proprietors sit reasonably easily in Agriculture as an occupational order, and in any case their number, both for males and females, is very small relative to the total size of the Agricultural order. House Proprietors fit less comfortably into the Building order but for males the number is again very small relative to the total size of the order. For females the number involved, though still small in absolute terms, is large relative to the total number of females in Building. Thus the figures for females in the Building order for the years 1851 to 1881 (this latter year not being affected since there is no category 'House Proprietor' 1881) are 645; 968; 332; and 58. If House Proprietors are excluded the figures become: 20; 12; 42 and 58, which seems more realistic. The overall distortion is, however, quite tiny.

A more significant break occurs in 1881. Before that year retired persons were included in their previous occupations; from 1881 retired persons (except for Army, Navy, Medical Practitioners and Clergymen) are enumerated in the 'Unoccupied' class. In 1891, the number of retired persons and pensioners was 13,000 or 2.3 per cent of the total working population. Other changes continued the trend towards a more exact occupational classification and some of these evade consistent treatment. For example, a separate category of Messengers and Porters was identified after 1891 but previously this group was simply included, without separate identification, with the number in the industry in which they were occupied. There is no way of identifying the number in these earlier years and we have, therefore, not attempted any re-allocation. A final important change was the exclusion, from 1901, of Students from the order of Professional Occupations. The term student always conveys some ambiguities. It is probable, for example, that it includes at this time student teachers who perhaps should still be included with the Professional category. We have, however, excluded all students from the Professional order in 1891 to keep it consistent with 1901 and 1911. The totals involved in 1891 were 5,080 for males and 4,746 for females.

One final point to notice is that there was a sharp fall in the Unoccupied order in 1891 for both males and females. The reason is that before 1891 all persons, irrespective of age, were included in the occupation returns. From 1891-1911 the returns only referred to persons over the age of ten. The change does not, however, significantly affect the various calculations in this article which are based on the number of occupied persons.

1851-1911 Males

The outstanding feature of the male occupational structure in Wales in 1851 was the extent to which it was dominated by just two (out of a total of twenty-two) occupational groups. About 35 per cent of the total population was engaged in Agriculture and a further 17 per cent in Mines and Quarries. The dominance of these two groups still continued, though less markedly, sixty years later. In 1911 these two occupational groups between them accounted for 43.55 per cent of the total occupied population, compared to 52.03 per cent in 1851. In this sense Wales was, therefore, still overwhelmingly a primary producing economy right up to the First World War—overwhelmingly because the demand to sustain employment in many sectors (transport, for example, and building) derived substantially from these two basic groups.

Three further points need to be made about these groups. In the first place the relative steadiness of their continuing dominance disguises very sharp changes as between the two basic primary producing sectors themselves. Indeed, between 1851 and 1911 their relative positions were almost totally reversed. In 1851 Agriculture accounted for 35 per cent and Mining for 17 per cent of the occupied population: in 1911 Mining accounted for about 32 per cent and Agriculture for about 12 per cent. But although the percentage decline in agriculture was more marked than the percentage increase in mining, this should not obscure the fact that the absolute decline in numbers in agriculture (from 135 to 96 thousands) was very much smaller than the increase in absolute numbers in mining (from 65 to 256 thousands).

The second point is that the decline which did take place in the dominance of these two groups (from 53 to 43 per cent), had already been effected by 1871. Thereafter the proportion of the total occupied male population in these two primary producing groups is remarkably steady (it falls further to 41 per cent in 1881 and then rises slowly to 43 per cent in 1911).

Thirdly, it needs to be emphasised that the relative growth of employment in Mining and Quarrying was not very marked for the first thirty years of this period: in 1851 17 per cent of the total occupied males were in this sector and this had increased to nearly 21 per cent by 1881. From 1881 to 1911, however, the occupational share of Mining and Quarrying markedly accelerated—25 per cent in 1891, 29 per cent in 1901 and 31.7 per cent in 1911. The quickening pace is perhaps even more evident in terms of the actual numbers employed—65,400 in 1851, 101,700 in 1881 and 256,250 in 1911.

Clearly, the absolute size and the scale of the change in Mining and Quarrying was sufficient to influence all else and hence requires a slightly more specific analysis. In 1851, 57.7 per cent (37,500) of the males enumerated under this order were employed in coal mines. At that time the North Wales coalfield produced about 1.5 million tons and the South Wales about 5 million tons so the spread was reasonably balanced. By 1911 the Mining and Quarrying order had become totally dominated by coal which accounted for nearly 86 per cent of the total number. And coal was itself by then dominated by the South Wales coalfield (where production was 50 million tons compared to 3.1/2 million tons in North Wales). Thus although more men were employed in the Slate industry in 1911 than in 1851, its share of the total 'in the order' was only 4.6 per cent in 1911. Iron mining which had accounted for 15.8 per cent of the order in 1851 had, by 1911, virtually disappeared with only 169 males employed.

The broad occupational structure in Wales was, moreover, significantly different from that of Britain as a whole, in the extent of the dominance by primary production. To compare the figures for Wales with those given in Deane and Cole for the British labour force it is necessary to include both males and females.[3] This greatly reduces the proportions employed in agriculture and mining (mainly because of the legal constraints on the employment of women in the fastest growing part of these groups, coal-mining). Even so, the much higher dependence of Wales on these primary sectors is clear: in 1851 over 42 per cent of all occupied persons (male and female) were in these groups in Wales, compared to just under 26 per cent for Britain as a whole. By 1911, moreover, the discrepancy had become still more marked: 36 per cent for Wales, 15 per cent for Britain as a whole. This was because in Britain at large these two groups declined almost continuously in relative importance from 1851 to 1911: in Wales, as was indicated above, the decline was halted, and slightly reversed, after 1881.

The change in agriculture and mining naturally overshadowed all other shifts in the occupied male population from 1851 to 1911. But there are other trends worth noticing. The total occupied male population more than doubled during these years, from 386 to 809 thousands. Against such a strongly expansionary background it is, therefore, not surprising to find that—in addition to agriculture—only four other groups experienced a decline in absolute numbers. These were Dress; Textile fabrics; Other General and Undefined workers; and Skins, leather etc. In the last of these groups (Skins, leather etc.) the absolute numbers were small (involving at the peak just $^{1}/_{2}$ per cent of the occupied male population) and the decline was tiny (there were 161 fewer male workers in 1911 compared to 1851). The decline of nearly 4,000 in the number of males in the Dress sector was more significant. In 1851 this involved 5.$^{1}/_{2}$ per cent of the total occupied males and was the sixth largest group: in 1911 only just over 2 per cent were so occupied. Similarly, the share occupied in Textiles fell from just over 2 to just under 1 per cent. In both these cases part of the explanation seems to have been a shift to female in place of male labour, since the number of women included in these occupations increased between 1851 and 1911 by more than the fall in the number of men. The decline in General and other Undefined workers—obviously a rather catch-all group—probably simply reflects the increasing accuracy of the census returns.

Apart from the large absolute increase in the number occupied in Mines and Quarries, the other major expansionary sectors before 1911 were Transport (Conveyance of men, goods and messages); Metals and Machines; Food, tobacco, drink and lodging; Commercial; and Professional. Between them these five groups accounted for over half (230,335 out of a total of 422,636) of the total increase in the occupied male population.

Since the increased numbers in Mines and Quarries accounted for a further 45 per cent, this points to another basic feature of the occupational structure which continued throughout the period between 1851 and 1911. Most of the occupational groups were, in the Welsh economic structure, insignificant in size. In 1851 ten of the 22 occupational groups each accounted for less than 1 per cent of the total occupied male population—which meant that in the whole of Wales there were less than 3,860 involved in each of these occupations. And it was frequently much less: for example in 1851 there were only 693 men occupied in the order concerned with Precious metals, jewels, watches, instruments and games, and only 1,152 in Chemicals, oil, grease, soap, etc. In 1911 there were again 10 of the 22 groups each accounting for less than 1 per cent (which now meant less than 4,230). They were mostly, but not all, the same groups: General and Local Government, and Commercial Occupations had climbed out of this group: Wood, furniture, etc. and Textile fabrics had fallen into it.

Despite the large absolute increase in the number of males occupied, however, the male activity rate[4] declined a little during this period. In 1851 87.08 per cent of the total male population aged over 10 was occupied;[5] in 1911 this had fallen to 84.80 per cent. In only two of the counties was this trend not repeated: in Carmarthen the activity rate was virtually unchanged over this period, and in Merioneth it rose by about 3 per cent. The uncertainties of the basic data, however, make it unwise to attach any significance to such minor variations or to the fact that two of the three counties showing the largest decrease (over four per cent) were the fast-growing industrial counties of Monmouth and Glamorgan.

1851-1911 Females

The most striking features about the changes in the female occupied population in Wales from 1851 to 1911 are associated with the aggregate number. In particular, the total number of occupied women grew more slowly (from about 126 to 216 thousand) than did the total number of occupied males (from 386 to 809 thousand). The increase of 71 per cent in the number of occupied women was noticeably out of line with the general increase in the population of Wales during these years (108 per cent) and with the increase of 109 per cent in the total number of occupied males.

It follows from this—but it is a social and economic fact of such significance as to deserve separate mention—that there was a decline in the proportion of women in the total occupied population. In 1851 the total number of females was 33 per cent of the total number of males: in 1911 it was 27 per cent, and thus the ratio of occupied males to occupied females rose from 3:1 in 1851 to 3.3/4:1 in 1911. There is little doubt that this change is associated with the rise in the relative importance of Mining. On the demand side, mining—especially after the legal prohibition of female employment underground—was overwhelmingly a male occupation: on the supply side, the daily need for baths and hot water in the home—often for several men in each household perhaps working separate shifts—placed especially heavy demands on women and constrained their possibilities of securing employment outside the home. This would only provide a partial explanation: any full treatment would have to consider many other factors. The present purpose, however, is less ambitious: it is merely to draw attention to the shift itself and to give a brief indication of its size and significance.

The broad downward trend in female employment opportunities is reflected in another indicator, the female activity rate. This fell from 28.24 per cent in 1851 to 23.63 per cent in 1911 (that is, a *change* of over 16 per cent). There were, however, strong county variations ranging from a 25 per cent increase in the activity rate in Cardigan (from 28.49 to 35.60) to a 25 per cent decrease (from 27.10 to 20.23) in Glamorgan. These variations are large enough to lend significance to the overall pattern of these variations. Seven counties, basically the rural heartland, showed an increase in their female activity rates: six counties, basically the new mining and industrial areas showed decreases. The particular importance suggested above for the part played by mining in reducing employment possibilities for women is reinforced by the fact that the two counties where the female activity rate fell most sharply were the two major mining counties of Glamorgan and Monmouth.

Two basic characteristics emerge, therefore. The first is that during the couple of generations before the First World War there was in Wales a definite decline in the relative employment opportunities for women. The second is that this decline did not show itself, indeed was generally reversed, in rural areas but was a marked feature of the more populous industrial and mining areas. Against this general background, the other major feature was the narrow range of occupations open to (or, at least, taken up by) women in Wales. To a degree greater even than that for male occupations, female occupations were dominated by two (of the twenty-two) groups. In 1851 sixty per cent of all females in occupations were either in Agriculture or in Domestic

Service: in 1911 these two occupations still accounted for 51 per cent. Besides the decline in the degree of predominance of these two groups there was a sharp shift in their relative importance. In 1851 Agriculture accounted for about 27 per cent and Domestic Service for about 33 per cent of the total number of occupied females: in 1911 Agriculture accounted for only 9 per cent and Domestic Service for 42 per cent. The real turning-point both for the dominance of these two groups and for the relative importance of domestic Service is, however, more accurately dated at 1891. In that year the combined share of Agriculture and Domestic Service in the total occupied female population still stood at 60 per cent and Domestic Service alone accounted for 55 per cent. Moreover, 1891 was easily the peak year in terms of the absolute numbers employed in Domestic Service. By 1911 this occupational order was already declining in absolute as well as relative terms, the number having fallen from 105 thousand in 1891 to 90 thousand in 1911. Thus by the latter date the female occupational structure in Wales was dominated by two, rapidly declining, groups.

The decline in agriculture is part of the normal process of an industrialising economy. However, part of the reason for the fall in the number of females occupied in agriculture between 1851 and 1911—the rate of decline of females was a little faster than for males—probably lies, as already explained above, within the census returns themselves. Part of the increase in the number of women in Domestic Service, and their decrease in Agriculture between 1851 and 1881 was due to farm servants being more accurately described. Similarly, our exclusion—on the grounds of consistency with later years—of the female relatives of farmers from the Agricultural order before 1871 has led to some under-statement of the number of females occupied in Agriculture in these early years, and hence to some under-statement of the full extent of the decline by 1911. It is important and reassuring to note, however, that if it were possible to correct this bias the effect would not be to alter, but to reinforce, the main point about the decline in the number of females in Agriculture before 1911.

In both 1851 and, even more markedly, 1911 there were two additional orders which were important in providing occupations for women. These were Dress (21.5 per cent in 1851 and 15.5 per cent in 1911) and Food, drink and tobacco (6.9 per cent in 1851 and 13.1 per cent in 1911). The four largest orders (Agriculture; Domestic Service; Dress; and Food etc.) thus accounted for 87 per cent of the total number of occupied females in 1851, and 80 per cent in 1911. The degree of occupational concentration was therefore even more marked for females than for males, a fact which was, obviously, equally reflected in the large number of occupational orders containing small absolute and relative numbers. In 1851, 16 out of the 22 broad occupational orders each contained less than 2 per cent (2,500) of the total occupied women, and this was still the case in 1911. Thus only two other orders besides the four already dealt with, are worth mentioning specifically. These are Professional occupations where there was a very large increase from less than 2,000 (1.5 per cent) in 1851 to over 18,000 (8.6 per cent) in 1911; and Textile fabrics where the numbers doubled between these dates to reach just over 7,000 (3.4 per cent) in 1911.

1921-71

During this period the perpetual problem of the formation of new occupations and the eradication or reclassification of old ones was accelerated. In particular, the Classifications of Occupations in 1921 and 1931 contained a large number of occupations which were either not listed, because they no longer existed, or were grouped together in the 1951 Classification. Such re-grouping means that a less detailed break-down is possible in the later censuses. This probably reduces the accuracy of the actual figures a little. However, the percentage figures are little affected since the major occupational orders in Wales were not touched by the reclassification, whilst the problems of comparison have been minimised by taking as the standard the later classification.

Three other general problems require mention. Firstly, the absence of a census in 1941 makes it difficult in some cases to trace the history of various orders. Secondly, the 1961 and 1971 occupational censuses were based on a 10 per cent sample and the results may thus have some sampling error, especially for the smaller orders. And finally, the figures of the various censuses refer to persons of different ages—the 1921 figures are for persons over 12 years old, the 1931 figures for those over 13, and those from 1951 on are for those aged over 15. This partly accounts for the fall in the total number of occupied males that took place at each census from 1921 to 1951, and for the fall in females in 1931, but not for the fall in occupied males from 1951 to 1971. Other factors were also at work however, such as the reversal of the migration flow—especially in the inter-war years when large numbers left Wales—the tendency for a larger number to pursue their education beyond the school-leaving age, and the change in the age-structure (males over 65, for example, constituted 4.1 per cent of the population in 1911 and 11.2 per cent in 1971).

All these factors are also important in helping to explain the trends in activity rates. If there is some room for doubt as to whether the male activity rate fell before 1911, there is no doubt about its decline over the next sixty years. The decline, moreover, was especially marked at the end of the period from 1951 to 1971 (the fall was from 86.02 per cent to 78.39 per cent). The decline was repeated in each of the individual counties over the whole period from 1921 to 1971 and neither the range nor the pattern of the county variations is of any significance. Activity rates for women, on the other hand, have risen during this period and again the change is especially sharp for the years between 1951 and 1971, when the increase was from 24.95 to 35.56, an increase of about 40 per cent. All the counties showed an increase in their female activity rates from 1921 to 1971, but there may be some significance in the fact that much the largest increases were in Monmouth (by 110 per cent) and Glamorgan (by 90 per cent): it would lend support to a hypothesis that female activity rates were low in industrial Wales when mining was a dominant industry, but the employment opportunities for women increased as the importance of the mines decreased.

1921-71 Males

The most dramatic shift in the structural make-up was the drastic fall in the relative importance of the primary producing sectors. In 1921, Agriculture, Fishing, Mining and Quarrying accounted for 42.3 per cent of the total males occupied; in 1971 their share had fallen to 10.5 per cent. The decline, and indeed the whole pattern of male occupations in the half-century after 1921, is dominated by one feature—the fall in the number occupied in Mining and Quarrying. In 1921 31.2 per cent of the male working population was so occupied; in 1971 less than one in twenty (4.7 per cent) was in this order. The full magnitude of the shift can only be appreciated by looking at the absolute numbers involved. Between 1921 and 1951 the pace of the decline was even faster than had been the rise after 1871.

The number in the occupational group fell by 165,000 in these years, and by 1971 238,000 fewer were engaged in Mining and Quarrying than had been the case fifty years earlier.

By 1971 the largest single occupational group had become Metal Manufacturing and Engineering, which had increased as a percentage of the total occupied males from 11.2 in 1921 to 20.5 in 1971. But, although this order covers a diversity of activities—and had indeed become three separate orders by the 1971 census—it had by no means replaced primary production as totally dominating the occupational structure of Wales. Indeed, one of the more prominent and significant changes during this period was the development of a more even spread of the workforce amongst the occupational groups. The four main occupational groups in 1921 (Agriculture; Mining and Quarrying; Metal Manufacturing and Engineering; and Transport and Communication) accounted for almost two-thirds of occupied males; by 1971 the share of the top four (Metal Manufacturing; Labourers, n.e.c.; Professional; and Transport) had fallen to less than half (46.5). The tendency towards greater occupational diversity should not, however, be overstressed. There still remained a number of groups in which the total number of occupied males was very small; in 1921 there were eleven orders each with less than one per cent of the total number: in 1971 there were still seven such orders.

An additional distinguishing characteristic of the period since the First World War is the significant proportion of the orders which experienced an absolute decline in numbers. To some degree this simply reflects the overall decline in the number of occupied males but it serves to emphasise an important contrast with the nineteenth-century experience Between 1851 and 1911 only four

Orders suffered an absolute decline in numbers, and of these only one—Agriculture (over 39,000)—fell by more than 5,000. Between 1921 and 1971 there was an absolute decline in ten of the Orders and several of these falls were substantial. Since the fall in one group—Mining and Quarrying (238,000)—was so massive, it is perhaps remarkable that there were also substantial falls in Agriculture (50,000); Clothing (6,600); Transport (24,600); Sales Workers (8,200); and Building (6,800).

The situation in the expansionary group is blurred because a significant number (32,100 and 6,800 respectively) went into the two residual groups, Labourers not elsewhere specified, and Inadequately described occupations. Of the rest, the greatest absolute increases were recorded in Metal Manufacturing and Engineering (61,600); Professional and technical (44,600); Clerical (19,600); Administrators and Managers (19,100); Service, sport and recreational (17,700); and Warehousemen, storekeepers, etc. (14,200). The growth of all except the first of these, moreover, suggested that the occupational structure of Wales was not merely breaking away from a traditional dependence on primary production, but was also beginning to share—though inadequately—in the mid-twentieth century shift towards the increasing importance of service occupations.

1921-71 Females

It is again the shifts in the aggregates which in many ways constitute the most interesting aspect of the adjustments in female occupations in Wales over the last half century. In particular, most of the broad trends which were noted for the period from 1851 to 1911 were not merely altered but decisively reversed. Before 1911 the total number of occupied women was growing more slowly than the general increase in population (by 71 per cent as against 108 per cent); from 1921 to 1971 the growth in the number of occupied women (81.6 per cent) was markedly greater than the general increase in the population (2.8 per cent). Before 1911 the proportion of women to men in the total occupied population was declining (from 33 per cent in 1851 to 27 per cent in 1911); after 1921 there was a sharp increase from 24.2 to 49.6 per cent in 1971.

It is likely that the twentieth-century increase, like the nineteenth-century decrease, was related to trends in the mining industry. The massive reduction in the relative and absolute importance of coal-mining had both a direct and an indirect effect. In direct terms it meant that an occupation which offered minimal opportunities for female labour had declined in importance, whilst indirectly the reduction in the household duties for women that were an integral part of coal-mining, increased the potential supply of female labour.

It is also noticeable that the female occupational structure changed much less than the male structure during this period. In particular the trend towards a more diversified occupational structure was less marked for women. Thus whereas the top four male occupational groups in 1921 accounted for nearly two-thirds (63.4 per cent) of the total occupied males, the top four groups in 1971 accounted for less than one-half (46.5 per cent). For women the top four groups in 1921 accounted for nearly four-fifths (79.3 per cent) and still contributed nearly three-quarters (73.2 per cent) fifty years later. Nor had there been much change in the composition of the leading female occupations. In 1921 the four most numerous orders were Service, sport etc. (44.5 per cent); Sales (15.1 per cent); Professional (10.6 per cent); and Clothing (9.1 per cent): by 1971 Service (24.6 per cent); Sales (14.0 per cent); and Professional (12.6 per cent) were still amongst the leading groups but

Clerical Workers had ousted Clothing Workers and had, indeed, dramatically leapt into second place accounting for 22.1 per cent in 1971 compared to only 5.8 per cent in 1921. The other big change had occurred in Service, sport etc. For although this was still the leading order in 1971, its proportional importance had been nearly halved, whilst the absolute numbers in this occupational group in 1971 was—despite the large increase in the total number of occupied women—almost exactly the same as it had been in 1921. Indeed, all this under-states the extent of change in this group. From 1921 to 1951 there was a sharp decrease in the number of women occupied in this group from 95,000 to 67,000 and it was only in the decade of the 1960s that the number recovered again to 95,000. These fluctuations were probably due to the other big shift concealed within the overall numbers of this Order: that is, the shift not so much in function—the main sub-groups were still Charwomen, office cleaners, maids, cooks—but in the place of work, moving out of private homes and into offices, hospitals, hotels, and other more public institutions.

Conclusion

The object of this short section is not to summarise what has gone before, but to bring out some broad tendencies in the occupational structure over the whole period of 120 years. The problems, already mentioned, of comparability between pre-1911 and post-1921 information on occupations necessarily limits the range within which such comments may be made with reasonable confidence especially in looking at individual occupations.

Nonetheless, it is clear that the male occupational structure in 1851 was dominated by primary production and that this dominance remained essentially intact until 1911—indeed, until 1921—because of the ability of the mining occupations, especially in South Wales coal, to absorb the numbers being released from agriculture and also additional workers to an extent which almost reflected the general increase in the male working population. But by 1971 neither of the primary occupations figures in the five largest Orders; they jointly accounted for only one in ten of all occupied males; and Agriculture had once again, as had been the case up to 1871, become a more numerous occupational grouping than Mining and Quarrying. Most of the decline into relative insignificance of the primary producing sectors has, moreover, taken place since 1951—the two decades before 1971 seeing an absolute decline of 73,500 in the numbers of men occupied in Mining and Quarrying and 44,000 in Agriculture. In the same two decades the largest increases were in Metal Manufacture and Engineering (48,000); Professional workers etc. (29,000); Administrators and Managers (13,000); and Service etc. (7,500). Thus it is only in the most recent period that the occupational structure for men in Wales has assumed a recognisably twentieth-century hue.

In the case of women's occupations, Agriculture and Clothing (Dress)—two of the big three outlets in 1851—had substantially and fairly persistently declined. Services, however, still remained as the largest single occupational order although, as already indicated, most of the women so occupied were more likely to be found in public establishments of various kinds rather than in private houses. The growing occupational sectors for women (Sales; Professional; Clerical—above all Clerical) had shown a persistent tendency to increase over the last half-century.

The other main points concern the aggregates and can be indicated by summarising what has been said about activity rates. Whichever of the measures (given in Appendix 3) of activity rates are used, the overall pattern is the same. For males, the activity rate is basically steady (perhaps falling slightly) from 1851 to 1921, but then falls quite clearly and sharply to 1971. But for women the behaviour of the activity rate is markedly different. There is a long period of clear decline from 1851 to 1921, followed by a major increase to 1971. The increase is all the more remarkable because the most obvious factors in any explanation of the decline in the male activity rates—raised school-leaving age and a higher proportion of the population over retiring age—also applied to women. Moreover, without this shift in the female activity rate there would have been a fall in the absolute number of the occupied population in Wales in the last fifty years instead of a slight increase from 1.094 million to 1.168 million. As a result there has been a dramatic shift in the ratio of male workers to female workers. In 1851 there were just over three occupied males for each occupied female; this rose to 3.3/4 by 1911 and continued to rise to just over 4 in 1921 and nearly 4.1/4 in 1931. The lack of census for 1941 makes it difficult to judge whether the reversal of this long-run trend was initiated or merely accelerated by the war: but by 1971 there had been a dramatic drop to just over two men for each woman in the total occupied population of Wales.

Notes

[1]*Guides to Official Sources, No. 1 Labour Statistics*, rev. edition 1958; *No. 2 Census Reports of Great Britain, 1801-1931*, 1951; W.A. Armstrong, 'The Use of Information about Occupation' in E.A. Wrigley (ed.), *Nineteenth Century Society*, 1972.

[2]It could be argued that there are, as indicated in the next section, other dates when substantial discontinuity occurs—such as 1871 or 1881. We have judged that, given the broad occupational structure in Wales at the time, the changes then introduced were not large enough to justify making a definite break in the

series. The appendix tables also try to indicate where the significant breaks arise between 1911 and 1921 by attempting to allocate the 1921 figures on the same basis as those for 1851-1911, and the 1911 figures on the same basis as those for 1921-71.

[3]P. Deane and W.A. Cole, *British Economic Growth, 1688-1959*, Cambridge, 1964, p. 143.

[4]There are at least two main ways of measuring activity rates. Some writers (e.g., C.H. Lee, *Regional Economic Growth in the U.K. since the 1880s,* 1971) give the number employed as a percentage of the total population. A disadvantage of this method for comparisons over time arises because social and legal changes tend to raise the normal age of entry into the work-force. Alternatively, the activity rate can be expressed as the percentage of persons in the labour force to the total population over school-leaving age (or other legal constraint on the age of starting employment). It is this latter formulation which is, unless otherwise stated, used in the present article. The disadvantage here is that because, over time, this age varies it might seem to introduce some inconsistency. On the other hand it can be argued that the activity rate should really show the number working as a proportion of those 'eligible' for work, and that legal and social changes over 'eligibility' are one of the factors determining shifts in the rate.

[5]Before the census of 1891 there was no compulsory minimum school-leaving age and no universal legal age restraints on employment. The censuses of 1891-1911, however, treated all those below the age of ten as unoccupied and we have used this as the basis for the entire period 1851-1911 (i.e., the activity rate is given by the number occupied as a percentage of the total population over ten years old). Since, at least before 1891, those who were employed younger than ten will be included in the numerator but not in the denominator, this gives the activity rate for the early years an upward bias. Hence it can only be said that the rate 'probably' declined between 1851 and 1911.

APPENDIX 1
OCCUPATIONAL DISTRIBUTION OF THE POPULATION, WALES 1851-1921

Class	Males 1851	Males 1861	Males 1871	Males 1881	Males 1891	Males 1901	Males 1911	Males 1921*	Females 1851	Females 1861	Females 1871	Females 1881	Females 1891	Females 1901	Females 1911	Females 1921*
1. General or Local Government	2,742	3,227	4,222	4,179	5,736	7,934	11,311	11,504	148	228	322	380	787	1,478	2,743	3,239
2. Defence	2,644	3,466	3,400	3,207	2,859	3,195	3,000	4,933	-	-	-	-	-	-	-	-
3. Professional Occupations	6,820	7,861	9,047	12,413	14,814	18,519	22,367	24,802	1,870	2,900	3,862	6,512	10,147	14,406	18,453	23,911
4. Domestic Offices or Services	5,259	5,587	6,133	10,240	4,848	11,459	14,792	8,024	41,948	68,817	83,896	88,221	105,390	88,878	90,496	78,481
5. Commercial Occupations	1,921	3,518	5,427	9,673	13,880	19,635	27,057	35,336	138	50	119	148	298	941	2,269	13,363
6. Conveyance of Men, Goods and Messages	16,144	22,937	26,547	36,644	52,027	69,751	85,481	94,401	496	301	318	416	434	652	683	4,214
7. Agriculture	135,443	131,330	111,815	100,023	98,999	91,668	95,966	94,739	33,748	18,023	13,541	10,731	9,294	12,359	20,181	11,355
8. Fishing	769	747	961	895	1,013	1,234	1,282	1,879	-	12	114	86	116	110	68	35
9. Mines and Quarries	65,398	77,348	89,656	101,675	144,705	188,958	256,250	278,003	1,816	1,485	1,986	1,320	802	343	268	175
10. Metals, Machines, Implements and Conveyances	35,659	47,945	53,727	55,503	62,451	68,033	90,845	100,889	2,127	2,652	3,134	3,710	4,549	2,411	3,525	4,586
11. Precious Metals, Jewels, Watches, Instruments & Games	693	926	1,037	1,121	1,449	1,751	2,191	1,274	10	47	75	91	133	181	286	50
12. Building and Works of Construction	26,102	32,225	33,603	39,871	44,040	52,048	59,958	61,040	645	986	332	58	66	35	27	173
13. Wood, Furniture, Fittings and Decorations	5,526	5,979	5,512	5,241	5,291	5,933	7,716	8,347	175	139	174	190	243	247	483	300
14. Brick, Cement, Pottery & Glass	1,341	1,576	1,608	2,133	2,803	4,440	5,096	3,040	244	467	644	707	678	498	484	483
15. Chemicals, Oil, Grease, Soap, Resin, etc.	1,152	1,384	1,837	2,161	2,409	2,414	3,331	1,793	52	51	104	123	156	190	373	99
16. Skins, Leather, Hair & Feathers	2,156	2,175	1,763	1,886	1,956	1,895	1,995	1,496	77	78	58	64	71	74	130	160
17. Paper, Print, Books and Stationery	1,095	1,435	1,944	2,513	3,360	4,193	4,966	3,824	143	189	288	520	825	1,331	1,933	1,272
18. Textile Fabrics	8,275	7,167	7,122	7,294	7,669	7,256	6,856	2,165	3,616	2,862	2,517	2,843	4,059	5,539	7,358	2,882
19. Dress	21,473	20,189	18,142	15,785	15,673	15,938	17,643	9,557	27,117	32,809	29,886	26,296	32,898	32,145	33,507	18,132
20. Food, Tobacco, Drink and Lodging	14,710	17,055	19,078	21,016	26,579	34,346	44,422	14,658	8,707	8,130	8,187	9,561	18,377	16,383	28,287	17,596
21. Gas, Water, Electricity, Sanitary Work	106	290	478	689	1,148	2,125	3,665	2,890	4	2	3	9	5	1	1	15
22. Other, General and Undefined Workers	30,530	33,161	61,274	55,477	62,253	43,024	42,404	115,813	2,781	2,413	3,320	2,771	2,580	2,222	4,126	32,631
TOTAL OCCUPIED	385,958	427,528	468,503	489,639	575,962	655,749	808,594	880,407	125,862	142,623	152,880	154,757	191,908	180,424	215,681	213,149
23. Unoccupied etc.+	208,835	227,617	246,268	299,435	103,898	118,407	144,895	123,643	468,259	515,066	558,189	633,702	475,895	583,427	696,687	792,497

* The figures for 1921 represent an attempt to redistribute the information from the 1921 census on the same basis as was used for 1851-1911.
\+ Children under 10 years of age are included up to 1881 but excluded from 1891 onwards.

APPENDIX 2

OCCUPATIONAL DISTRIBUTION OF THE POPULATION, WALES, 1911-1971

Class	Males 1911*	Males 1921	Males 1931	Males 1951	Males 1961	Males 1971	Females 1911*	Females 1921	Females 1931	Females 1951	Females 1961	Females 1971
1. Fishing	1,282	1,879	2,379	1,334	730	470	68	35	18	3	-	20
2. Agriculture	102,371	95,480	92,510	79,457	61,230	45,130	20,192	11,355	8,606	10,267	6,470	7,620
3. Gas, Coke and Chemicals	1,342	5,011	3,489	9,408	11,440	12,090	229	102	81	1,348	1,420	1,020
4. Metal Manufacturing and Engineering	94,436	98,558	81,449	112,430	142,370	160,120	3,839	4,527	1,627	7,345	13,910	19,550
5. Mining and Quarrying	256,250	274,682	234,554	110,000	79,470	36,500	268	146	32	32	20	60
6. Woodworkers (+ Cork & Cane)	24,325	20,575	17,770	19,667	17,580	17,330	493	170	72	225	300	470
7. Leather Workers, Furn Dressers	9,057	5,544	4,897	3,325	2,130	1,620	1,007	211	132	1,011	800	1,390
8. Textile Workers	6,856	1,876	1,291	1,892	1,530	2,850	7,358	1,629	2,237	2,106	2,050	2,120
9. Clothing Workers	8,030	6,342	4,718	3,131	1,930	2,220	32,464	19,436	10,447	13,156	11,710	13,130
10. Food, Drink and Tobacco	8,549	8,824	8,878	7,534	10,930	9,170	1,976	2,609	1,912	2,831	3,150	3,690
11. Paper and Printing	4,966	3,824	3,768	3,170	3,940	4,850	1,933	1,272	1,120	1,291	1,700	2,410
12. Building and Contracting	35,928	38,735	43,227	63,098	30,690	31,900	20	100	42	81	20	80
13. Glass, Ceramics, Cement	5,096	3,040	2,070	2,901	2,580	2,040	484	483	146	498	560	590
14. Makers of Other Products (Rubber, Plastics etc.)	50	5,671	3,833	2,695	6,450	9,950	10	216	160	1,395	3,940	5,240
15. Painters and Decorators	6,652	8,019	8,503	12,113	12,410	11,820	2	82	85	397	540	480
16. Stationary Engine and Crane Drivers	14,826	20,203	20,965	22,472	26,990	25,970	-	-	23	150	130	170
17. Labourers (n.e.c.)	23,145	39,264	42,371	67,736	77,120	72,350	77	446	131	17,988	5,260	6,150
18. Transport and Communication	89,720	88,674	94,774	86,167	74,660	64,080	2,679	2,920	2,597	5,353	4,800	5,830
19. Warehousemen, Storekeepers, Packers, Bottlers, etc.	212	5,727	6,880	12,972	18,190	19,870	6	1,294	1,552	4,416	6,470	8,480
20. Clerical Workers	16,695	21,746	25,986	36,715	45,320	41,300	2,763	12,303	13,179	45,393	63,600	85,420
21. Sales Workers	49,683	59,026	77,211	60,996	58,440	50,780	15,995	32,191	34,165	42,219	52,180	54,050
22. Services, Sport and Recreation (including Personal Service)	20,393	21,730	25,877	31,960	34,680	39,510	106,719	94,827	98,234	67,059	67,590	95,230
23. Administrators and Managers	-	9,578	4,510	15,681	21,480	28,680	-	3,323	198	1,357	1,190	2,410
24 Professional, Technical Workers, Artists	21,282	22,117	23,829	37,326	56,720	66,140	16,854	22,536	23,580	30,334	39,530	48,850
25. Armed Forces	3,000	4,933	2,746	20,776	11,640	7,450	-	-	-	641	230	290
26. Inadequately Described Occupations	4,448	9,349	34,187	8,567	18,390	16,200	245	936	5,763	2,465	7,980	22,480
TOTAL OCCUPIED	808,594	880,407	872,672	833,523	829,040	780,390	215,681	213,149	206,139	259,361	295,550	387,230
27. Retired and Unoccupied	144,895	123,643	95,533	135,455	154,470	215,095	696,687	792,497	773,655	779,844	759,050	701,430

* The figures for 1911 represent an attempt to redistribute the information from the 1911 census on the same basis as that used for 1921-1971.

APPENDIX 3

WALES: ACTIVITY RATES, 1851-1971

1. 1851-1921[1.]

	1851	1861	1871	1881	1891	1901	1911	1921
Males	87.08	87.60	89.15	83.84	84.72	84.70	84.80	83.12
Females	28.24	28.95	28.94	26.48	28.74	23.62	23.63	20.09
TOTAL	57.57	58.13	58.96	55.15	56.97	54.36	54.89	51.58
TOTAL[3.]	44.00	44.32	43.98	40.99	43.34	41.54	42.30	41.16

2. 1911-1971[2.]

	1911	1921	1931	1951	1961	1971
Males	97.02	95.45	92.30	86.02	84.96	78.39
Females	27.26	23.06	21.52	24.95	28.13	35.56
TOTAL	63.03	59.21	56.68	54.42	55.50	56.02
TOTAL[3.]	42.30	41.16	41.59	42.05	42.53	42.75

NOTES:

1. Total occupied (10 and upwards) ÷ Total aged 10 and upwards.

2. Total occupied (15 and upwards) ÷ Total aged 15 and upwards.

3. Activity rate calculated as total occupied ÷ total population (cf. Lee, *op.cit.*, Table 17, p. 245, where he gives some figures for employment as share of total population).

14. THE MYTH OF MINERS' SOLIDARITY

(A talk originally given to a *Llafur* meeting in Swansea in 1975 after the two victorious miner's strikes of 1972 and 1974. It was held in the South Wales Miners' Library and, at that time, many Llafur members were miners. Alas, the world we have lost!)

Giving this talk on this subject before this audience, could be described as a foolhardy act. The British miners have, twice in three years, stood solidly and successfully together in major confrontations and a number of the South Wales miners who played a major role in these Triumphs of Solidarity are present tonight. In a small (minor?) way I can imagine how Lloyd George must have felt when, at the height of the Boer War in December, 1901, he attempted to present to the audience at a public meeting in Birmingham the case for the Boers. But although I don't have the protection of Lloyd George's oratorial skills, nor even a policeman's cloak to cover my retreat, I have the surer support of knowing that my audience knows where my sympathies and my intellectual convictions lie, and that the Miners' Library is a citadel of neither the Conservative Party nor the Coal Board management.

There are few ideas more deeply entrenched in Labour History than the notion that the miners have been a spearhead of the Labour movement. Their dominant influence is seen largely to arise from, and to reflect, their solidarity as a group. The miners have been—it is assumed—well-organised, have acted together, have been ready to make sacrifices to gain their ends—and these ends have normally been radical, if not revolutionary.

These assumptions are not much questioned. Partly because it has been convenient for the natural opponents of these views—those on the political right—to accept the role they give to the miners. Indeed, the whole picture is, if anything, even more firmly entrenched in the mythology of the right than of the left. The miners—red in tooth and claw—are the bogey-men which good Tories use to bring to heel their recalcitrant children of all ages.

Nor have many attempts been made at explanation: to explain the unique and leading position which these entrenched ideas and attitudes have bestowed on miners. Those attempts which have been made[1] stress—quite rightly—the normally isolated nature of mining communities which sets them apart from the rest of society and makes them a tightly-knit and united group. There is a tendency to conclude that all this tends to make miners, industrially and politically, radical in outlook. In Britain there is, no doubt, much substance in this—but it should be noted that it does not necessarily follow. Gaston Rimmleger,[2] for example, demonstrated that—over a longer period—the Saar miners, although similarly isolated and close-knit, had formed a relatively peaceful and docile sector of the workers in Germany. He attributed this to a long tradition of State paternalism which made the Saar miners (although a socially distinct group) well-integrated into the general society and especially sensitive to the opinion of society about them. Because of this the strong group cohesion, instead of leading to aggression, became in their case a source of disciplined industrial conduct. In the currently fashionable euphemism for social virtue—they were 'men of moderation'. The broader point being made, however, is this: whilst it is possible, using a reasonable mixture of observation, assumption and deduction, to establish the normal isolation and cohesion of communities of miners, and even demonstrate their own consciousness of this separation, it by no means follows that the expression of these characteristics has to take a radical form. This is, of course, a *general* point: that is, the abstract concept of a definite working-class interest—even if this conception is based on impeccable assumptions and irreproachable logic—is not *itself* sufficient to induce the working-class, or any sector of it, to act on the basis of this notional interest. To return to our more specific case it seems reasonable to conclude that, whilst there are bound to be reservations over the complete Rimmleger analysis, the essential point is unassailable: there is no compelling mechanism which unavoidably translates the isolated nature of mining communities into rebellious industrial and political behaviour.

The assumptions about the miners' role in the development of a Labour movement could, therefore, be challenged more or less head-on. The present objective is much more limited: the aim is to raise the prior question as to whether the substantial geographical separation of the industry produced the overwhelming degree of unity in thought and action amongst coal-miners which is normally suggested. Did they support each other so unswervingly and tenaciously? Was miners' solidarity a myth?

Before attempting to answer these questions, a few preliminary comments are needed. Any full discussion of this issue would need to be preceded by a fairly precise definition of 'Solidarity'—preferably in a form which would make it operationally testable. The evidence about the actual behaviour and attitudes of the miners could then be brought against the accurately specified concept of Solidarity. Then—wherever possible—measurement and, where necessary, judgement could be made as to how well they conformed to the standards set. It needs to be said straight-away that what follows is much more rough-and-ready, much less satisfactory. This essay will simply point towards some evidence of behaviour and attitudes amongst miners in the past and ask whether this tallies with the rather vague concept of solidarity which we all have in our minds. The vagueness of the concept is only—but, perhaps, significantly—reduced by calling on the brief dictionary definitions. By solidarity we have in mind then, 'a community of interests, feelings and actions', 'a oneness of interests and aims'. The stress on *interests* is, to anticipate some of the later discussion, illuminating, or so it will be suggested. In addition, the miners are generally attributed with having provided substantial leadership in the development of the labour movement as a whole. The entire issue of working class solidarity and the contribution to it made by the miners is altogether too wide-ranging to be tackled in one brief essay. But a few—fairly random—comments will be made to suggest that there, too, there are grounds for not taking too much for granted.

A second introductory comment would be this: a general presumption of the essay is that the mere provision of evidence of disagreements over policy issues cannot normally be taken as indicating a lack of uniformity of interest amongst the miners. Obviously any significant group can—probably *must*—have internal differences of opinion over the policies to be followed, the means whereby to achieve whatever ends have brought them together. This is true of all kinds of groups from political parties to church fete committees. But it does not *necessarily* mean that they are therefore lacking in solidarity, nor that such solidarity is thus under-mined. It may be (depending on a whole range of imponderables—like the length, the intensity and the significance of the particular issue), but it does not *have* to be.

In general, then, evidence of policy differences will be excluded. This carries with it two serious difficulties for the general argument being set out here. Firstly, it prevents the use of the material which would apparently provide the most persuasive and most readily-available evidence about breaches in the solidarity of the miners. Disputes over policy were the most vocal, the most publicised, the most fully articulated and usually the most colourful of the disagreements amongst the miners themselves. For example, there was open hostility for much of the 1890s between William Abraham (Mabon) [the long-established and—at the time—much respected leader and the first miners' M.P. from South Wales], and William Brace, the thrusting firebrand and prophet of the emergent Miners' Federation of Great Britain (M.F.G.B.). Moreover, the antipathies were not merely personal: they symbolised a deep division of opinion amongst the miners of South Wales. The episode had an early and dramatic initial climax (there were others later in the decade), when Mabon took Brace before the Queen's courts for defamation of character in August 1893. The embarrassing public display of policy differences, heightened by apparent personality differences, could not, however, be taken as a reliable guide to the solidarity of the miners of south Wales. The long, cruel strike of 1898 overwhelmed such policy and personality disagreements. In its bitter aftermath Mabon and Brace joined forces to create the South Wales Miners' Federation (the 'Fed') which soon came to epitomise solidarity on the coalfield. And yet within a decade the pattern was largely repeated. The difference was that it was now Mabon and Brace standing shoulder to shoulder as the Old Guard, whilst a new breed of Young Turks (led by Stanton, Vernon Hartshorn and Noah Ablett) had emerged, a breed made all the more effective (dangerous?) because some of them had been given a taste of formal education at Ruskin and/or the break-away Central Labour College. Again fierce policy disagreements were involved and so were personal and inter-generational differences, but—noisy and, indeed, vicious as they sometimes were—they are only in a very superficial sense indicators of solidarity shortcomings.

Their exclusion, however justifiable, nonetheless raises a serious difficulty, and one which again threatens to engulf the argument with tortuous semantic problems. The difficulty arises because it is by no means easy to draw a clear line around policy disagreements. For one thing, the very dramatic and newsworthy quality of, say, a struggle over leadership tends not only to overshadow, but to absorb other differences, differences that do reflect real problems over the essential community of feeling within the union. For another, there is no doubt that these leadership struggles sometimes reflect more fundamental and permanent differences of interest amongst different groups of miners. And, again to anticipate a little, it is the existence of such differences of interest which is being suggested as the most important constraining influence on maintaining an overall unity within the mining community.

One last point needs to be made by way of prologue. But this one is much more straightforward. It is simply to say that most of the examples used will be drawn from South Wales. In addition, most of the cases cited will be drawn from the period before 1914, and certainly before 1939. In each case the limitation has mostly been imposed by the limitations of the author's knowledge. But it is asserted that neither the arguments nor the conclusions apply only to pre-1914 (or pre-1939) South Wales. Similar examples could certainly be obtained from the other British coal-mining regions. Nor did the problems cease with nationalisation. The formation of the National Union of Mineworkers and the legitimacy, privileges and benefits apparently bestowed upon it by the National Coal Board (N.C.B.) might seem to have institutionalised solidarity. And any doubts raised by the hesitancy of its exercise in the 1950s and 1960s, again seemed to have been rendered redundant by the recent heady triumphs of 1972 and 1974. It is part of the contention of this paper that the united action of the early 1970s rested on fragile foundations which would be under-mined if the N.C.B. retreated, and was allowed to retreat, to management's historic insistence on stressing regional differences especially for wage determination.

(As an aside, perhaps a brief contemporary comment could be slipped in here since it is directly relevant to my main theme. There are many strands leading to the recent national coal stoppages but one crucial thread was the existence of the national power-loading agreement. One feature of this was that wage advances in the high productivity coalfields were directly tied to those of other coalfields. So areas like Nottingham had an immediate interest in supporting the wage demands from other areas. All this provided the essential cement for the unity of the miners in the early seventies. Having come this far, I might as well desert my historical brief still further and slide—briefly, rashly—into the future to make one bold prediction. It would surprise me very much if the N.C.B. in the years to come does not proceed to dismantle or modify the national power-loading agreement in order to split up the areas by reducing the degree of common interest between them).

It was necessary to embark on these lengthy preliminary comments. Without some indication of how the decks had been cleared some of the major limitations and presumptions of the analysis would have been obscured. One further major assumption must be made explicit. The approach of this paper rests heavily on the belief that, in the absence of any plausible and possible ways of measuring solidarity, its existence and strength can best be tested by looking at the evidence about a number of key relationships within the mining community. Six categories of relationship have been identified:

1) relationships between leaders and leaders;
2) relationships between leaders and men;
3) relationships within the mining community of a particular coalfield;
4) relationships between the mining communities of different coalfields;
5) relationships making for common national action amongst miners;

and

6) relationships between miners and other groups of workers.

It is not pretended that the list is exhaustive but it is claimed that even a relatively cursory look at some of the evidence under these heads raises serious doubts about any presumption that there has existed a more or less monolithic degree of solidarity amongst British miners.

The examination of the evidence under the first two categories, relationships between leaders and leaders and between leaders and rank-and-file, is particularly perfunctory. This is not because of any lack of evidence. On the contrary it is because, as has already been argued above, most differences within these categories reflect policy judgements and provide no sound indicator of essential unity or disunity. Of course, while any particular dispute is in progress it is likely to make for factions within the group which will probably reduce its unity of purpose. And the particular way in which these disputes work themselves out can—especially at times of crisis—reduce the group's solidarity of action. The treatment of these relationships is being truncated, therefore, not because they are considered unimportant or trivial. These issues can, indeed, have significance for the expression and exercise of solidarity. Where they do so, however, the contention is that more than mere personal differences have been involved, and that the most important of these deeper sources of dissension are picked up in the other categories which have been suggested.

All this can, with some economy, be illustrated for each of these categories by looking at some aspects of the Cambrian Combine strike of 1910-11. The Cambrian strike was ultimately a strike over abnormal places, which was an issue of general significance and concern in South Wales. There is little doubt, however, that the clash between the local Cambrian leaders and the coalfield leaders of the S.W.M.F. reduced this essential unity. The local Cambrian leaders attacked the Old Guard with more zeal than tact, and the frequent and gratuitous offensiveness of their remarks were not calculated to stimulate the enthusiasm with which the existing Executive members pressed the case of the Cambrian colliers. Such considerations clearly constituted part of the explanation for the very poor response of the coalfield to the levies which were imposed to raise funds for the strikers. The poverty of the response was in itself, of course, *also* a commentary on the general limits to solidarity—as the stoppage progressed there was a growing stream of protests from individual lodges against the levy.

The gulf between the Cambrian men and the national (British) leadership was even greater, and was expressed with a directness that had an even more damaging impact on general solidarity during the crisis of the stoppage. Harvey (of the Derbyshire miners) and Thomas Ashton (the mild general secretary of the M.F.G.B.) had been sent to Tonypandy in March 1911 by the national executive as peace-makers. They must have considered, quite reasonably, that their credentials had been firmly established with the men since, from at least January, the financial mainstay of the strikers had been a grant of £3,000 a week from the M.F.G.B. Despite this, however, Harvey and Ashton were greeted in Tonypandy by a crowd which made its hostility uncomfortably explicit. All this undoubtedly hardened the reluctance of the general body of miners to lend support to the Cambrian men. 'Anything is better than the state of anarchy and red riot such as prevails in Tonypandy today', it was said—not by one of the coalowners but by W.E. Harvey of the Derbyshire miners. The final breach came at a national conference in June when only the Welsh delegates opposed a resolution under which the national union completely wiped its hands of the dispute.

It would seem plausible to use such illustrations to conclude that disputes between different leaderships or between the leaders and the rank-and-file provide evidence of a lack of solidarity. They certainly show that such differences weakened the miners' position if they surfaced during periods of crisis. None the less it is contended that they do not constitute the core of the problem, and even less do they provide a satisfactory explanation for any lapses from solidarity. Such explanations are rather to be found in the existence of specific obstacles to the attainment of unity amongst miners both within a particular coalfield and as between different coalfields, as well as some explicit additional barriers which discouraged common national action being taken.

The slow emergence of anything like a stable, reasonably permanent and comprehensive trade union organisation in each of the coalfields should have alerted historians into recognising and emphasising the prime fact that the path to unity within each coalfield was necessarily beset with obstacles. Some of the barriers were common, and commonplace. There was, for example, the simple, natural reluctance of men to pay union dues. There was also the very real fear of union membership leading directly to suffering for a miner and his family: the more or less naked use of oppression and intimidation was fairly general in the nineteenth century and, in particular circumstances and places, lapped over into at least the first four decades of the twentieth century. In addition, there were always problems involved in any attempts to bring together in a single organisation all the miners in a given coalfield. The size of the problem, of course, varied from coalfield to coalfield. For South Wales, for example, the difficulties were particularly acute because of the exceptionally large size of the coalfield and also because the valley formation tended to separate off the different districts. Not until the 1890s was South Wales able to hold out serious hopes of providing some permanent central organisation. And not until 1898, with the formation of the S.W.M.F., was the single union for the coalfield made an effective reality. Even then the constitution retained a great deal of the power (and half the subscriptions) for the 20 districts which made up the Federation.

Even so, there were other more serious obstacles to unity, more serious because they provided objective criteria over which real differences of interest could, and would, emerge amongst different groups of miners. Thus in South Wales, even if discussion is limited to the broadest categories, the existence of quite significantly different types of coal sold in different markets governed by different conditions tended to make for divergence between those mining house coal, those mining steam coal, and those mining anthracite. Fortunately for unity, steam coal became persistently more dominant in South Wales down to 1914, a trend which helped to reduce the significance of these divisive influences. A further divisive factor, which again fortunately dwindled in importance after about 1870, was the existence in the industry of at least two distinct types of firms: those the primary function of which was the production and sale of coal and those which, although major coal producers, were mainly interested in selling iron. The differences of interest amongst the two groups of miners (the earnings of one group being mainly decided by variations in the iron market: that of the other group by changes in the coal market) made joint action much more difficult.

There were other, more subtle but no less formidable, barriers to unity. The steam coal trade in South Wales spread geographically over time. Thus, for example, the earliest developments were in the Merthyr valley in the 1830s, from whence the trade spread into the Aberdare valley in the 1840s and 1850s and into the Rhondda in the succeeding decades and so on. Each newly-developing region, partly in order to attract labour to raw, bleak areas, offered higher cutting-rates for working the various seams. As a result there were perceptible earnings differences between the different groups of miners. But the Rhondda men were not willing to see any funds towards which they had contributed being used to support, say, the Aberdare colliers on strike to 'level-up' their wages to equal those of the Rhondda men. Nor would Aberdare men cheerfully support Rhondda strikers who were resisting the attempt of a coalowner to 'level-down' their wages to those prevailing in Aberdare. Such considerations drove substantial wedges between the various districts within the coalfield.

It is, moreover, quite mistaken to look upon miners as being a more or less homogeneous group in relation to their work. This is not just a matter of finding a few unusual jobs:

coalmining, in common with virtually all industries, can throw up such bizarre-sounding jobs as Washery bed labourer, Washery slurry lump and Endlass lad. There were also various significant divisions between, for example, surface and underground workers, or between craftsmen and labourers. It would be possible to sectionalise the workforce in quite complicated ways. For our purposes, however, we need only to concentrate on the basic division which was between those on piece-rates and those paid by the day. The earnings of the former were directly linked to productivity (the more coal they cut the more they earned) whereas the day-wage men simply found themselves working harder for the same pay. Piece-workers were the coal-cutters, the aristocracy of the industry—most of the day-men were generally lower-paid. In the expansionary period of the industry the problems posed by the existence of such divergences were considerably reduced because the newer, rawer recruits—those straight from the farms of Cardigan or Dorset—could be given the less well-paid jobs; and also because the younger day-men could have a reasonable expectation that they might eventually be given a stall and themselves become piece-workers. None the less the differences occasionally come to the surface. Thus the 1893 strike in South Wales had numerous under-tones; it was in part an attempt to win over the Welsh district unions to the English union, the Miners' Federation of Great Britain, and it was in part a revolt against the Sliding Scale. But one major, distinguishing characteristic was that it was a strike, especially in Glamorgan, initiated by the Hauliers. Moreover, one of the particular features of the strike was the willingness, in a number of pits, of the piece-work colliers to take over the work previously performed by the day-wage hauliers. Indeed, strike-breaking activities sometimes went even beyond this: at Ebbw Vale, for example, the marching bands of hauliers, the main means by which the strike was spread, were physically beaten off by the local colliers (and iron workers). This was not an entirely spontaneous action on the part of the colliers; they were marshalled by the Ebbw Vale Iron Steel & Coal Co., but the available evidence suggests they were willing enough to act. All this was—of course—quite exceptional, but the attitudes which it betrays were perhaps more general. At all events, it would be very difficult to think of any occasion before 1914 on which the more prosperous face-workers took any industrial action mainly to support the lower-paid men. Indeed, in Northumberland and Durham, before 1908, it could be said that the shorter hours of the face-workers to some degree directly depended upon other groups—including boys—working much longer hours.

What is being suggested is this: we can take, as an overall indicator of substantial obstacles to solidarity, the relatively slow growth of a strong, stable union in a particular coalfield, such as South Wales. We can find further confirmation of these problems in the continuing difficulty, as long as membership was voluntary, of keeping up the strength of the union.[3] And when we look for *explanations* we are confronted not only with such more or less autonomous factors as, to give a summary indication, apathy, fear and geographical barriers; but also by real divisions of interest within the mining community. The focus of these divisions can, as has been seen, shift over time. In addition, the nature of the divisions is far from fully exhausted by the examples that have been given: in Lanarkshire, for example, problems of solidarity were much exacerbated by Irish-Scots (and hence Catholic-Protestant) clashes. Not until 1944 did a single union for Scottish miners emerge.

Much the same pattern is repeated when we look at relationships between coalfield and coalfield. There is again a layer of more-or-less obvious autonomous obstacles to such unity. There are clearly extra problems of organisation, communication, size and geography, but these need not be enumerated. It is more germane to our present purposes to note that there are again objective barriers to unity and that these emerge in a still starker form at this level. The M.F.G.B. was actually launched in South Wales, at a meeting held in Newport at the end of 1889. Despite this, the bulk of the South Wales colliers (together with those from Durham) withdrew almost straight away when a resolution condemning the sliding-scale system of wage-regulation was passed. The disagreements over sliding scales were, however, only the proximate cause of the split which really reflected a much more enduring division between those coalfields which found their major markets overseas and those which were more dependent on home sales. The particular way in which this difference affected the behaviour and attitudes of miners in different coalfields shifted over time, but the source of division lasted at least until the Second World War. (Since that time the division between coalfields on the basis of the market they served has perhaps simply been replaced by a division between those coalfields—or districts—which have been expanding and those which have been contracting; and, even more recently, between those of high productivity and those of low productivity.) The operation of the exporting/home market division was seen in its starkest form after the government imposed an export tax on coal of 1s. a ton in 1901. The miners in areas like South Wales and Durham pressed for national industrial action to secure its removal, but for most of the coalfields the tax did not seem to represent a strong enough attack on their interest to justify a strike. Such a highlighting was accidental: but recognition of that should not obscure the more important point that the division which was embodied was a constant obstacle to joint action. In the inter-war years, for example, the clear difference in the severity with which the general economic depression hit different coalfields—with exporting areas like South Wales being particularly badly affected—necessarily emphasised the divergence of interest between districts. This contributed to the total absence of effective national movements for a full decade after 1926.

The way in which conflicting interests could exist between different coalfields is dramatically illustrated by attitudes towards securing an eight hour day. There was from time to time, both within and between coalfields, division over whether this was best secured by industrial or political action. In addition, since there was much variety in the customary length of the working day there was also much variation in the degree of enthusiasm with which an Eight Hour Day was sought. These considerations represented mere tactical differences. The opposition of the miners of Northumberland and Durham however was quite different. Their resistance to any legislative action was total. In these districts the hewers already worked less than eight hours a day (boys and other day-men working eleven hours or more). Miners' M.Ps from the North-east (Thomas Burt, Fenwick, John Wilson) not only failed to lend support to efforts to secure an eight-hour day by legislation but actually spoke in the House in support of coalowner opposition to Bills introduced by the M.F.G.B. For over two decades the Eight Hour Day question was a source of deep division amongst the miners themselves.

The existence of important objective factors blurring the basis for inter-coalfield solidarity is obviously closely related to the next broad category: the problems of securing common national action. A pervasive illustration is provided by the major operational difficulty, in the days of district agreements, of getting the miners in the different coalfields in a position to act together and at the same time over wages and hours. Agreements tended to expire at different dates which inhibited common action: but any national action for national ends demanded exceptionally dedicated unity since the coalowners were implacably opposed to anything that smacked of national agreements. Any attempts to change matters were thus bound to involve clashes somewhere or other. In other words, if the miners wanted (as they mostly did) to get agreements expiring at the same time so that they could, if necessary, take common action, then there was a price to pay. The question was who was prepared to pay it? The issue arose starkly when South Wales did eventually join the M.F.G.B. after the 1898 strike. In 1900 there had been unanimous acceptance of a resolution, moved by Scotland and supported by South Wales, that wage agreements should be made to terminate simultaneously in the various districts of the Federation. In October 1902 the Southport conference of the M.F.G.B. had gone on to resolve that no district should enter any agreement which could not be terminated at the end of 1903 (when the agreement for the Midland coalfields, the core of the original federation, terminated). Unfortunately, the current South Wales agreement ended in December 1902 and the Welsh coalowners totally refused to negotiate a new agreement for one year only. If the agreement was to be confined to one year the coalowners would only accept the existing sliding-scale arrangement. They well knew that the Welsh miners could hardly agree to prolong the sliding-scale, because the acceptance of South Wales into the M.F.G.B. had been conditional on the Welsh miners ending the sliding-scale system as soon as the existing agreement ran out.[4] The Welsh negotiators were certainly in a dilemma: it seemed they had to choose between a new agreement, getting rid of the sliding-scale—as they had pledged the M.F.G.B. to do—but letting the agreement run for three years (when M.F.G.B. policy allowed them only a one-year arrangement); or letting the old discredited sliding-scale run on for a further year. They finally chose the former course. Indeed, despite all the shadow-fighting, there was never any real doubt (right from the beginning) that South Wales was more than ready to be wooed away from standing for a one-year settlement. There was much recrimination, however, and three special meetings of the M.F.G.B. were held before the Federation accepted (without agreeing to) the action of South Wales. Ben Pickard, the President of the M.F.G.B., was especially bitter and poured scorn and mordant scepticism on Mabon and Brace as they lucidly and penitently explained the Welsh dilemma.

There was, of course, another choice. South Wales could have pressed the issue to a strike—for no one thought the Welsh owners were bluffing. It has to be said that little serious consideration was given to this possibility although it was clear that a successful stoppage was almost certainly the only way in which South Wales could have redeemed both of its pledges to the M.F.G.B.: to end the sliding scale and to negotiate an agreement which would run for a year only. Neither Mabon nor Brace saw any sense in striking against an agreement which gave them very solid gains and was only objectionable because of the time clause. There is every indication that the Welsh miners, with memories of the cost and suffering of 1898 still green, on this point agreed with their leaders. Nor was the reluctance to take positive action confined to South Wales. The districts which were pressing the Welsh miners to stand firm would not, as was made clear, come out themselves in support. The immediate reason for this was that their own existing agreement with their employers forbade such action: but even without this it is tolerably certain that the other districts would not have put Rule 20 into operation. Their help would have been limited to finance. The reality of the barriers to joint action was under-lined when, a couple of years later, the situation was reversed and the Midland districts came to re-negotiate their agreement. They accepted a three year term even though the Welsh agreement now had only a year to run. No further serious attempt was made before 1914 to secure the co-incident termination of agreements in the various districts—even though this was an essential pre-requisite for any sustained common action amongst British miners.

The failure of the miners on this issue indicated the persistent realities of differences amongst the districts and the natural reluctance of any particular sector to bear the brunt of the substantial cost that would be involved in any attempt to depart from district arrangements. Of course, they also represented the determination of the owners' resistance to anything resembling national agreements. Such opposition must have been anticipated and certainly makes no difference to the general point: namely, that the desire for common and continuous national action amongst the men was never strong enough to win it for themselves.[5] So far as it was obtained it came as a by-product of an external factor—national emergency in the form of two world wars. After the First World War the miners—in exceptionally unfavourable conditions—were unable to hold on to the prize of national settlements; after the Second World War its retention might be said to be due to the removal—by nationalisation—of the opposition of the coalowners. Indeed, it would really be quite possible to argue that the Coal Board, despite its designation of 'National', has on the crucial issues of wage-rates, costs and prices been as evasive about national formulations as were the old coalowners. Such a discussion, however, would be for a different context: but mention of the possibility does under-line that the sources of disunity presently being rehearsed were inherent in the economic conditions of the industry and could not be swept away even by substantial institutional change unless it was accompanied by shifts in attitudes away from a simple dependence on the crude (and inadequate indicator) of short-term profitability.

For the present purposes, the really crucial question is: how often has there been concerted national action amongst British miners? In 1912, 1921, 1926 and—1972 and 1974. Of course, it can and will be correctly asserted that miners have been the most strike-prone of all the occupational groups in industrial Britain. It is not this fact but the common implication that this embodies a general willingness to act together to press for their rights that is being questioned here. In the 1950s, for example, over 70% of all stoppages in Britain took place in the mining industry, where there were some 16,000 separate stoppages. In assessing the nature and strength of miners' solidarity, it may be more pertinent to draw attention to, especially as it is commonly overlooked, the parallel fact that during this period there were no national mining stoppages—indeed, there were no major district stoppages. The suggestion is that the pattern should at least excite speculation about the kind of solidarity which is suggested by such behaviour.

In this connection it is worth noting, in passing, that the constitutional arrangements of the miners' unions have, especially before 1945, generally tended to work against speedy, decisive, common action. The old M.F.G.B. was, as its name described, a federation and the aspect of federalism which was given clearest expression was that which limited the powers of the centre. In most of the important issues ultimate control was reserved for the various districts. The position has been modified somewhat since the formation of the N.U.M., but the fundamental fact remains that the processes of the union are, at each stage, dominated by highly democratic principles: and it is not easy to fashion a large democratic institution into a major instrument for radical action. The intention of this comment is not to attack, criticise or even to defend the constitutional arrangements. It is rather to describe the mechanism and to indicate that its nature suggests that if the miners did indeed play the active, aggressive and united role which is implied by the more sweeping formulations of the solidarity concept, then they did so despite a union organisation and constitution which hampered such an approach.

The constitutional, and other, constraints which have been briefly cited as constraints on common action amongst miners, naturally placed still stronger barriers against miners taking joint industrial action in support of other workers. Certainly, the one great institution created for this purpose, the Triple Alliance founded in 1914, was generally ineffective.[6] It is not, indeed, easy to find cases, other than those in which the miners themselves were in the vanguard and calling upon workers in general for support. A fact which perhaps can simply be taken as under-lining the miners' role as leaders of the industrial working class. It is undeniable that such leadership did often extend into the political sphere where it had a solid objective basis. The geographical isolation of the industry necessarily worked to give the miners a greater degree of influence in shaping and pressing for general working-class legislation. Even in this respect, however, it would be necessary to register the fact that miners at the beginning of the twentieth century were notably slow and reluctant to shift their political allegiance from the Liberals to the Labour Party.[7]

Beyond providing some gentle provocation, the intention of this brief essay has been to question some of the assumptions which lie behind what has, for brevity, been termed the myth of miners' solidarity. This, like most historical myths, no doubt has its uses but it also has its dangers. Certainly, to make too facile an assumption that miners naturally and automatically strove together in unison, gave each other instant and unquestioning support, eagerly espoused radical ideas and policies, and much more, is quite simply at variance with many of the facts and objective conditions. Much more to the point, a distorted picture of effortless harmony merely devalues the contributions, the struggles and the sacrifices of the miners. These aspects have not been depicted here but they lurk in the background. The immediate purpose has been to examine some of the barriers to, and limits of, solidarity—but not, in doing so, to deride the notion of solidarity or belittle what has been achieved. On the contrary one implicit question has been: if solidarity is as easily come by as the myth suggests, then what virtue lies in its attainment? It is essential to recognise that there were, and are, substantial barriers to solidarity; to resist the tendency to treat miners as a homogeneous group, which can then be represented as some lumpen mass; to accept the existence within the mining community of distinct groups with strong, and sometimes incompatible, self-interests; to admit that miners were not—are not—immune from the powerful seductions of apathy, lethargy, the quiet life and the lure of the *status quo*. The recognition of such factors, as well as the strength and power of the opposition, are necessary prerequisites if the real attainments are to be appreciated and nurtured. To present the existence of solidarity amongst miners as if it were a free good is both a huge distortion and a disservice. Like most social objects which are valued and valuable it has had to be striven for and continuously reconstructed.

Notes

[1]One of the most wide-ranging is by Siegel & Clark Kerr, 'The Inter-industry Propensity to Strike: An International Comparison', in Kornhauser, Dubin and Ross (eds.), *Industrial Conflict*, N.Y. 1954.

[2]'International Differences in the Strike Propensity of Coal Miners: Experience in Four Countries', *Industrial and Labour Relations Rev*, 12.3. April, 1959.

[3]This can be illustrated from the experience of South Wales. The union, for example, exerted direct pressure, on employers as well as non-unionists, by threatening strikes to force men to join. Often the threat was enough but between 1898 and 1904 there were 68 actual stoppages on this issue in South Wales. There was also much unofficial intimidation—often by women. Non-unionists were turned out of lodging-places, were paraded through the streets in long white shirts, were black-leaded and generally tormented. Even so there were sharp fluctuations in union membership which tended to decline in periods of poor trade and declining wages. The problem was, of course, most acute in the desperate years after 1926 when only a very courageous campaign checked, and then reversed, the spread of company unionism. David Smith, 'The Struggle Against Company Unionism in the south Wales Coalfield, 1926-39', *Welsh History Review*, 6, 3, June, 1973.

[4]This was an opportunity lost. After 1898, South Wales was determined to end the sliding-scale, and the M.F.G.B. had been insistent on this condition. Everyone on the miners' side took this as an unquestionable starting point. Yet if their minds had not been so closed, the continuation of the sliding-scale in South Wales for just one more year, was probably the only way—and certainly much the cheapest way—of securing a situation in which all the M.F.G.B. agreements could end together. In Scotland, quite fortuitously, the current agreement was for no specific term but would be ended on three months notice. Human nature being what it is, the fortuitous nature of the flexibility thus open to the Scots did not prevent them taking a high moral tone over this issue first with the Welsh and, in 1904, with the English districts.

[5]The apparent exception was, of course, the national stoppage of 1912. But although this was comparatively short and sharp—and, significantly brought in the government to press the owners towards a quick settlement—what emerged was not an effective national minimum wage, but a series of district minima.

[6]P.S. Bagwell, 'The Triple Industrial Alliance, 1913-22', in Briggs and Saville (eds.), *Essays in Labour History, 1886-1923*, vol. 2, 1971, pp. 96-128; G.A. Phillips, The Triple Industrial Alliance in 1914', *Economic History Review*, xxiv, 1, 1971, pp. 55-67.

[7]Roy Gregory, *The Miners and British Politics, 1906-14*, 1968.